ONE EARTH MANY WORLDS

A Philosophical Essay on Holopoetic Cosmology

Acknowledgments

Very special thanks to Michael W. Fox, John B. Cobb, Jr., and Henryk Skolimowski for forcing me to read, think and write. Special thanks to Paolo Soleri and Arnes Naess for inviting me to work with them. And, thanks to Paul Shepard, R. Buckminster Fuller, David Klein, and Neil Evernden for commenting on the work through its changes as an abridged dissertation.

Books by Alan Wittbecker

Poetic Archaeology of the Flesh
Topopoetics: Making Good Places
Eutopias Or Outopias
Eutopias: Making Good Places Ecologically & Culturally
Eutopian Essays
RE: viewing turning thinking
Good Forestry from Good Theories & Good Practices
Global Emergency Actions
Domiture: Coevolution of Nature & Culture (OP)
Global Government
Redesigning the Planet: Foundations
Redesigning the Planet: Local Systems
Redesigning the Planet: Regions
Redesigning the Planet: Global Ecological Designs

ONE EARTH, MANY WORLDS

A Philosophical Essay on Holopoetic Cosmology

Second Edition

Alan Wittbecker

Clio Press
Mozart & Reason Wolfe Ltd.
2016

One Earth Many Worlds
Second Edition, Paperback – Published 2012
Published by Clio Press, M&RW Ltd.
Post Office Box 370
Tallevast, Florida 34270
Mozart@ReasonWolf.com

Publisher's Cataloging in Publication Data

Alan Wittbecker One Earth Many Worlds

Includes Index.
 1. Cosmology. 2. Anthropology. 3. Philosophy. 4. Ecology.
I. Title.

ISBN-13: 978-1518768347
ISBN-10: 1518768342

One Earth Many Worlds, 1st Edition Hardcover © 1983

Book Design by Rian Garcia Calusa

Printed in the United States of America

Second Printing
2 3 4 5 6 7 8 9 10

Contents

Abstract

The universe has been the object of investigation and speculation for thousands of years. The varied circumstances of most cultures resulted in unique models of the universe. These cosmologies have been limited to historical places and by human perception. Modern technological cosmology, beyond being another kind of order, more linear and abstract, is wrongly considered to be the evolutionary successor to traditional cosmologies, and is displacing them rapidly. Where human understanding is still underdeveloped, humanity cannot afford to suppress the diversity of thought necessary for adaptation to the diversity of environments, or to eliminate ecosystems and the societies adapted to them. The ecological, social, and political problems of today do not have simple, disciplinary solutions. The problems are cosmological and must be solved on that level. But, a single cosmology cannot solve all problems in all places. A framework that protects local cosmologies as important functions, that is fit around them, not as a replacement, but as a means of preservation, understanding, and integration, is proposed. This holocosmological framework has many of the same functions—order, explanation, justification, and integration—as local cosmologies.

Cosmologies of select cultures are examined for common threads, such as sacredness and cyclicity; special attention is given to representative cosmologies: Archaic, classical, mechanical, and evolutionary—and basic features are excerpted. Ideas from philosophical thought are fit into the framework, which is outlined with the useful medieval distinction of cosmic levels: Macrocosm, mesocosm, and microcosm. Cosmological ideas are framed in such a way that they are consistent with scientific findings and theories. General themes of cosmological significance, such as self-making, ordering, and wholeness, are distilled from philosophy and physics. Further themes, including participation and interrelatedness, are discerned in the realm of physical order and carried through the level of organic order, where new characteristics emerge: Growth, reproduction, and evolution, for example. At the human level of complexity, perception and consciousness form logical universes with still different characteristics—vagueness, uncertainty, and complementarity—that must be considered. Human beings interact in specific places on earth, which reflect different languages and cultures. A broad epistemology, that takes up animism, taoist objectivity, organic dialectics, and systems theory, leads into a theology of the earth. An ecological model of knowledge is proposed, on which a relative ethics and a theory of rights are based. This 'panethics' is qualified by its ontological equality, reverence, right action, and understanding.

The holocosmological model is aesthetic and uses metaphor at all levels. The structure and function of metaphor, and its role in philosophical and scientific description, is presented, using the concepts of holography as a metaphor for metaphor. Important metaphysical themes, such as participation and caring, are brought together in a discussion of the role of language as expression and limitation. Poetic language is justified as the primary expression of knowledge of human and ambihuman nature; it is found to be particularly appropriate for cosmology, with its ability to impart wholeness, ambiguity, reference, and interrelatedness. Poetry weaves the themes and threads of cultures into a holocosmology. Literally, poesis is "making" and holopoesis is making the whole universe.

This poetic framework is a holopoetic cosmology, where the highest wisdom is "letting be" (beyond necessary utilization), and where compliance and caring are derivations of the most binding human emotion, love. This framework is necessary for placing historical cosmologies in a global context, a context that we need to understand to see how human cultural patterns are unfolding with the wild patterns of nature and how all these patterns must be limited or constrained so that the planetary development is harmonious and healthy. The holocosmology can fit and protect local images. The holocosmology can provide ways to understand the global aspects of civilizations embedded in a wild, living planet, and suggest ways to develop joyously and wisely.

Figure 1.
*Gaelic Coin
World Tree.*

Introduction

KOSMOS

Who having consider'd the body finds all its organs and parts good,
Who, out of the theory of the earth and of his or her body
understands by / subtle analogies all other theories,
The theory of a city, a poem, and of the large politics of these States;
Who believes not only in our globe with its sun and moon, but in
other / globes with their suns and moons,
Who, constructing the house of himself or herself, not for a day
but for all / time, sees races, eras, dates, generations,
The past, the future, dwelling there, like space, inseparable together.
Walt Whitman, *Leaves of Grass*

The cosmos described by Whitman is derived from the Greek idea of
kosmos, which is the noun form of the verb, *kosmeo*, which means to
"arrange" or "set in order." The history of the word suggests that human
order was applied to the organic world and the universe. The word has
aesthetic and moral connotations. One adjective, cosmetic, means the
composition of the face in a proper order that is pleasing to the eye. In
early Greek usage what was beautiful was also morally admirable. Homer
used *kosmos* to mean moral action. A cosmos is that which has order, from
a human face to all of nature. This work is a cosmology, a study of the
cosmos. Works from the disciplines of the physical and social sciences
and from the humanities are analyzed for insights into the common
themes of wholeness, order, interrelatedness, change, and value. A basic,
metaphysical synthesis is constructed from the distillations of these
themes, and a new perspective on the basic processes of the universe is
presented that interrelates all of the themes. This approach is not based
on experimentation, nor on new information; it is a way of looking at old
information, and then forming a series of deductions from principles and
facts. For example:

Plato held that the universe was living.
Whitehead considered the universe as a valuing process.
Spinoza made pantheism egalitarian, i.e., nonanthropocentric.
Francis deposed man as monarch of the universe.
Lamarck reversed the chain of being.
Lao Tse reversed the values of beings.

Darwin considered everything related, changed historically.
Lorenz, Fox and others demonstrated the complexity of animals.
Leopold made man a biotic citizen.
Schweitzer conceived of a reverence for life.
Laszlo extended that reverence for natural systems.
Stone argued that natural objects be given legal rights.
Salk concluded that only wisdom will ensure human survival.
Novalis and others thought poetry the best expression of wisdom.

But nowhere is there a holistic account of value. Nowhere is there an account of a cosmology that is capable of assuming these insights. For example, Leopold argues only that we ought to think of land as having rights; he does not say it has rights or that we ought to defend them. Stone does not argue that natural objects have natural rights. Spinoza and St. Francis are most useful for insights into the equality of beings, but their systems of thought are not used in this work. Odum and others saw that the insights of ecology went far beyond that of a science, but few of these have been worked into a systematic cosmology. There are numerous frames of reference—anthropological, cultural, linguistic, philosophic, historical, scientific—that can be related through common themes.

Theoretical physics, in the views of some, leads back to insights from mystical traditions that propose images of nature that are spiritual rather than mechanistic (refer to Bohm, Wheeler, Capra, Heisenberg, and von Weizsacker). Physics and mysticism have been contrasted in several books, for example, *The Tao of Physics*.

Ecology and mysticism can be linked in a similar way. For instance, Zen does not make the distinction between man and nature; it teaches that humans are part of a constant flow, in which no part dominates; the ecologist teaches that organisms are linked in an interdependent ecosystem. Much ecology is pressed into the mathematical molds preferred by contemporary fashion and the politics of science. Even so, ecology contributes to our understanding of the phenomenal world. Some interpretations of biology give purpose and will a greater role in evolution than natural selection (refer to A. Hardy, du Nouy, E. Sinnott, C. Morgan, and W. Wheeler). All social systems operate in an ecological context, so a knowledge of ecohistory is necessary to understand human history. Anthropologists and environmental scientists draw on primitive and folk cultures to discover values found in myth and ritual and for ideas on how to maintain healthy ecosystems and to develop healthy participants.

Order is a basic problem in cosmology. Besides investigating general meanings of order, this work will examine new theories of order. In 1967 N. Prigogine postulated a new ordering principle (N. Prigogine, *From Being to Becoming*. San Francisco: Freeman, 1980), order through fluctuation. His ordering principle will be seen to be a part of a universal principle proposed in the late 1800s. A core notion of self-organization tendered by Maturana and Varela (1973) is *autopoiesis*, the characteristic of living systems to renew themselves and to regulate the process so that structural integrity is maintained. Upgrading (anabolic) and downgrading processes (catabolic) run simultaneously. Pribram found self-reference to be a key notion in brain functions. Eigen and Winkler see chance and necessity as complementary processes. Many of these theorists extend their ideas to every level and class of existence. Like the "true believer" described by E. Hoffer, or the Marxist convert described by K. Popper, the theorists' eyes are open and they see everything in terms of their theory. For example, Eric Jantsch sees dissipative structures in everything, from God to ideas. While it is not bad to apply a metaphor wherever it will fit, it is improper to interpret it too literally. Jantsch's single-vision leads to conclusions that are contradictory and dangerous. For example, in applying the concept of fluctuations to ecosystems, he concludes that the human destruction of habitats is beneficial to evolution. The errors in this kind of rank metaphorization will be examined in greater detail.

The two general schools of philosophy described as Process Philosophy and Phenomenology are particularly appropriate to a cosmology that intends to be consistent with the findings of ecology and humane ethics. These schools form the basis of this cosmology. Philosophy is also concerned with the whole, the totality of all possible meanings. Martin Heidegger grounds philosophy in the earth and being (throughout, 'being' will not be capitalized; it is treated like the 'tao'). Maurice Merleau-Ponty grounded philosophy in the human bodily dimension. The body is the basis for metaphysics, an access to being as well as an expression of it. Philosophy is tied to a comprehensive anthropology—everything perceived and expressed is anthropocentric and anthropomorphic. All philosophy becomes human first, before it is communicated.

Phenomenology approaches understanding through lived experience. It admits values and meaning in the world. It is capable of dealing with the essential ambiguity of nature, and it can accommodate ecological necessity within its framework. Many techniques of phenomenology are used to refine the perspectives of this work. One of the shortcomings of phenomenology, as recognized by Heidegger and Merleau-Ponty, was that a truly creative language was needed at the limits of description, where prose failed. This work extends the effort toward a creative language for philosophy and anthropology.

Understanding Traditional Cosmology

Cosmology incorporates a complete set of ideas about the nature and composition of the universe used by a cultural system. This idea of the universe provides people with an orientation in their cosmos. Melville Jacobs (in *Campa Cosmology*, by G. Weiss) offered a catalog of ingredients that could be included in a world view: Epistemology, prepsychology, logic, a theory of disease, the supernatural, geography, climate, history, zoology, astronomy, biology, myth, music, and theology (Immanuel Kant's distinction between cosmology and theology is not considered valid here; cosmology also considers the supernatural world behind appearances). The contents, limits and functions of cosmology have not been rigorously defined in science or literature. This introduction formulates an expression of what cosmology is and what it does, then generally examines cosmologies to determine common traits.

Definitions
What is the world like? How did the world get the way it is? And what is the role of humanity in the world? All cultures ask and answer these questions. Some of the questions can not be answered from direct observation. And so many of the answers are not limited to observable events. Ideas concerning humanity and the nature of the universe tend to form a coherent system in which ideas are integrated or rejected over days or centuries. Culture includes all of the expectations, understandings, beliefs, and commitments that influence the behavior of human groups. The classical definition of culture was put forward by Sir E.B. Tylor in 1871: "Culture . . . is that complex whole which includes knowledge, belief, art, morals, law, custom, and any other capabilities and habits acquired by man as a member of society." Cosmology forms part of the ideological system of culture. Cosmology is a collective image of the universe. Ezra Pound stated that the image is an emotional and intellectual complex in an instant of time. He used the figure of a Chinese ideogram as an expression of a complex image created by throwing groups of elements together without predication, which is a characteristic of assertion. The image includes beliefs about the origin, structure and destiny of the universe.

Image. Human behavior depends on constructed images. Images of the environment structure reality. We are not only shaped by our buildings, as Winston Churchill recognized, but by our wildernesses and gardens, our images. Images may be of events, places or ideas. Images may come from experience or from artistic expression. The arts manipulate images by their very presentation; they may be clear or vague, certain or uncertain, local or global, rigid or flexible.

Goethe, Whitehead and others understood that the factual aspect of images cannot be separated from value. As Kenneth Boulding notes, "For any organism or organization, there are no such things as 'facts.' There are only messages filtered through a changeable value system."

There are three levels of image: Self, humanity and the cosmos. The image of humanity is the world. The world—from the German word meaning man-image—may be added to haphazardly or through accumulation in a well-defined way. It may be transformed to incorporate new images. As the world becomes more complex, its image becomes more complex. No longer is space just sacred or profane. The ideal landscape became the middle region, the garden between the complete order of the city and complete chaos of the wilderness. The garden is cultivated from the wilderness as a middle landscape (although now the city expands at the expense of gardens and wilderness). The garden is a human order, but not usually sacred. Not only poets, but politicians and economists created the image of the rural ideal. In traditional Chinese social classification the farmer was ranked below the scholar, but above the artisan and merchant. Jefferson wished for Americans to be husbandmen in a like manner.

The early Sumerian temple tower, with a hieratically organized city surrounding it, became the model for the Hindu world mountain Sumeru, for the Greek Olympus, for Aztec temples, and even for Dante's Purgatory. The king was the central human representative of power. The Sumerian city was organized in the design of a quartered circle. This design has been a favorite for many cities and utopias, besides many cosmologies.

People create an image of the world, in which the most sacred part, a mountain, building or grove, is the most central. The image of the center of the earth, *axis mundi*, running through the middle place, may often give a moral or physical strength. In fact, the image of the center, and its cosmic importance, may be necessary for a culture. The image generates hope and confidence.

Cosmology is derived from the values and patterns of human society. The basic image of a cosmology can be stated as a series of basic principles. For example, twentieth-century American cosmology can be characterized by these statements: "The universe is mechanical; man is master; men are equal; and men are perfectible." Contrast these statements with those of other cosmologies (shown in Figure 2).

Navajo	Dahomey	Yaruru
Universe is personal and orderly	A basic duality (man-god)	Static and internal
Events are primary (not actors)	Impersonal fate rules	Man is sensible to wants of others
Family comes first	There is hierarchy (god-man)	All beings equal)gods, dead, men)
Men quest for harmony	Imperfect is part of duality	System is good, but evil exists

Figure 2. *Contrasting Images*

The set of ideas is common to a culture, although some ideas may be shared among other cultures. Most cosmologies have to be understood in a cultural context, which means that they are not intelligible without reference to a particular culture.

Place. A cosmology is part of a culture, which exists in a particular location with a unique history. Most cosmologies are in place in a particular territory. This is particularly true of the Campa, in a tropical forest in Peru, and the Ituri pygmy, in a tropical rainforest in Africa. These peoples do not, and could not, live with the image of an ocean or desert. Many features of a cosmology exist specifically in one place. Ascribing mythic significance to land strengthens identification with it. Nomadic tribes have a core region that is vigorously defended; modern nations have strict boundaries necessary for their integrity. Humans have a habit of structuring the world with their own group at the center. This ethnocentrism is evident in small tribes as well as in large empires, such as the Roman or Chinese. The center of a cosmos is usually the place of living, the locality of the group creating the cosmology. Ethnocentrism seems to be universal. Even if the center of the world is relatively featureless, myths are created to give it special significance; a sacred event may give sanction to a rock or tree. The center becomes sacred. Temples may be built on the spot to mark it.

Even when different cultures meet, the best explanations may not prevail, although good myths are sometimes borrowed. That is because a cosmology orders reality in a special place. The theory of quanta would be meaningless to the Campa, regardless of how the concept was introduced, because it has no importance to the order of things.

Functions

A cosmology explains and orders the universe. It also dictates and justifies the behavior of its adherents. By explaining reality, cosmology binds the human and ambihuman, and the past and the present, into a meaningful whole.

C. Levi-Strauss emphasized that tribal cultures brought the full power of the human brain to bear in expressing a cosmology (in *Structural Anthropology*, 1963). The 'savage' mind is as logical as the modern. Levi-Strauss thought that mythology was explanatory, a product of the observation and reflection of reality. Myths often were created, however, out of inherited ideational pieces through fitting together (bricolage). But, thought proceeded through understanding, with the aid of distinctions and oppositions (Levy-Bruhl's opinion was that participation was more important than logical thought, and the participation is unavoidable). Cosmology serves to explain appearances, if not in observable events, then in terms of a hidden reality. These two realities make up a totality that is explained. Usually the present is explained as the result of past events.

Malinowski argues that the primary function of mythology is to justify human activities, in order to have those activities continued. Unless a cultural phenomenon satisfied a basic human need, it would not be repeated. The human needs that he listed were all physiological: Metabolism, reproduction, comfort, safety, growth, and health. But not all needs are physiological. At the other extreme, Jeremy Rifkin considered only psychological needs were satisfied by a cosmology. But there are also social needs, in a spectrum of needs, to be considered, such as social status.

A Holopoetic Cosmology Framework

Worlds have been built by peoples over so many thousands of years that it is not necessary to start from raw sensations. Human beings see that a world exists, greater than any human experience of it. And societies create cosmologies that reflect the knowledge and place of each society.

The earliest human beings, finding themselves at the center of their experience, considered themselves at the center of the universe. Successive increments of knowledge have decentralized humanity from the center. With the observations of Copernicus, Galileo, Brahe, and Kepler, the earth was no longer the center of the solar system. Several hundred years later, astronomers calculated that the solar system was not the center of the galaxy. Later still, Hubble discovered that the Milky Way was part of a cluster of galaxies among billions. Some theorists are questioning whether our universe may not be one bubble universe among many.

After Charles Darwin, humanity was not considered central to the earth, but as an evolved form among many forms, part of an ecological system. With exploration and communication, human groups realized that they were not necessarily the center of all existence. Cosmologies have had to expand to some extent.

The feeling of displacement in the universe, with each wave of knowledge, comes from an insistence on positioning. But, humanity is where it always has been, on earth.

Understanding the human place in the universe is the basic problem for all cosmologies. The question of humanity's place in nature should be rephrased as "what is the self-image of humanity?" There are many descriptions of the human image that science and theology cannot provide. The vocabularies of science, religion and politics are more concerned with prediction and control. The vocabulary of art has to do with image.

The explanation of the universe in the earliest cosmologies is essentially mythical. As explanation became more scientific, the cosmologies changed. In the face of psychological decentralizations and ecological catastrophes, the explanation must be metamythical and metascientific. It needs to be poetic. Beyond being just true or false, poetic language can change and inspire human behavior. The human species in fact is poetic—self-making. Humanity makes itself, but not by unmaking other species and taking their places. Living does not need a purpose beyond living. As John Steinbeck saw so clearly, the biologist learns that the first rule of life is living: "The dryballs cannot possibly know a thing every starfish knows in the core of his soul and in the vesicles between his rays." (David Burnor, "Ed Ricketts: 'From the tidepool to the stars.'" *Coevolution Quarterly* 28: 14-21.) With the planet-wide explosion of information, a holocosmology requires a poetry to make the images of identity necessary for human health, and hence the health of the planet.

However, human cosmologies are limited and contradictory. All cosmologies cause destruction and waste; all produce the opposite (evil or enantiodromia) of the good intended. Archaic and modern, occidental and oriental, worldviews are complementary but not complete. The very circumstance that makes each cosmology unique—being in a unique place—ensures that each is limited. Often, a cosmology is accepted as unquestioningly as a language, technology or place. The ideology forms part of the personal identity of the members of a society. Even in cultures with alternative cosmological explanations, individual choice is determined more by social and educational levels than by rational comparison and evaluation.

Many of the problems of human societies can be rooted in their cosmologies, in their images of the universe. But the solution cannot be a uniform cosmology of the earth. The strength of anthropology has been to describe the similarities between cultural groups, but the strengths of cultures lie in the diversity of values, in the fitness to particular places. What is required is a holocosmology, to preserve the differences in a whole image of the earth, a holocosmology created from the distillation of conflicting methodologies into a manyness and openness. It cannot be a rigid shell to contain everything, but rather a flexible bond between human and natural groups.

We must find a way to affirm the metabolism of nature as our own. Each individual is part of a world that extends around the self. There are different, partial worlds. We may see trees on a house site as encroaching, where a Dakota Black Elk may see them as standing peoples, with equal rights to the land. The self is related to each world in different ways. We may see plowing fields for seeds as an act of mastery and exploitation, where another may see it as an act of tender involvement, bringing forth potential.

The study of these worlds is a holocosmology, which embraces a knowledge of earth and of dwellings of humanity. It is as the geography described by Thomas Arnold (1842), stretching one hand to history and the other to geology and physiology; it is that part of a domain of knowledge where students of physical and moral science interact.

The study of cultural ecology—human adaptation to nature—has been neglected in many endeavors. The dilemma of the world reveals the extent of the neglect. Culture is a sum of descriptions of reality, through language and technology. Ideas of culture will be critically examined. Culture codifies reality through expressions, which can be preserved and transmitted through generations through language. Language is a major element in the formation of thought. It is a means to program our perception of the world. Different languages program events differently, therefore no philosophy or belief system can be considered entirely apart from language, or language entirely apart from place.

Philosophy, poetry and science are embodied in language, which is embodied in perception, which is embodied in human action. As Heraklitus noted, the world is in flux and so are the concepts to deal with it. But the earth, the human world, is always anthropomorphic. The human time scale for climatology is conditioned by a human lifespan; so is physics, as Kohler points out. Storms in part of the earth often affect conditions elsewhere, although even with weather satellites this is not always obvious. To a localized people it is even less obvious. As Goethe pointed out, all our human facts are theories—composites of perception, memory, logic, and faith.

Instead of one world, there are many private geographies. These experiences come together to make up a social reality. The learned geography of the world is unified by ideas, art and logic. Each human being inhabits an autonomous, private world; these worlds are very different and deserve respect. We need to recognize the autonomy of consciousness. We construct our normality from information from the senses, which are tuned by culture. There is a cultural bias that prevents us from knowing how much we are contributing to the world we take in. Inside human consciousness is a bit of place consciousness. Humans are embedded in places. The nonhuman consciousness senses the interdependence of all living things and tries to bring them inside. The current ecological consciousness is a system effect. We are imbedded in the ecosystem and subject to its processes—nature still heals herself. Since the entire system determines our fate, we ought to apply our consciousness towards its health.

Paul Shepard and others have written that relationships are as real as the objects that result from them. Ecology attends the overall pattern of relationships, beyond the details. Ecological knowledge can provide reasons for allowing diversity and disturbance in ecosystems; it can offer suggestions for human responses. Ecological principles can be subducted into a cosmology. The concepts of nature and ecology require new conceptual definitions. They are major philosophical problems.

As philosophy attempts to describe the world and discover the order of nature, it must go into mathematics, astronomy, physics, chemistry, and biology. The scientific method, however, fragments the world. The mystic or artist feels the world as described by scientists and it is whole again. Most modern cosmologies are based on physical science. Older cosmologies were based on feeling. The new biological paradigm, combined with process philosophy and phenomenology, supports a new cosmology of feeling and imaging.

Play

The whole universe is at play, wearing different masks of itself. Even at the most basic levels of its field, motion is play. A new philosophy, a new cosmology, must not be limited by a scientific attitude; it must incorporate a taoist attitude. Taoists were keen observers of nature. Needham describes taoism as the only system of mysticism in the world that is not profoundly antiscientific. And yet taoism is playful. The tao flows playfully. Tao is used either as a noun or verb in the earliest writings. As a noun it means way or word; as a verb it means to lead or to tell. Chuang Tzu compares words to a fish trap or rabbit snare. The tao that can be spoken is not the constant tao. It is used in the same special sense as being. Taoism has much in parallel with modern philosophies. So much so that taoism has been used as a metaphorical approach to science, physics, psychology, and brain research (See *The Tao of Science, The Tao of Physics, The Tao of Psychology,* "The Tao of the Brain."). Western Philosophy must also learn to play. Needham compares the tao to the logos of Heraklitus, which has similar root meanings. He also emphasizes the organic nature of the taoistic thought and compares it to process philosophy. These philosophies are profitable directions to follow.

According to Huizinga's *Homo Ludens*, philosophy was born in sacred play; it was an attempt to solve the most basic puzzle of the universe. Philosophy began in a theological play mentality. In Hindu myth, the self of the universe perceives all existence as a form of play. Modern philosophy addresses the same puzzle. Heidegger calls for humanity to live authentically, in the knowledge of discrepancies between anticipation and context. Authenticity means living in ambiguity to Heidegger. Living in ambiguity is like play, a coordination of actuality and possibility, of events and ideas. To be ambiguous means to wander about, whereas ambition means going about. The play of life includes sickness, aging and death. Philosophical activity is a kind of play; thinking just to think, without having change or revolt as a purpose. Human activity is a play, in place within a community of nature.

Play is the creation of meaning for an animal that can experience it. This play function can also be termed poesis, or making. Poetry has vital functions—ritual, entertainment, persuasion, prophecy, competition—that are needed to make a cosmology. In archaic cultures, poetic language is still the most effective expression. It is the vehicle of morality, justice and wisdom; it puts rituals and myths into words. Poetic language plays with the images of cosmology. The creation of a cosmology is a form of play that adapts its creators to the earth.

Mythology
The first humans lived under the stars but on the earth and tried to reconcile the differences with explanations. The first explanations were mythical. The latest have been scientific, although these cosmologies share the same patterns as the mythological ones. Three basic religious cosmologies, and their scientific counterparts, can be distinguished: The Steady State theory, the standard Big Bang, and the Pulsating Universe theory. The first tenet of the Steady State theory, championed by F. Hoyle, is that the universe has always existed. The Ojibwa people of the Great Lakes region of North America have a steady-state cosmology; they have no creation tale and many mythical characters are immortal. The Big Bang theory hypothesizes that the present universe can be traced to a single event. Zoroastrianism, Judaism, Christianity, and Islam share the same general scope of a linear, historical path from beginning to end (Whether or not the universe ends after the big bang depends on how much mass it possesses; if it has little mass then it may expand indefinitely; with much mass it may be closed and contract; evidence favors the former as of 1981). The pulsating universe resembles Hindu mythology, where Shiva spins out the universe as he dances, until he tires and the universe runs down and all life vanishes until he begins again; this dance is billions of years long.

Similarly, in Norse mythology, the universe ends in the Doom of the Gods, where the battle against chaos is fought in vain, warriors and gods are crushed, and all life extinguished. But a new earth is born, the sons of Odin and Thor restore order, and humanity is regenerated.

Cosmologies are created with poetry and myth. Mythology provides individuals with identities and frameworks for decisions and values. A new world order is primarily a mythological problem, not just a psychological, geographical, economic, or political one. Even ecology is still circumscribed compared to a cosmology that can take up the insights of ecology, the results of scientific models, the values of religion, and the expression of poetry—and can offer descriptive and prescriptive fundamentals of the human and ambihuman condition.

This work attempts to synthesize organic conceptions and themes into an outline of a cosmological frame. The new frame requires a new mythology. As innocent as that sounds, it cannot be rigid, it cannot be exclusive or perfect. Aldous Huxley warned of some of the dangers. "The Marxist calls himself scientific and to this claim the Fascist adds another: he is the poet—the scientific poet—of a new mythology. Both are justified in their pretensions; for each applies to human situations the procedures which have proved effective in the laboratory and the ivory tower. They simplify, they abstract, they eliminate all that, for their purposes, is irrelevant and ignore whatever they choose to regard as inessential; they impose a style, they compel the facts to verify a favorite hypothesis, they consign to the waste paper basket all that, to their mind, falls short of perfection" (in *Ape and Essence*, p. 5). A holocosmology must be based on 'known' truths, without rejecting unfashionable ones. It must be open to change and addition.

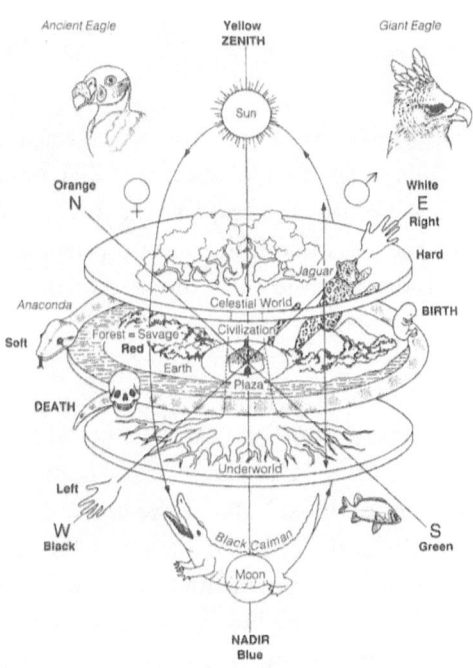

Figure 3. *Amazonian Cosmos.*

Part One: Many Worlds

Joseph Campbell describes the inspiration of civilization around 5200 years ago in Mesopotamia (in *The Masks of God: Primitive Mythology*). The whole cultural syndrome—writing, mathematics, taxes, calendars—appeared within a relatively brief time. This new order of humanity was the conscious creation of temple priests, according to Campbell. The inspiration was based on the discovery of planetary motions and on the ideas that the laws governing these motions should be the same as those governing the life and thoughts of men. This idea has been carried through classical, medieval and modern civilizations, with little modification. Now, the laws are considered limiting factors more than forms to be obeyed. The recognition of the cosmic order of stars fulfilled a psychological and sociological need to bring the parts of a differentiated universe and community into orderly relations. Plato described a universal order to be followed in building an earthly one. Campbell notes that the Egyptian term for that order was Ma'at, the Indian Dharma, the Chinese Tao.

Levels of Order

The whole city, and not just the temple, was conceived as an earthly imitation of the cosmic order, a sociological middle cosmos, established between the macrocosm of the universe and the microcosm of the individual. Through the priesthood, the one essential form of all was made visible. The cosmos is divided into three orders that are related directly.

- Macrocosm
- Mesocosm
- Microcosm

In the Hermetic writings, the hierarchical structure of the cosmos resembled that of an organism: Cell-tissue-organ-body. The idea of microcosm is stated succinctly as: "Man is the universe in miniature" or "As above, so below" (from the Emerald Tablets of Hermes Trismegistus). Man, as microcosm, embodies the qualities of the universe. From a central position in the chain of being, the human serves as nexus between the world of spirit and of matter. A microcosm is shown by two intersecting triangles overlapped, one based in spirituality, the other in sensuality, so that sensuality decreases as spirituality increases (as in Figure 4).

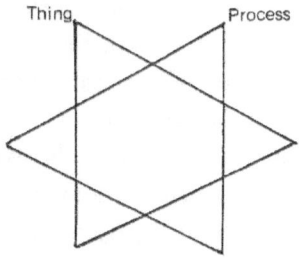

Figure 4. *Triangle Metaphor*

The pattern of the cosmos is intrinsic at all levels of creation, an effectual potency that informs the hierarchies of existence from galaxies to microbes. The potential is not always actualized. If humanity is considered to have a moral imperative to implement the latency of the cosmos, then the institution and maintenance of natural order becomes the fundamental objective of any moral code. Cosmology and worldviews address the human relation to nature: Wilderness and cities; conceptions of vertical and horizontal dimensions; perceptions and attitudes about near and far places. The universe is revealed by scientific observation. But understanding of the microcosm is restricted by our preconceptions of the macrocosm. This idea is not complete, however. Self-understanding, knowing, self-image, and feeling are left out. These attributes have to be considered somehow.

Functions of Cosmology
Cosmologies have at least four functions in human society.
- Order (an aesthetic function)
- Explain (intellectual and scientific)
- Justify (political)
- Integrate (emotional and ecological)

Each of these functions is described more fully.

Order
Cosmologies derive from lived experiences and give them meaning and direction. The complex associations described by a cosmology furnish rich symbolic experiences. Nothing is quite what it seems. Black Elk perceived that tepees were round like the nests of birds (who share the same

religion), set in a circle (as the sun and moon and seasons go), the nation's hoop (J. G. Neihardt, *Black Elk Speaks*. New York: Pocket Books, 1959).

The process of the universe seems to be toward different individual orders, i.e., experience. Experience is personal history. Order constitutes a matrix through which a person perceives the environment. Objects, events and values are assumed in an ordered view of the world. But individual perspectives are not strictly individual phenomena; they are products of the interaction of people and places. Experience is partly a function of the orders of place and people. Orders may be analyzed into:

- temporal/spatial order: the physical scale and rhythm of a place. For instance, time is perceived at a faster rate in cities than in rural settings.
- economic: things of different rarities or sizes are valued differently. In many modern societies, they are assigned monetary amounts according to value.
- emotional: events or places in which people participate become personally ordered, with or without political or religious overtones.
- cultural: the myths, rituals and stories of a society are ordered. People also produce maps and public orders.

Explanation

C. Levi-Strauss thought that mythology was explanatory, a product of observation and reflection of reality. Cosmology serves to explain appearances, if not in observable events, then in terms of a hidden reality. These two realities make up a totality that is explained. Usually the present is explained as the result of past events: Mythologies are attached to animals and personalized beings (mountains, trees) in nature. By explaining reality in this way, cosmology binds the human and ambihuman, and the past and the present, into a meaningful whole. Cosmology attempts to explain the human order in terms of physical, biological and cosmic processes.

Justification

B. Malinowski argues that the primary function of mythology is to justify human activities, in order to have those activities continued. Unless a cultural phenomenon satisfied a basic human need, it would not be repeated.

Cosmology dictates and justifies the behavior of its adherents. The position of women and men are ordered in cosmology. For the Isneg of the Philippines, all religious matters are handled by women. Great Lakes people (in the USA) have male and female shamans, without distinctions. Other groups separate males and females completely. A cosmology also determines intercosmological relationships. It was assumed by the modern mechanical cosmology that the modern civilized view culminated from the primitive. Thus, modern cosmology justified exploiting or removing 'primitive' cosmologies (much as those groups considered themselves superior to other less-favored groups). By granting human sovereignty, modern cosmology justified usurping the habitats of plants and animals for plantations and recreation boating.

Integration
Particularly in agricultural societies, cosmologies are gauged closely to seasons. They are also tuned to the limits of the local ecology, within their knowledge of interactions (the long-range ecological consequences of drainage, irrigation or overexploitation contribute to the deaths of cultures). Cosmologies can integrate peoples to each other, as well as to places and ideas. Integration is accomplished by a shared image.

Figure 5. *Logo of SynGeo ArchiGraph.*

Traditional Cosmologies
Archaic Cosmology

This is the account of how all was in suspense, all calm, in silence; all motionless, still, and the expanse of the sky was empty.

This is the first account, the first narrative. There was neither man, nor animal, birds, fishes, crabs, trees, stones, caves, ravines, grasses, nor forests; there was only the sky.

. . . Only the Creator, the Maker, Tepeu, Gucumatz, The Forefathers, were in the water surrounded with light. They were hidden under green and blue feathers, and were therefore called Quetzal Serpent." Maya, From The Popol Vuh: Beginnings (J. Rothenberg and G. Quasha, eds., *America A Prophecy*. New York: Vintage Books, 1974, p. 13.)

This is a description of the Mayan cosmos (circa 800 AD). Similarities can be discerned between this and other archaic cosmologies: The distinction between the sacred and the profane, the meaning of the cosmos for humans, their adaptiveness to nature, and their personal aspects.

Sacred & Profane
Human groups have traditionally ordered the universe into two realms: the sacred and the profane. Places without special significance, that do not partake of the sense of the center, that are beyond, are profane. The center, as point, place, locale, or vague area, is sacred. What is known and mythologized is sacred. The lived place is sacred. The familiar is sacred. Sacred space is where sacred experience occurs, that is, the manifestation of a wholly different order, not of the human world. Most pre-modern civilizations organized space around a sacred center. The areas outside their world were considered profane wilderness. Peoples as literate as the Greeks and Chinese structured their worlds this way (see Figure 6).

The prevalence of sacred corners or sides is almost universal. The worldview and cosmology of a culture, including orientation to vertical and horizontal dimensions and attitudes about the universe and world, are manifested in various forms in the places that people create. Culture and environment have a coherence that exists at many levels of functioning, perception, cognition, behavior. (cf. Norberg-Schulz). The cosmos can be considered as vertical or horizontal. Most cosmologies structure space vertically; perhaps because of the pervading influence of planetary motions. Then space is layered. Those peoples in starless worlds, such as the Mbuti pygmy of the tropical rainforest in the Congo, tend to develop a horizontal cosmos.

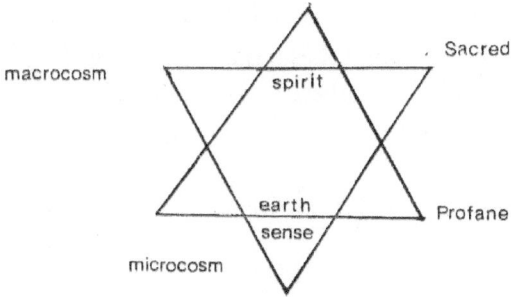

Figure 6. *Division of Space*

In the village layouts of the South Nias Islanders of Indonesia, there is interplay of political, religious, and cosmological values. Religious values are organized around series of polarities: sky/earth, male/female, upriver/downriver. Opposites are represented by two brother deities, who are associated with the upper- and underworlds. The siting, layout and design of a village fits with values. Villages are usually sited on hilltops, representing the upperworld; the chief's hut is represented as upperworld, and the ordinary people are associated with the underworld (Rapoport, 1969). In Fiji the east wall is for chiefs; in Madagascar the northeast corner is most sacred and the north is for notable guests. In China the Northwest corner is most sacred, although the whole house is considered sacred. Ritual space distribution is found in Arab, Mongol, Lap, and Indian houses, among others.

The Zuni, an agricultural group in the southwest United States, live in a highly structured world of zones. The universe is divided into zones for ritual purposes. These zones are oriented toward the center, the Zuni pueblo. By contrast, the neighboring Navajo, who are sheepherders, live in scattered hogans, each of which is a center. The sacred center is a dispersed cluster.

Meaning
Humans have evolved under the influence of the cosmos, from galactic to terrestrial to internal rhythms. Processes on earth are geared to cosmic rhythms. The solar system has its own periodicities. Daily and seasonal cycles are evident in all life on earth. The circadian rhythm, a 24-hour

periodicity, is one of the most evident in living beings. Apparently all functions in the human body exhibit a daily rhythm, from the dividing of cells to kidney functions and mental acuity.

Cosmologies bring nature and humanity into a coherent system. In many earlier cosmologies, the characteristics of basic substances in nature were extended to human nature. Besides being identified with personality traits ('he is fiery' or 'all wet'), substances were linked with space, colors, and animals, as illustrated in Figure 7.

Culture	Direction	Color	Human	Substance	Weather
Pueblo	north	blue		mountain	
	west	yellow		mountain	
	south	red		mountain	
	east	white		mountain	
	zenith	dark			
	nadir	rain-bow			
Oglala Sioux	center				
	north	white			wind
	west	black		rain	thunder
	south	yellow			summer
	east	red	wisdom		
Chinese	center	yellow	desire	earth	
	north	black	fear	water	winter
	west	white	sorrow	metal	autumn
	south	red	joy	fire	summer
	east	green	anger	wood	spring
Indonesian	center	grey		earth	
	north	black	rigid	fire	
	west	yellow	luxury	gold	
	south	red	avaricious	mountain	
	east	white	comprehend	wind	

Figure 7. *Cosmological Correspondences*
(Pueblo, Sioux, Chinese, Indonesian)

Although some arrangements seem arbitrary to outsiders, they probably seem appropriate within a culture. The associations establish significant relationships among the total phenomena of nature. A cosmology orders phenomena.

The schema shown relates characteristics of nature or human nature to direction. In the beginning, color and actions of nature are related to direction, as for the Sioux. The Indonesian scheme includes human qualities. The Chinese relates inanimate elements to emotions. Classical and Medieval European civilizations made similar connections.

The Oglala Sioux, Black Elk, described the relevance of the sacred pipe, how it was made and what it meant. He described the four ribbons on the stem as the four quarters of the universe (see figure 4), but noted that they were only one spirit, represented by the eagle feather, which was like a father. "Is not the sky the father and the earth a mother, and are not all living things with feet or wings or roots their children? And this hide upon the mouthpiece here, which should be bison hide, is for the earth, from whence we come and at whose breast we suck as babies all our lives, along with all the animals, and birds and trees and grasses. And because it means all this, and more than any man can understand, the pipe is holy." (Neihardt, *Black Elk Speaks*, p. 37).

Adaptiveness

Archaic worldviews have been considered primitive survival mechanisms. Their representations were considered dim. It has been assumed by the modern mechanical cosmology that the modern civilized view culminated from the primitive. Thus modern cosmology justified exploiting or removing primitive cosmologies. But the anthropologist Levi-Strauss claimed that archaic thought patterns were highly disciplined intellectual structures designed to make the world coherent and meaningful.

A proper cosmology is adaptive because it aids survival in the ambihuman world. It offers a sense of security, belonging and purpose. By organizing humanity in the natural world, it touches him socially and politically. Old cosmologies have had the function of preventing society members from breaking the stability of a societal relationship with a vulnerable habitat.

Even peoples considered primitive have integrated worldviews. These societies can instruct modern ones in fitness to the environment. Reichel-Doklmatoff claims that most rituals of the tropical American Indian tribes are concerned with ecological balance (though not self-consciously, necessarily, from 'Cosmology as ecological analysis,' *The Ecologist.* 7: 4-11). The recital of myths is of great importance; myths provide a cognitive matrix for life. The cosmological myths of the Tukano do not describe their place in nature in terms of mastery of a subordinate environment. Instead the Tukano learn that they are part of a larger system that transcends individuals. Survival and maintenance of the quality of life are possible only if all other lives are allowed to evolve according to their specific needs, which are described in myths and traditions.

Personal Nature

The natural world is seen anthropomorphically. Or perhaps, since human beings are seen as relatives of all that is, cosmomorphically. Archaic cosmology was wedded to shape (*morphos*), more than to language (*logos*). The anthropomorphism is the only way to understand the mother and father and kin. Anthropomorphism leads to some kind of understanding of the ambihuman. We understand other beings by expanding ourselves, not by shrinking them. (Anthropomorphism as it is used here is concerned with the projection of experience into other beings, not with making other beings into humans.) Everything has a spirit; the social life of humans and other beings is not separate. A core of anthropomorphism is necessary as a way of understanding nonhuman views. This core actually sponsors diversity in individuals and species. Symbolic associations and transformations are made between diverse entities. All events have some cosmological significance. Toynbee concludes that worship of nature unites people because it is not "self-centered." Anthropomorphic thought increases the dimensions of the human intellect. Language itself is anthropomorphic. By rejecting anthropomorphism, the experience of others is restricted, and the scope of self-knowledge is reduced (cf. Paul Shepard). Narrowness of experience is a source of human insecurity. The feeling of security is necessary for a fitting cosmology.

Otto Rank suggested that our concepts of nature were supremely anthropocentric (in Ernest Becker, *The Denial of Death*. New York: Free Press, 1973), but they are anthropomorphic instead. In anthropocentrism, humans desire to make everything conform to images of themselves; the "stink" of humanity clings to everything. In ancient China, humans found justification of their worldviews in the matrix of nature. Perceived cruelty in nature justified real cruelty in humans. The idea that man is the most important part of the universe is the central idea of anthropocentrism. But anthropomorphism is an expression of perspective. These two approaches will be contrasted later in more detail.

Archaic cultures thought of nature as presence: Phenomena are personalized for storage as narrative (instead of scientific categories); intersubjectivity is the prime mode of experience—noise in the woods at night is the voice of a living being, a person. The aural/oral world is not so much spread out to the eye as a dynamic, unpredictable event-world, highly personal, polemic, less interiorized and solipsistic.

In oral societies thought is not advanced by genius, but by everyone together. The early life-world belonged to shamans and poets because it was constructed out of archetypal images favored by mystery, poetry and art. Memory in an oral noetic culture is never verbatim; this is especially true of epic singers; but oral memory is tenacious and accurate, locked in themes.

These poets, with stores of thousands of phrases, are rhapsodizers, or stitchers as the Greeks called them (from *raptein*, meaning to sew together). This kind of composition features complex meters, but not rhyme. The oral world was polemic. Truth was the possession of a personal relationship (quite different from an empirical truth, the nonrelational verification of fact). Plato's expulsion of the poets from his ideal society was a rejection of oral learning; the step toward the abstract idea of forms (cf. Jantsch and Waddington). The exciting vision of narrative was replaced by motionless forms. Visual images may just be an ethnocentric bias of literate societies. The evidence of imagery is private, unlike the voices and scents that everyone could verify. Nonliterate societies may have had strong auditory, olfactory and tactile images, however.

Most preliterate and some modern cultures are event-worlds, constructed by sounds. For a human being, voice is the paradigm of all sound; to it all sounds tend to be assimilated: We hear the voice of the sea, of thunder, wind, engines, and of all existence. The concept of view, as in worldview, is visually grounded. Most early cultures probably did not have the concept of worldview. In Greek and Latin, there are words for hope or outlook, but not worldview. Other words meant order or house. The Greeks took knowing as something like seeing (intuition), but also thought of the world as a harmony, something heard. But gradually vision dominated.

Classical Worldview

Thales:
> Never was Nature, with her fluid powers,
> Reduced to scale of days or nights or hours.
> Thus every form by law she will create;
> No violence she uses to be great.
>> Goethe (Peter Salm, *The Poem as Plant*. Cleveland:
>> Case Western Reserve, 1971, p. 44.)

The first rational attempt to describe the nature of the universe is attributed to Thales. Although his ideas were apparently affected by Egyptian or Babylonian mythology, he formulated them in a nonmystical way. Having noticed movement in everything, he thought that the world as a whole was permeated by a life force. Possibly he noticed that water was necessary for life. In any case, he named water as the first principle.

The philosophy of Anaximenes was also dominated by the idea of a single, basic substance, the isolation of which was required for a cogent account of reality, since the whole world must have emerged from it and differentiated itself. He concluded that air was the basic element and explained physical events through condensation and rarefaction.

Heraklitus retained the idea of a basic substance, fire, but subsumed it to the *logos*, the unity of things in their structure. The visible world was that in which the true essence revealed and hid itself at the same time. "Nature loves hiding," as Heraklitus said. The essence revealed itself in signs. The cosmos was the "same for all" and "one and common" only for those who were awake to read the signs. It was private and impoverished for those who were asleep, i.e., unconscious. The unity of changes, and "everything changes," was the logos, which governed all. Wisdom was knowledge of the logos.

There were other physical cosmologists. For instance, Anaximander's one originative substance was the apeiron, the boundless, infinite basis of the four elements. His order was spatial structure, and not the dynamic, temporal order of Heraklitus. After the physical cosmological approach of the Milesian thinkers, others applied their insights to the unity of the arrangement and theological aspects of things. The Pythagoreans became concerned with the structure of the world. Number became the basic principle; the ultimate substructure of matter was spatial configuration: Triangles! Plato characterized the Pythagorean impulse as almost emotional, while Aristotle described their 'strange principles' as arising from religious grounds and concluded that, in spite of the abstractness of their principles, they concerned themselves wholly with nature. The Eleatic philosophers, beginning with Parmenides, attempted to reach the first principle as being, as the one, devoid of plurality. Ultimate being was changeless and timeless. Melissus argued that the universe was internally whole and infinite; there was no nonbeing or void.

Empedocles, trying to observe the tenets of the Eleatics, explained all natural processes in terms of the combination or separation of the four elements (as in Anaximander), due to the opposing influences of love and strife (similar to Heraklitus). Love and strife were not only dynamic principles, but were physical masses, thereby making the mind and body homogenous. Nothing came into being or perished; there was only mixture and separation. In his cosmology, Anaxagoras held that the four elements were aggregates of seeds. An infinite number and variety of seeds was scattered in the cosmic process. Seeds grew into things, by like attracting like. For Parmenides or Empedocles, nothing had being but the basic substance, true being or the elements. But Anaxagoras made being the common possession of all things.

Leucippus, Epicurus and Democritus stripped the seeds of their variety. The atomists maintained that matter was composed of indivisible, changeless, homogenous minima; only differences in arrangement and position accounted for the variety of the world. The void had been reinstated to allow motion, becoming and perishing. (The atomistic void was truly empty, as the Pythagorean void was not.)

Plato also assumed that the constituents of nature consisted of the four elements—air, fire, earth and water (Plato, *The Collected Dialogues*. New York: Pantheon, 1961). These elements were logically linked to human personality (the four humors) and disease. In fact, humanity was part of a cosmic order that was divinely created. Plato wrote in the Timeaus: "God, wishing to make this world most nearly like that intelligible thing which is best ... fashioned it as a single, visible, living creature" with sense and reason. In Plato's theory, the God did not create matter but only fashioned it according to an ideal pattern. The world was not fashioned perfectly. Instead, it was fashioned as a living creature, with mind and reason that moved towards the realization of an ideal form; all the forms contained within it also were in the process of becoming, of realizing their essence. The visible reality was changing; the perfect forms lay beyond. Perfection was at the end of the process (cf. Whitehead).

In the "Gorgias" (507D-508A), Plato stated that "communion and friendship and orderliness and temperance and justice bind together heaven and earth and gods and men and that this universe is therefore called Cosmos or order." The Greek kosmos originally meant order, then later 'good order' and universe. The *polis*, the classical city-state, was a place where the citizens depended on and maintained the whole, which cared for and outlasted the individual. The stoics declared the cosmos to be the great city "of gods and men." The citizen became related to the cosmos as a whole, in the same way. The Greek idea of nature was based on an analogy with the human body, with thoughts and feelings. The universe was a kind of living organism. Thus, the Greeks also kept an anthropomorphic perspective toward cosmology.

Plutarch speaks of the orderly digestion that the complex term cosmos signifies, the way it organizes the variety of the world in a systematic arrangement. Cosmos is an organic whole which incorporates all items of nature in a single orderly scheme. It also conveys Cicero's notion of universe: all things turning in unison or 'that which rolls as one' (*versus* is past participle of *vertere*, meaning 'to turn about').

The history of arts, sciences and politics might be written as variations on the theme of world order. Romans borrowed the term *kosmos* and translated it as *mundus*, which meant toilet ornaments and farm implements as well as universe. Cicero defined mundus as universe, as the common home (*domus*) or city (urbs) or state (civitas) of gods and men (*De Natura Deorum*, ii, p. 154).

Gnostic & Medieval Cosmology

The ideas of Plato and Aristotle were represented throughout medieval Europe by Augustine, Abelard, Boethius, and others (Kaufman, *Philosophical Classics*). The forms were translated into a Christian context as Providence, the plan for the universe in the Mind of God. Humanity was still considered part of the total world, vital and spiritual. The spiritual order encompassed nature and humanity, and individual and society.

Although traditional Christianity accepted the unity of humanity and nature from classical Greek thought, the gnostic movement in the first three centuries of Christianity recognized an estrangement between humanity and nature, a loss of the cosmos. The gnostic attitude was a complex dualism, between man and world and between God and world; man and God were separated by the world. The spirit of man was not part of the world; neither was the world part of God. The gnostics believed that a lesser being, the demiurge, created the world out of ignorance and passion. Valentinus wrote that it was out of fear of Adam's greater power, that the angels ruined the work of the world into which Adam was thrown. Although the world was still a cosmos, an order, it was a miserable one, alien to human aspirations to know God, the light in the dark vastness. Cosmic law was recognized only as the limit on human freedom; no longer worshipped as the expression of reason. Providence, once identified with logos, was replaced by hiemarmene, oppressive fate.

Hans Jonas concluded that the cosmos was contrary to life and spirit for the gnostics (H. Jonas, *Philosophical Essays*. Englewood Cliffs: Prentice-Hall, 1974). The stars, once the most divine example of harmony, were alien and pitiless forces. Humanity was locked in servitude to cosmic designs. Knowledge, as gnosis, was power to overcome the world, a magic weapon to defeat the power of planets. The opposition of gnosis did not attempt to comply with the laws of the cosmos or to integrate humanity into the whole, as did Stoic wisdom. It was knowledge to extricate the self from the world. The divinely ordered cosmos collapsed. The new cosmos was inhabited by demons.

For the rest of medieval Christianity, the universe was immense, but had definite limits. The earth was infinitesimally small, a mathematical point in the center. The cosmos was ranked vertically; up and down were absolute. Earth was the lowest place; stars were the highest. The sky was not a vacuum, but filled with light or the frames of constellations. Place for Gnostic and Christian was a pleroma, a fullness.

Mechanistic Cosmology
With the gnostic idea of God being totally transcendent, there was no reason for the universe to be more than mechanical. The "Ancients," as Isaac Newton called them, stressed the importance of the science of mechanics in the investigation of nature. Mechanics was rational and practical. But with Newton, it became a metaphor for the operation of the world. The cosmos resembled a well-organized machine, running effortlessly by precise mathematical laws. Living creatures were automata, incapable of experiencing pain or pleasure. Francis Bacon and Rene Descartes shared this mechanistic view. The world was conceptualized as Leucippus' atoms moving through the void according to laws. God was the omnipotent creator, again, but standing outside of the world. Humans were free to examine the clockwork put in motion by God. Bacon interpreted Genesis to mean that God had given man dominion over nature (Latin translation changed the Hebrew *rahe*, humane stewardship, into *domino*, rule over, which was left ambiguous). Knowledge was equated

with power over animals and things.

With Bacon, the opposition of man and nature was restated in a secular form. Dualism was applied everywhere. Descartes put a "ghost in the machine" to explain the duality of mind and body. Hobbes posed the individual against society. The human machine was a part of the social machine, which was the way social order was maintained.

The industrial revolution decreased contact with the natural world and objectified what was left. As a result of drastic changes in the production of economic goods, other political, social and even psychological changes occurred. The form of government involved democratic control. Human relationships were based on economic allegiances instead of kinship, and were formed in societies, not communities. Money became a symbolic representation for the value of labor and land. Land and labor became commodities. R. Redfield noted that in folk society technical order was subordinate to moral order. During urbanization, old orders were shaken, then rebuilt on new levels; self-consciousness became a factor. In industrial society, the technical and moral were separated. Consumers and workers held a new worldview.

The two great myths, progress and nationalism, arose with the industrial cosmology. Aldous Huxley described progress as the theory that one can get something for nothing (in *Ape and Essence*), that the gain in one field is not even paid for in another. Progress assumed that all consequences could be foreseen, and that the ideal ends in the future justified the most abominable means, robbery, murder, or cheating. Primitive groups only obstructed the march toward paradise. Then, nationalism was the theory that the state was the only true god; all others, especially, other states, were false. Conflicts over prestige or power were crusades for the Good and the True.

Modern Philosophical Cosmologies

Throughout the latter part of the 19th century, thinkers were beginning to question the mechanistic concept of nature. The romantics expressed a reaction against mechanism. Although Darwin's theory of evolution depended on mechanistic imagery, it placed humanity back in nature (Charles Darwin, *The Origin of the Species*. London: Murray, 1859). The idea of evolution restored the ideal of humans as part of a totality; humans were part of a complex ecological system. The use of the word "ecology," by Ernst Haeckel in 1870, implied that the natural world was a place to live, a house, rather than a machine to control.

Ironically, Darwin's ideas were used by the myth to support the mechanistic rape of nature by technology. The theory seemed to support the most selfish and aggressive assertions of class, nation and race. Natural selection in a forest justified ruthlessness in a factory. Darwin drew ideas and support from Malthus. Marx used Darwin's ideas to confirm the theory of class struggle. Acts of greed and aggression asserted nature's fundamental, violent laws, which were to be respected.

But responses showing the opposite have been increasing. Patrick Geddes noted that the mammalian impulse to nurture the young, intensified in humans, made the family the model for larger forms of cooperation. The geographer, P. Kropotkin, pointed out that the evolutionists had overlooked the factor of mutual aid. Kropotkin was also an advocate of the minimal state. After rejecting a position in the Russian Geographical Society, he devoted his life to a society in which knowledge and wealth were shared by all. He maintained that progress occurred by people working together, not through competition. In *Fields, Factories and Workshops Tomorrow*, he argued for self-sufficient local economies and an integrated urban and rural society with decentralized industries.

A number of naturalists wrote with a religious view towards nature. The writings of Emerson, Thoreau, Whitman, R. Jefferies, W. Hudson, and others combined a sacred vision of nature with the observational methods of mechanistic science. Later naturalists like Muir, Burroughs, Seton, and G.B. Grinnell stressed the ethical problems of the mechanistic approach. The logical consequence of complete domination of nature might be the complete destruction of humanity. Some philosophers searched for a paradigm more consistent with ecological and cosmological views. Process cosmology and ecological philosophies offer the strongest support for a holocosmology. Yet, even these positions have weaknesses that must be accounted for.

Process Cosmology

In *Process and Reality: An Essay in Cosmology*, Alfred North Whitehead attempts to answer the cosmological problem "What does it all come to?" He argues that the impoverishment of our conceptual universe led to the disaster of physicalism and to no metaphysics at all. Whitehead developed a model of reality that weaves physical and psychic aspects of nature into a coherent unified whole, thus avoiding the aesthetic and logical difficulties in other theories. His process metaphysics accepts change as a fundamental characteristic of the universe and takes value as part of the meaning of actuality. Whitehead's philosophy recognizes the dialectical character of process, the interpenetration of opposites, the significance of levels of organization, the importance of community, and the irreducible character of awareness. His process philosophy asserts that being and becoming, permanence and change, have *coequal footing* in reality and are insistent aspects of experience.

All of Whitehead's notions—actual occasions, facts, purpose, process, system, creative advance, feeling, societies—form an interlocking, coherent cosmology. He emphasized that every one of these notions was explicitly formulated by Locke or Descartes, but neither one put them all into one system. Instead, each substituted alternative notions, which eventually lead to the Humean extreme. He criticized modern philosophy for losing sight of stubborn fact in the heat of inductive formulation.

Each formal notion—Existence, Obligation, Ultimate—has its own category. Whitehead regarded his categories, not as dogmatic statements of the obvious, but as tentative formulations of the ultimate generalities, from which true propositions applicable to particular circumstances can be derived. Thus, philosophy is an experimental adventure through descriptive generalizations, against the background of a systematic universe. Every proposition refers to a universe exhibiting some general systematic metaphysical character. Whitehead writes: "Apart from this background, the separate entities which go to form the proposition, and the proposition as a whole, are without determinate character . . . every definite entity requires a systematic universe to supply its requisite status" (Ibid, p. 16). Whitehead asserts the doctrine that the ultimate claim of existence is the breadth of thought reacting with the intensity of sensitive experience, and that the development of "self-justifying" thoughts has been achieved by the process of generalization from particular topics, of imaginative schematizations of those generalizations, and then renewed comparison with direct experience—the ultimate test.

Creativity, an ultimate principle in Whitehead, relates the many and the one in a manner productive of the pulsations of process which are the actual entities. "There is a rhythm of process whereby creation produces natural pulsation, each pulsation forming a natural unit . . ." A deductive metaphysical system requires primitive ultimate concepts, undefined. "The sole appeal is to intuition" (Ibid., p. 32). Whitehead conceives the 'ultimate' as creativity, a universal process of creative activity, which while transcending each individual actual creature, is not itself actual, but is made concrete in the individual. This secures the concept of a connected universe and its character as self-creating activity. Creative activity is considered as activity toward some end. God is a unique actual entity from which the element of "telos" in the universe is derived. God serves as the "foundation of order," the "goal toward novelty," and the "solution of aesthetic problems" (Ibid., p. 28).

Process is the fundamental feature of that which is really real and in its primary sense process is the coming to be of the individual actualities. Process is the expansion of the universe, any stage of which is an organism. The organism is an incomplete process, however. The organic process describes each actual entity: "It repeats in microcosm what the universe is in macrocosm" (Ibid., p. 327). It repeats the hermetic equation referred to earlier.

In the philosophy of organism, the traditional notion of an entity as the unchanging subject of change is replaced by the actual entity, which is not only the subject experiencing, but the superject (A technical term in Whitehead; the opposite of subject. For Kant, the world emerges from the subject; for Whitehead, the subject emerges from the world as superject of its experiences). So it is not substance that is permanent, but form, which only suffers changing relations. The actual occasions perish subjectively, but gain objective immortality.

Another implicit assumption of traditional philosophy, that perception, consciousness or thought are the basic ingredients of experience, is repudiated by Whitehead. They are inessential for organismic actual experience, physical or mental. The doctrine of the philosophy of organism is a reformed version of the subjectivist doctrine, togetherness. This unique togetherness is derivative only from the experiential togetherness in the actual occasion. Whitehead calls togetherness a generic term, presupposing the notions of creativity, one, many, identity, and diversity. The actual occasion as an organism in process will be examined in the next three sections.

Actual Occasions

Nature, for Whitehead, consisted of patterns whose movement was essential to their being. These patterns are analyzed into events or occasions. The basic unit in Whitehead's philosophy is the unit of experience, the actual occasion.

- raw materials of science are occasions of experience
- an occasion of experience has duration
- an occasion of experience is a unity
- its content is infinite and undenumerable
- experience is an event that has characteristics

But Whitehead has to postulate a serial and sequential ordering of events (actual occasions), leading to a complication of a world comprised of an ill-defined multiplicity of events. Emphasis on serial notion restores unity to the world. When describing prehension, future or creativity, Whitehead implies a one-way dependence among actualities. (Sometimes they seem to be mutually implicative, but Whitehead never makes it clear which they are.) One important feature of the doctrine is that: "the ultimate physical entities of science are always vectors indicating transference" (Ibid., p.364), that is, being is becoming (Whitehead translates Heraklitus as "All things are vectors, i.e., flow").

An actual entity arises out of the actual world through a process in which objectivity is transformed into subjective immediacy. Data are integrated with feelings. A datum is appropriated and enjoyed. Through complexity, there are physical feelings, as well as conceptual, propositional, and comparative. An intense experience is an aesthetic fact, according to Whitehead. Everything enjoys "prehensions," absorbing what is outside being inside. A plant prehends sunlight, making it part of its behavior. All events mind, in that sense. The human mind is just complex enough to prehend propositions, since it is a society of events.

Actual entities are the final things of which the world is made. Besides the eternal objects, what is permanent for Whitehead is the value achieved in an entity whose self-creative process combines the world in a perspective. The product of the self-creative act, being, is permanent; the activity, becoming, is not. An event has two sides, individual self and signification in the universe, that work dialectically. Becoming is for the purpose of being (signification) and being is for the purpose of becoming. Objectivity is the permanent aspect of reality. Process is the changeable aspect. Objects grow together to create a novel subject. Value is achieved through an ongoing process in nature, not a static one. Thing and entity are concepts essential to reasoning about the world.

Any set of occasions, combined into a unity, is a nexus. Nexus are macroscopic entities. A nexus with social order is a society. Nexus and societies range in degrees of complexity: Organisms, persons, cities, and ecosystems. Among nexus different levels of order emerge, with novel characteristics, greater abstraction and greater intensity. There are structured societies, like molecules, and complex structured societies, like chairs and tables; there are complex structured societies with living, regnant nexus, like organic bodies. A society is a self-sustaining environment for its members. A structured society provides a favorable environment for subordinate nexus within it. An animal body is an entirely living nexus, and "each animal body harbours a living person" (Idem, *Process and Reality* (corrected edition). New York: Free Press, 1978, p. 107), Whitehead concludes. He considers that the growth of a complex, structured society exemplifies the "general purpose pervading nature" (Ibid., p. 100).

Organism

Whitehead replaces material mechanism with the idea of "organic mechanism" (Idem, *Science in the Modern World*. New York: Free Press, 1967, p. 116), but later drops any reference to mechanism. An individual entity, whose own life history is part within the life history of some, larger, deeper, more complete pattern, is liable to have some aspects of that larger pattern dominating its own being, and to experience modifications of the larger pattern reflected in itself as modifications of its own being (Whitehead, *SMW* p. 156). The term organic suggests the doctrine of modification of parts in forming a whole.

All well-unified wholes are organic; all wholes are involved in organic wholes. The notion of part and whole is derived from extensiveness, which is the pervading generic form to which the morphological structures of the world conform (*PR* p. 287. Cf. Sheldrake). In discussing the reciprocity of part and whole, Whitehead uses the terms organism and environment. There is internal relatedness between organisms and environments. Biology is the study of larger organisms, whereas physics is the study of smaller (Ibid., p. 150). Life refers to complexes in which parts are modified according to principles derived from the whole. Organism can refer to molecules and ecosystems, or to any general sense of organic unity. Each individual organism is only a partial, however. They are like Arthur Koestler's concept of the holon, which will be used later. From above each is a whole; from below each is a part.

Whitehead discerns two meanings of organism, interconnected but intellectually separable.

- The microscopic meaning, concerned with the formal constitution of an actual occasion as a process of realizing an individual unity of experience.
- The macroscopic meaning, concerned with the giveness of the actual world as stubborn fact, which limits and provides opportunity for the actual occasion.

The macroscopic process is the transition from attained actuality to actuality in attainment, while the microscopic process is the conversion of conditions "which are merely real into determinate actuality" (Idem, *Process and Reality* (corrected) p. 326). The macroscopic transforms the actual to the merely real; the microscopic teleologically effects the change from real to actual.

Organisms are historical processes. In human experience, "we essentially arise out of our bodies which are the stubborn facts of the immediate relevant past. We are also carried on by our immediate past of personal experience" (Ibid., p. 197).

Whitehead regarded organism as a universal principle, applicable in every field of reality from metaphysics to ethics. Everything that exists has its place in the order of nature. This does not mean that reality is an organism or that everything is reduced to biological terms. It does mean that every thing resembles a living organism since its essence depends on the pattern in which they occur, and not on its components.

Process

Nature is not only organism, it is process. The activities of an organism are united into the being of the organism. Beyond being merely relations of relations, with there never being anything to relate to, organisms (for convenience in argument, actual occasions will be referred to as organisms) are pulsations of process, natural units of fact (Idem, *Modes of Thought*. New York: Macmillan, 1938, p. 120). For example, since subatomic particles are part of a field, and they are internally related within the field, they cannot exist without the field. The field, or electromagnetic society, provides the order required for producing individual actual occasions. The coming-to-be of organisms, i.e., process, is a fundamental feature of reality. The organism is what it does. The relata are entities, not just external relations between nonbeings. The process of nature is not merely rhythmic change, it is a creative advance, producing new forms everywhere. The organism undergoes a process of evolution in which it produces new forms in itself. "There is an all-embracing fact which is the advancing history of the one universe," Whitehead states (Idem, *Adventures of Ideas*. New York: Macmillan, 1933, p. 150). Although he characterizes evolution as a one of the "great generalizations of science," (Idem, The Function of Reason. (Boston: Beacon Press, 1958), p. 6.), he considers the concept overused; applied to everything, it looses its meaning.

Yet, Whitehead himself wonders why (Ibid., p. 5) when inorganic things like rock persist longer than the longest lived trees, any complex organism, with only a "faint" survival power, emerges at all. This seems to be an example of the inapplicability of the concept of adaptation to inorganic bodies. Whitehead also questions why the trend of evolution has been upwards and concludes that this trend cannot be explained by a doctrine of adaptation to the environment. In place of adaptation, he proposes the function of "Reason," (Ibid., p. 8), which directs the "attack on the environment" (Ibid., p. 8). Whitehead shares the same theme of strife as T. H. Huxley. Reason promotes the art of living with its three-fold urge: (i) to live, (ii) to live well, (iii) to live better. Reason is presented as the great counteragency to entropy (although Whitehead does not use this word specifically), the slow descent of nature "towards nothingness" (Ibid., p. 33). Embodied in humans, reason "saves the world" (Ibid., p. 34). And it civilizes the attack. Mental experience introduces novelty into nature. The urge to live is directed toward the attainment of an imaginary end. Through art, reason introduces a higher appetition. Art is the most important means for modifying the environment.

Everything has a place in the order of nature. Nature is an organism and a process. Whitehead held that there could not be empty space or time, without process. (This idea fits well with the conclusions of Pagels, Bohm and others that space is a sea of virtual particles.) Substance and activity are one; this is basic principle of Whitehead's cosmology. Process is a rejection of the idea of substance. Descartes described substance as an existent thing which required nothing other than itself to exist. Whitehead saw the independence of substance as fatal to a metaphysics of experience, where the world is an ecosystem, an intertwining of all things in a philosophy of organism. Whitehead contrasts his cosmology of process with the predominant scientific materialism. (Even his vocabulary is designed to free thought from the presumptions of scientific materialism.) His cosmology is generally consistent with the tenets of modern physics (relativity and quantum mechanics), which has also abandoned the cornerstones of materialist cosmology: Chunks of matter and absolute time.

According to David Bohm, Whitehead adopted discontinuity,

indeterminacy and indivisibility from quantum theory; discontinuity, the invisible transition between states, dispenses Newtonian motion; indeterminacy is unavoidable with prehension; indivisibility assures the world of wholeness. In fact, all parts of the universe are connected; any "local agitation shakes the whole universe" (Idem, *Modes of Thought*, p. 188), although the distant effects are minute. Whitehead's cosmology is also consonant with the important principles of ecology. Ecology recognizes that the earth is the home of all [known] beings and that these beings interpenetrate together in nature. The cosmos is encountered is significant. Perceptual knowledge is the apprehension of significance, and significance is the "relatedness of all things" (Idem, *An Enquiry Concerning the Principles of Natural Knowledge*. Cambridge: University Press, 1919, p. 12).

Throughout his works, Whitehead protests the "bifurcation" (Idem, *The Concept of Nature*. Cambridge: University Press, 1920, p. 30) of nature into two systems of reality, body and mind, which are ontologically separate. This bifurcation has been extended to humanity and nature, also. For Whitehead, humanity is a part of nature. The common attributes assigned to a Cartesian body are really internal relationships (between organisms or within nexus). He proposes only one kind of togetherness for all of nature: in the "experiences of subjects" (Idem, *Process and Reality* (corrected) p. 167). Everything is either subjective experience or subjectively experienced. There are no absolute perspectives, since any actual occasion is always a possible datum for another actual occasion.

Adventures with Ideas
Whitehead is a complex and sophisticated thinker. He abhors the bifurcation of nature by others, yet his own cosmology seems to be compounded with dualities. The bifurcation of substances becomes the bifurcation of aspects: there is that which is apprehended in awareness and that causing awareness; there are mental poles and physical poles; there is an extensive continuum that exists and is not actual; the cosmos is complete (in potential) and incomplete (advancing in organisms), and it is continuous and discontinuous, spatio-temporal and nonspatio-temporal. He recognizes that the cosmological construction is left with "the final opposites, joy and sorrow, good and evil . . . freedom and necessity, God and the World" (Ibid., p. 341).

Whitehead seems to find it necessary to divide the cosmic process into two characteristics, extensiveness and aim. Extensiveness means that the process is spread through space and goes on in time. In fact, he considers extensiveness more basic than the arbitrary factors of four dimensions or "electromagnetic laws" (Ibid., p. 91). Extensiveness is the binding of the physical world by relatedness. Pervaded by aim the cosmic process requires transcendence. New qualities are eternal objects. Eternal objects are lures for the process. They attract the process toward its realization. Thus Whitehead combines Aristotle's unmoved mover, directing the process through love, with Plato's perfect forms that exist in a perfect reality presupposing the cosmic process. Nowhere is this more apparent than when he lists the four phases wherein the universe accomplishes its actuality: (1) a conceptual origination, (2) a physical origination, (3) a perfected actuality, derived from the first two, and (4) the love of God for the World (Ibid., p. 351).

This bifurcation is also extended to communities of occasions, as objects and eternal objects. M. Grene notes that Whitehead needed recourse to the doctrine of eternal objects and considered that a radical incoherence. Whitehead postulated eternal objects as a lure for production of novelty. The eternal objects require God (everything must be someplace), as he requires them (Ibid., p. 257). God has a dual nature: as primordial, conceptual prehension of entire multiplicity of eternal objects; and as consequent, physical prehension of finite actual occasions. He grades the entire multiplicity of eternal objects for appropriateness; for instance, so that a tree remains a tree and does not become a stone (although trees petrify). The subjective aim of actual occasions is initiated in God (Ibid., p. 244). God lures the advance of actual occasions with eternal objects. God evaluates eternal objects for intensity of experience in actual occasions, but how is this seeming determinism better than the mechanical variety? How does the pre-established potentiality differ from a clockwork creator? Furthermore, if God is an actual occasion, how can he be nontemporal? And if God is nontemporal, how can he be part of the process of nature? Does the idea of God, the eternal object, exist in God the actual occasion? Is God an eternal object? God is an actual occasion, one of the complex, interdependent drops of experience. John Cobb states that "God is seen as envisaging all the eternal objects as well as all actual occasions" (in *A Christian Natural Theology*, p. 196). Whitehead's concept of God is general enough to permit many interpretations, but will not be used in a framework for cosmologies.

In Plato's *Timaeus*, the cosmic epoch is traced back to disorder, the primal chaos. Whitehead identifies this reasoning as the "evolutionary doctrine of the philosophy of organism" (*Process and Reality*, p. 95). Whitehead explains evolutionary process in terms of teleology, orienting change toward a goal. In a universe of purpose, life can be treated too easily as a means rather than an end. The role of purpose in the universe will be discussed in a following section. While organisms exhibit purposive behavior, it is unlikely that ecosystems, evolution or the universe do. He also seems to stress the conflict of organisms in living, less than the cooperation and kinship. He states that, whether for the general good or not, "life is robbery" (Ibid., p. 105). His view seems quite close to T. H. Huxley's view. The relationships of beings in an evolutionary universe will be examined in the section on evolutionary ethics. Whitehead hypothesizes no limits to the complexity of process. Yet, there may be limits, just as there are limits on the complexity of atoms and particles. Many of these matters will be discussed more fully in later sections. Whitehead does not discern any stages to the creative process of nature, like Morgan or Smuts. He argues that the characteristics of life are self-enjoyment, creative activity and aim, but the inorganic world possesses all three. This argument is not fatal to an ecological ethics, since new values and feelings emerge at different levels of societies, and it is these that need to be preserved or conserved. Internal relations occur on all levels of existence. And internal relations are constitutive of the character of nexus and actual entities. Feelings and values extend from the microscopic through the macroscopic. What is undeniable in Whitehead is that life is not separate from matter, that mind is not different from nature. Philosophical facts and scientific facts are historical. Theories rest on historical facts. Cosmologies rest in historical ideas. No one can grasp what nature is until one knows what history is.

Whitehead's properties of events may be redefined to fit with the holistic perspective being proposed.

- Events occur (in sequence or serial)
- events have aspects that define STEM field (location, energy)
- each event is associated with a net of events.
- each event involves a sorting decision (similar to Whitehead psychical assessment and decision).
- possible events are limited by conditions (momentum-energy along a geodesic in Whitehead).
- the process is probablistic under local conditions.
- groups of events may be self-organizing and self-sustaining

The basic character of Whitehead's metaphysics is aesthetic, from the actualities to the categories. The foundation of the world is found in aesthetic experience, rather than in cognitive experience, as with I. Kant. Pure feeling is as basic as pure reason. All orders are therefore aspects of aesthetic order. The essential order of experience is aesthetic. An actual fact is a fact of aesthetic experience. Even a physical theory of wave mechanics can be described in aesthetic terms as a union of repetition and contrast. Aesthetic principles apply from quantum vibrations to complex societies.

Philosophy begins in human experience. Whitehead's theory of fact is a theory of value. Value is a basic cosmological factor; there is no such thing as a valueless actual occasion. Whitehead uses the word value for intrinsic reality. However, there is also no such thing as a "bare" value; there exist only individual feelings of value.

Process philosophy is compatible with many other kinds of thought and expression. Philosophy is mystical, for mysticism is direct insight into depths as yet unspoken (*Modes of Thought*, p. 237). But the purpose of philosophy is to rationalize mysticism with verbal characterizations. Philosophy is akin to poetry, according to Whitehead. It may use poetry to point to the ineffable, silent truth. As organisms were incomplete truths, so the characteristics of the process are imperfect truths.

Ecophilosophy

Henryk Skolimowski proposes an ecological humanism to combine two concerns: ecology as a study of nature focusing on a devastated environment; humanism as a philosophy of man focusing on devastated men. Ecological humanism is only one tenet of an ecophilosophy.

Ecophilosophy is life-oriented; committed to nature, life, human values, it is spiritually alive for Skolimowski. Evolution is the spiritualization of primordial matter. Spirituality is a state of being where the world is experienced in a state of grace. Reverence, compassion and love are forms of spirituality. The quest for meaning is a spiritual quest, which is also a public quest as great civilizations knew. Ecophilosophy insists that the human project is a rediscovery of human meaning. The life process is a knowledge process. The epistemology of life is an articulation of ecophilosophy, according to Skolimowski.

Ecophilosophy aligns itself with the economics of life. Economic forces determine society, but they can be directed. Ecophilosophy exhibits political awareness: of population, diet and waste. Ecophilosophy addresses the well-being of society. Society (as a mode of being) has a life of its own. The social contract is cooperative. Society is the nexus of individual visions. Ecophilosophy vocalizes individual responsibilities. Human rights are respected, but obligations must be equally urged. It is volunteeristic, but within the constraints of natural order and understanding of the cosmos. Ecophilosophy entails health-consciousness. Humans are complex fields of force that are maintained through effort. To be healthy is to be on good terms with the cosmos. In the taoist view, also, sickness is a symptom of disharmony with the universe. Taking care of health means taking responsibility for the focus of the universe that is the self. Human values are derived from the process of the unfolding cosmos. Ecophilosophy engenders ecological consciousness. It advocates judicious use and reverence for nature. It heralds the age of stewardship. Ecophilosophy is global and comprehensive: Skolimowski represents it as a process philosophy that is integrative, hierarchical and normative. It is self-actualizing with regard to the individual and symbiotic with regard to the cosmos.

Ecophilosophy has an ecotheology: God is in process of becoming. "We are fragments of divinity in status nascendii," says Skolimowski (Ibid., p. 86). Sacredness is acquired. Divinity appears at the very end of the process of spiritualization, not at the beginning. This idea of divinity was first proposed in modern times by S. Alexander, in a slightly different form, after that of Plato.

Ecophilosophy expresses concern with wisdom. Wisdom consists in the exercise of judgment, based on qualitative criteria, in conflicting situations. Facts are judgmental. As Garrett Hardin notes, without wisdom, compassion and empathy will destroy the object of attention, not improve its circumstance. The message of ecophilosophy is that humanity can affect the elements of individual, society, spirit, ecology, and political life by affecting them all together.

Limits of an Evolution Paradigm. Skolimowski identifies a new moral order to address values. One should behave:
- to preserve unfolding of evolution
- to enhance life, as a condition of evolution
- to enhance the ecosystem
- to enhance capacities of the highest form: consciousness, creativity and compassion.
- to enhance human life.

Points two through five follow from one. But we really do not understand enough about evolution to enhance it or preserve it. So we will have to act as if we were wise, as was recommended by H. Vaihinger (in J. Salk, 1973) and A. Koestler (in *Janus: A Summing Up*, p. 4.) or J. Salk (as will be argued later in more detail). Skolimowski claims that his moral imperative accommodates other imperatives:
- Promethean transcendence

- Kantian human morals (achievement)
- Ecological preservation of habitat

In fact, the first imperative assumes that there is a point of ultimate perfection for humanity. But Promethean transcendence is too costly a mistake to continue; Roszak characterizes it as tragic. Kantian morals are too limited. of ultimate perfection for humanity. But Promethean transcendence is too costly a mistake to continue; Roszak characterizes it as tragic. Kantian morals are too limited. And ecological preservation is impossible in the strict sense.

Skolimowski claims that the universe is evolution-centered, not God-centered, man-centered or matter-centered. But the evolution he describes is nevertheless concerned with the final goal of the cosmos. He shares with Whitehead a view of a cosmic end. Rifkin notes that for the past century the theory of evolution has served as the centerpiece of the cosmological order. Concepts and nature and cosmologies are concerned with the meaning and structure of existence. Rifkin concludes that evolution was a cosmology used to explain and justify the industrial age. The hierarchy of the universe paralleled the feudal social hierarchy. The myth of plenitude can be related to the feudal social order, in which there is no room for maneuvering up or down, since all niches are filled. Evolution is used as the rationale for inventing what can be imagined and using what is invented.

Ecophilosophy assumes that humanity has the knowledge to support a stewardship of the earth. And knowledge is not limited or perhaps even centered around evolution. In keeping humanity at the top of the ladder of evolution, Skolimowski subscribes to the new anthropocentrism. He believes that the universe is as it is, in its size and age, "in order to enable life to evolve." Humans are the "crowning glory" of the universe; "it is us." "Man is of utmost importance," he says, and, "The sacredness of man is uniqueness of biological constitution" (Eco-philosophy, p. 73). There is no evidence for purpose to evolution or goals for evolution, as will be argued in more detail later. These sentiments apply to all beings more or less. Ecophilosophy is too anthropocentric. Although Anthropomorphism is a valuable tool of understanding, anthropocentrism is unjustified.

The Anthropic Principle Since the initial conditions of the universe, and even its physical laws, are not known, the deductive method cannot be used; therefore, the anthropic principle is invoked by some. The anthropic principle was introduced by R.H. Dicke in 1961 ("Dirac's Cosmology and Mach's Principle." *Nature*, 1961 192: 440), as a result of his study of Dirac's discovery of numerical relations of measures of force, time and mass. Dirac found several instances where the order of magnitude was integral power of 10^{40} (gravitational force: 10^{-40}; number of massive particles: 10^{80}; age of universe in atomic units: 10^{40}).

Dicke thought that a causal connection might be founded on Mach's principle. Mach had proposed that the inertial mass of a particle was determined by its gravitational interaction with distant matter. According to this principle, the weakness of gravity is related to the enormous amount of distant matter, and the whole determines the parts.

The size, homogeneity and age of the universe all exist to support life. The big bang theoretically had arbitrary, small-scale perturbations that developed into homogeneities and galaxies. Galaxies would not have arisen if the recessional velocity of matter were not equal to escape velocity. Collins and Hawking concluded that galaxies are necessary for life. Dyson distinguishes the following states bearing on organic evolution: The sheer size of the universe is such that the fall-in time prolongs the life of universe to hundreds of billions of years; The energy output of the sun, and revolution of planets create special environments for life; there are all kinds of critical sizes: galaxy, sun, earth, ecosystem, primate brain, and human (*Disturbing the Universe*).

The earth is suitable for life because:
- solar radiation has stayed within certain limits for 4 billion years
- the biogeochemical cycles of oxygen, carbon, nitrogen, phosphorus, sulfur, water have stayed within certain limits
- the environment has been constant enough for organic evolution, but variable enough for natural selection to be challenged.

Dicke sees that man has appeared at a "privileged moment," that certain conditions are necessary for human existence, and invokes the anthropic principle, that humans are necessary for the prehuman stages to exist. This anthropic principle implies the existence of a divine plan. This argument entails a misunderstanding of necessity and existence. Although the current conditions are necessary, it is not necessary that they had to occur. That humanity exists on earth shows only that they did occur, not that they had to occur. If humanity did not exist then the universe would probably be much the same. There are plenty of sentient species on earth. This problem will be addressed in more detail in the section on Gaia.

Biotechnology & Time

Jeremy Rifkin proffers a cosmology to supercede the evolution-centered cosmologies of others (in *Algeny*). He observes that humanity is moving from the age of Pyrotechnology to the age of Biotechnology, from a world forged in fire to one combined in the test tube (But then everything is translated from fire in a way. The etymological derivation of the word green comes from the Greek word meaning to burn, heat, melt, or shine, derived from the Sanskrit, *ghar*). The industrial age depends on fossil fuels, a burning of the past. This amounts to a stealing from the future. Rifkin states that with fire, man melts down the inanimate world and reshapes it to a world of pure utilities. The metaphor for the age of Pyrotechnology is alchemy. The philosophical metaphor for Biotechnology will be algeny. Alchemy may be derived from the Arabic, meaning perfection. But algeny is a bastard composite of Arabic and Greek roots. Alchemy clings to notion of transforming and perfecting nature by imitative procedures. Apparently, the algenist also views the living world as potential, an arena where organisms seek to complete themselves.

Algeny is concerned with engineering living forms. This bioengineering is an attempt to speed up the conversion of living matter into economic utilities for economic growth. Rifkin lists three stages in the unfolding of the Age of biotechnology: Genetic engineering; understanding the cybernetic relation of gene, cell, organism and environment; and engineering the entire ecosystems. Each step requires an increase in human responsibility. In Darwinian evolution humans competed for self and family and tribe; in biotechnology, for all life. Perhaps the responsibility should be trimmed to not interfering in what we cannot guarantee control of.

From Evolution to Information. The Newtonian model of nature as the movement of particles by force is replaced with the informational model as the storage and transmission of information in a system. In ecophilosophy, evolution was the reason for cosmology. In algeny it is information.

The processes of life are directed by programs, original and self-programmed. Life is no longer the Darwinian aggregate of parts assembled into wholes, but a code printed into a computer. P. Grasse (Ibid) states that information forms and animates the living organism. Evolution is a process by which information is acquired and modified. Rifkin characterizes the new temporal theory as seeing organisms as adapting or failing to adapt to changing temporalities. Darwin's theory was spatially conceived, with temporal overtones. The new theory is almost exclusively temporal.

Truncated Cosmology. Rifkin himself has a limited view of cosmologies; he considers that they all share the same themes, that of mirroring the daily activity of civilization and that of elevating human behavior to cosmic importance. Cosmologies make the strange environment familiar. They bring universe in line with local world. They were more effective when shrouded in myth and discovered, not consciously created. Now, their creation is conscious. He groups all cosmologies as part of a campaign to inflate the human species at a cost to other species. But many archaic cosmologies are a form of fitness and limitation. Most try for adaptation before domination (cf. Reichel-Doklmatoff). He states that cosmologies are a way of hiding the unimaginable: voids, gaps, size; they relieve apprehension. They make the world manageable by limiting it. They make the world comfortable and small. Rifkin claims that humanity inflates its daily activity into principles of nature and that this is a rationalization to legitimize social and political activities, yet forgo responsibilities.

Rifkin further states that cosmologies are a repudiation of nature, not a representation of it. They are expressions of the desire to negate everything alive. They do try to control and explain, but not always kill; what about those that give life to rocks? He thinks that morality supports the cosmology; good and evil are descriptions of following the natural order. But morality is simply a set of rules for living together. If living togetherness is extended to all beings, then morality is extended and not contradictory to nature or supportive of an ugly cosmology.

Rifkin noted that nature was conceptualized to conform with four basic psychological needs; the needs for immortality, self-containment, dissociation of identity with nature, and justification of behavior. Ironically, Malinowski considered only physiological needs in his discussion of cosmology. As has been discussed, cosmologies do far more than justify human needs.

Desacralization. Both pyrotechnology and biotechnology desacralize nature. Nature is separated into two categories: things outside of human control and things within it. The former category is treated as sacred. That which cannot be anticipated and manipulated becomes and remains sacred. And this attitude is just the opposite of that of archaic cosmologies, where the known is the sacred. Sometime since the advent of the modern era, the concept of the sacred has been reversed. In the archaic view, the familiar was sacred. When modern cosmologies made the familiar trivial, it became profane. The quality of sacredness was given to the unknown, wilderness, or the lives of children (but not adults). Modern cultures show reverence toward that which cannot be dominated. So reverence for nature diminishes as control escalates, in the industrial cosmologies. The familiar needs to be resacralized and the unknown allowed to remain sacred.

Desacralization is the severance of empathetic association, a renunciation of indebtedness toward nature. There is no acknowledgment of the suffering and destruction inflicted on beings by humanity. Lorca acknowledges it (*News of the Universe*, pp. 110-111).

> Beneath all the statistics
> there is a drop of duck's blood.
> Beneath all the columns
> there is a drop of sailor's blood.
> Beneath all the totals, a river of warm blood;
> a river that goes singing
> past the bedrooms of the suburbs,
> and the river is silver, cement, or wind
> in the lying daybreak of New York
> The mountains exist, I know that . . .
> The ducks and the pigeons
> and the hogs and the lambs
> lay their drops of blood down
> underneath all the statistics;
> and the terrible bawling of the packed-in cattle
> fills the valley with suffering
> where the Hudson is getting drunk on its oil.
> I attack all those persons
> who know nothing of the other half,
> the half who cannot be saved,
> who raise the cement mountains
> in which the hearts of the small
> animals no one thinks of are beating,
> and from which we will all fall
> during the final holiday of the drills.
> I spit in your face . . .
> And you are earth, swimming through the figures of the office.
> What shall I do, set my landscape in order?

Rifkin notes that cosmologies read like an accountant's credit and debit sheet; as more of nature is brought under control things are moved from the sacred column to the profane. Desacralization allows more complete control. It deadens things and silences the voices of existence. It drains the prey of aliveness to make it palatable. It denies fundamental likeness and relationships.

Information is no more appropriate than evolution for the basis of a cosmology. The use of information continues the tradition of gross quantification. [awre Add Goldsmith on information here] Information eliminates the idea of fixed individuals and species. But information can be used to justify saving individuals and species, since that information is unique.

The Prefailure of Biotechnology. Rifkin is right about biotechnology: It may have much to offer, but the costs have not been calculated. As a cosmology, it shares the problems of all goal-directed cosmologies: There is a value vacuum between goals; time is the essence; space is an obstacle; and relationships are ignored.

Rifkin points out that Darwin was influenced by the ideas of his culture; evolution arose right after capitalism. He exaggerates in saying that Darwin dressed up nature with an English personality and form of government. Bertrand Russell did point out that the theory was an extension of laissez-faire economics to the living world, suggested by Malthus' theory of population. The cosmology of biotechnology is still economic in a primitive sense. Only the myths have changed to include greater manipulation. It is still concerned with utility, growth and efficiency, as short-term goals. The problem with efficiency is that it is defined within such narrow limits. True efficiency means continuity over long periods of time, as with natural processes. Long-term exchanges in nature are not efficient in the industrial sense. The large sense of economics is the measurement of nature. All cosmologies have some economic impact.

Evolution Bungled. Rifkin describes evolution as Social Darwinism only, then posits the new evolution in terms of information. If evolution is the accumulation of information, then the scientist advances the development of life on earth. But this would be true only on a static earth. The fate of all individuals is to die, of all species to be extinct. Where then is the advance? Thinking that each species is better informed than previous species, Rifkin thinks that this justifies the search for knowledge in man. Limits are then unnatural. Knowledge is considered information. Understanding is ignored. This argument is wrong. The psychological need for mystery is ignored.

Is it information or feeling that animates? What information is being transferred in experiments on the pleasure centers in primates? Each species would be better informed only if the environment were constant. It is not. Therefore each species cannot be better informed. A living organism is not seen as a permanent form, but a network of activity continually informing) this is different from Whitehead's perspective, where the form is permanent, part of the process). Rifkin mentions that Prigogine views evolution as a tendency of living systems to advance to increased complexity of organization. The interactions of organisms, especially predator/prey may require more complexity for survival. But organisms only adjust to their environment, not to goals of complexity. Sharks do not need to be more complex. Rifkin sees evolution as a movement striving to complete itself. But it is complete. It strives only to produce feeling, experience of beings.

Time is made the dominant factor in Rifkin's characterization of the new evolution. He gives time greater independence from space, supporting his view with out-of-context ideas from ecology, physics and process philosophy. (The ideas of Whitehead support the opposite.) The fragmentation of time has little advantage over that of space or energy. The concepts of space/time/energy/mass are related in an indivisible field. Without space, there is no time; without energy, no space. One group of evolutionists has shown that separation in space is as effective as separation in time for change.

Structure does not determine function; the two mutually arise. Rifkin concludes that a bird is a bundle of temporal programs. The temporal theory introduces mind into all things, woven from a larger pattern of mind. This concept of mind will be addressed later. Mind pulsates with purpose and intention, but evolution does not. Rifkin thinks the idea of nature as mind is indistinguishable from nature as fields. This difference will be discussed later, also.

Ecological Cosmologies
Ecological Resistance
John Rodman distinguishes four perspectives in ecology:
- Resource conservation, which in America has been an aspect of resource development. Wilderness is regarded as a kind of land use where a scarce resource is conserved by being managed.
- The Nature Moralist's perspective that grows out of the humane movement and radical animal liberation. Their notion of human virtue is justice; the right of all animals to exist.
- Wilderness preservation by any means. The problem with the California condor, for example, which has been proposed to be bred in captivity, is that the species is thought to be abstracted

from a complex habitat. But most species cannot be abstracted.

- A fourth world of perception and action Rodman calls Ecological Resistance.

Ecological Resistance is action that precedes theory; a central principle is that diversity is good. Other principles are: The struggle between monoculture and diversity, as exemplified by J.S. Mill, who defended biological diversity against threat of humanized planet, W. Indian blacks against European racists, women against patriarchy, and the multifaceted personality against totalitarian technology; different levels of experience, from cosmos through polis and psyche mirror one another (the hermetic tradition again); relationship between levels of experience is of a metaphoric mirroring, not superstructure or base or cause and effect (the ecosystem could be considered a base model perceived as common gestalt). Ecological Resistance also involves a ritual affirmation of the myth of microcosm; acts are not undertaken in a spirit of calculated self-interest (of individual, society or species), or of moral duty, or to prevent profanation, but because a threat to the biosphere is a threat to the self.

Of the four perspectives: Resource Conservation has no justification for speciesism, because it is an economic treatment with a short time scale, limited to humans. Wilderness preservation links primordial experience or an encounter with the holy to a transient aesthetic; it is an aesthetic view. Nature Moralism imposes a species-specific morality of rights and duties.

But, Ecological Resistance is unclear about the balance of nature. It offers a participatory image of humanity, as an integral part of food chain, an organic cycle of birth and death, and a microcosm. Prudence, justice and reverence are part of the good life; integrity includes them. Jantsch endorses Rodman's ecological resistance, as going beyond precaution, reverence and morality. But resistance is a limited stance.

Human nature does not find meaning in an absurd world, but discovers its structure through interaction with the ambihuman order. Human identity exists partly in relation to nature; the destruction of one involves the other. An act of ecological resistance is an affirmation of the integrity of the naturally diverse self and world. The meaning of such an act is not exhausted by success or failure in linear sequence of events. One is aligned with the ultimate order of things by ritual action. Rodman's ideas of right action—the concept has its roots in Buddhism— are appropriate for a holocosmology, and can contribute to it, but as a cosmology, it is not holistic enough.

Deep Ecology & Ecosophy

When Arne Naess presented his deep ecology alternative in 1972, he contrasted it with the shallow ecology movement, which he characterized as fighting against resource depletion and pollution—the objective of the shallow form was the health and affluence of people in developed countries, more than the health and richness of life in the planet. Deep ecology takes its inspiration from the science of ecology. Deep ecology is inspired and fortified by ecological knowledge derived from experience, rather than logic. Its tenets are normative. Its value system is only partly based on scientific research. As a science, ecology describes the interrelationships of organisms and environments, that is, the experience of living together in the biosphere. Ecology is not a reductive discipline and is not readily amenable to complete quantification. Even scientific ecology is an integrative discipline that extends beyond the boundaries of science. Ecology can be considered an amphibious discipline, with the authority of science and the force of moral knowledge. Studied through its components and relationships, ecology is a way of seeing, a perspective of the human situation in its interconnection. It is a 'subversive' subject, in Paul Shepherd's words, normative and sensible, offering what Theodore Roszak calls a 'sacramental' vision of nature.

The technological paradigm of the shallow form has reached its limits. Data and information developed by hard studies have undercut the paradigms that guided their investigation. When a paradigm shifts, perceptions change, as in the understanding of a metaphor. Deep ecology forms part of a new metaphor that is more appropriate to the unity and interrelatedness of the earth; and it may be more personally fulfilling as well.

Deep ecology is a movement that goes beyond a concern with pollution and resource use to consider humanity in a relational, total-field image. The movement promotes human equality, conservation, and local autonomy. In principle, it proposes a biospherical egalitarianism, the equal right of all beings to live in place without undue interference. It adds a normative dimension to ecology in a philosophical framework of 'ecosophy,' literally the wisdom of the house. Naess characterized deep ecology in his article thus:

- Relational total-field image (knots in a field of intrinsic relations)
- Biospherical egalitarianism (key words: respect, understanding, right to live and blossom, space and crowding)
- Principles of diversity and symbiosis (where diversity means live and let live rather than either/or, and symbiosis means

coexistence)
- Anti-class posture (key words: exploitation)
- Fight against resource pollution and resource depletion (ecologists as informants)
- Complexity, not complication (there is multiplicity and lawful factors; and division of labor, not fragmentation)
- Local autonomy and decentralization (to strengthen local regions and encourage self-sufficiency).

The platform of deep ecology addresses the well being and flourishing of human and nonhuman (the intrinsic value) of life, as well as the richness and diversity of living forms. The platform of deep ecology developed over several decades and has been presented in numerous publications. The platform has eight planks:

1. The well-being and flourishing of human and nonhuman life; all beings have value in themselves (synonyms: intrinsic value, inherent value). These values are independent of the usefulness of the nonhuman world for human purposes. Life includes individuals, species, populations, habitats, and all human and nonhuman cultures. Deep concern and respect for cultures. Ecological processes should remain intact.

2. Richness and diversity of life forms contribute to the realization of these values and are also values in themselves. This considers that ecologically, complexity and symbiosis are conditions for maximizing diversity. Simple species contribute to richness and diversity of life. The history of life presupposes an increase of diversity and richness.

3. Humans have no right to reduce this richness and diversity except to satisfy vital needs. Vital need is left vague to due requirements of different cultures in their locations.

4. The flourishing of human life and cultures is compatible with a substantial decrease of the human population. The flourishing of nonhuman life requires such a decrease. Richest countries are not expected to reduce their "excessive interference" with nonhuman world overnight. Stabilization and reduction may take time but is extremely serious.

5. Present human interference with the nonhuman world is excessive, and the situation is rapidly worsening. The slogan of "noninterference" does not mean not exploiting species for human use. Wilderness areas should be expanded.

6. Policies must therefore be changed. These policies affect basic economic, technological, and ideological structures. The resulting state of affairs will be deeply different from the present. Continued economic

growth is incompatible with principles 1-5. Current growth is not sustainable. Things are valued in the current economic system because they are scarce or have a commodity value. Waste and consumption become sources of prestige. The implementation of deep changes requires global action as well as local. Government interference, especially developed world, accomplishes nothing. Appropriate technology can advance cultural diversity and independence.

7. The ideological change is mainly that of appreciating life quality (dwelling in situations of inherent value) rather than adhering to an increasingly higher standard of living. There will be a profound awareness of the difference between big and great. Quality of life is considered vague because it is nonquantitative. It cannot be quantified, but there is no need to do so.

8. Those who subscribe to the foregoing points have an obligation directly or indirectly to try to implement the necessary changes. There is room for different opinions about priorities, however.

Policies must be changed to reduce economic growth and to appreciate 'life quality,' which cannot and need not be quantified—this implies that we personally have an obligation to try to implement necessary changes. The platform addresses not only ethical concerns, but scientific, cosmological, economic, and political ones as well. The platform differentiates deep ecology as a perspective from the world view of industrial culture (Figure 8).

Deep ecology emphasizes biological equality. When Charles Elton transformed the "Great Chain of Being" into a chain of eating, ecologists realized that the bottom link of the food chain, plants, was the most important. Humanity is part of the food chain, although it appropriates a large amount of the productivity of most ecosystems. The exploitative competition of humans in ecosystems is an important part of biogeochemical cycles. Humanity cannot unparticipate by choice. Deep ecology argues for diversity. In nature, variety emerges spontaneously, as the capacities of species are sorted by the environment. Variety provides flexibility in systems. The diminution of variety through human interference may debase the wholeness and stability of systems. Furthermore, aesthetic, ethical, and utilitarian reasons all support the efforts to conserve the diversity of nature.

Deep Ecology Cosmology	Modern Industrial Cosmology
Nature has intrinsic worth	Nature is a human resource
Harmony with nature	Pan-dominance of nature
Population fit to nature	Unrestricted growth
Limits to use of resources	Unlimited resources/substitution
Appropriate technology	One-way progressive technology
Intelligent frugality	Unrestrained consumption
Homeorhetic economy	Unsustainable economic growth
Local/regional control	Global management
Cooperative relations	Competitive, destructive relations
Spiritual/material goals	Material goals

Figure 8. *Contrast of Industrial and Deep views.*

Deep ecology incorporates a broader scientific method that might be called patient practice. There are ways of dealing with the earth that are not scientific or technical; they are aesthetic or ethical. These alternatives are not incompatible with traditional science. Where the methodology of traditional science is limited and wasteful, promoting technologies that ignore or destroy values with blind quantification, the methods of deep ecology are traditional and conservative.

Deep ecology, more than just a popular movement, is based on a formal philosophy that differs dramatically from the silent (also turgid, limited, destructive) philosophy that underlies, like a procrustean bed, the actions of science and technology so adored and embraced by industrial models.

Naess offers the specific term ecosophy to describe the theoretical basis of the deep ecology movement. Ecosophy is a philosophy of ecological harmony. Naess defines it as a "personal code of values and view of the world," which guides one's decisions and grounds the acceptance of the principles of deep ecology.

An ecosophy contains both norms (value judgments) and hypotheses. It is like an Aristotelian or Spinozan system, that is, a set of verbal expressions with a variety of descriptive and prescriptive functions, than a general systems theory or formal philosophy. The format of an ecosophy is based on Spinozan philosophy, although Naess finds Spinoza too complex to serve as a patron saint of ecology, and urges that the movement uses him as a source of inspiration. Adherence to Spinoza's system is consistent with a karma-yoga, a person externally active on all levels of existence, according to Naess.

Because of its normative and personal aspects, the philosophy only occurs in individual instances; Naess's own version of ecosophy is referred to by him as Ecosophy T (See Figure 9 for part of the expression of Ecosophy T. Note that the Norms [N] are exclamations and the Hypotheses [H] are declaratives; from his book Ecology, Community and Lifestyle). Because an ecosophy is a 'total view' (intuitive and coherent), it cannot be separated into its components, e.g., epistemology, ontology, ethics, aesthetics, or political philosophy. There are no incorrect total views, which is one reason why Naess does not reject radical ecology, ecofeminism or other ecological philosophies.

H6: Life resources of the earth are limited

H7: Symbiosis maximizes Self-realization potentials under conditions of limited resources

N5: Symbiosis!

...

H1: The higher the self-realisation attained by anyone, the broader and deeper the identification with others.

...

H3: Complete Self-realisation of anyone depends on that of all.

N2: Self-realisation for all beings!

N1: Self-realisation!

Figure 9. *Excerpts from Naess' Ecosophy T.*

This kind of set of expressions can be used in numerous arguments about behavior in various situations, from strategies for protest to restoration policies. As a philosophy, ecosophy asks different kinds of questions from traditional philosophy. Traditional philosophy asks how conservation can be deconstructed, or under what conditions a pre-emptive nuclear strike is ethical, or whether a tree falling in the forest makes a sound. By contrast, ecosophy asks how things fit together, what actions would reverse the catastrophic destruction of species and habitats, what kinds of technology are appropriate for local conditions and traditions, or how the vital needs of the human population can be satisfied indefinitely, without unnecessary destruction or conversion of ecosystems.

As a philosophy, ecosophy investigates the normative aspects of living together, that is, ethics, and the maintenance of the affairs of communities, that is, economics and politics. As a noetic discipline, deep ecology provides information on the state of nature, recognizing that human beings are participants in nature, as well as participants in human societies.

Despite its reasonableness and openness, deep ecology (and ecosophy) has been attacked from different perspectives. In asking how deep is deep ecology, George Bradford, and later Ariel Salleh and other, criticize the failure of deep ecology to critique political systems, such as democracy, and to emphasize gender differences. Specifically, they and others criticize deep ecology for (with responses in parentheses):

- Failure to extend the concept of interrelatedness to technology; global capitalism is taken for granted (a number of deep ecologists, such as Rothenberg and Fox, have addressed interrelatedness and technology)
- Failure to understand that egalitarianism is a projection of human sociopolitical categories (deep ecology understands that all words and symbols are human artifacts)
- The concept of wilderness as devoid of human presence is an ethnocentric concept (although a few argue that all wilderness should be nonhuman, most suggest numerous gradations of human presence—personally, I believe that humanity should not be present in every wild ecosystem; possibly 35% of the land area had little or no human presence for millennia)
- Failure to consider humans as animals in wilderness/human distinction (being based in ecology means that humans are animals first then cultural beings)
- Blind acceptance of the premise that there are too many people, e.g., hunger is the problem of maldevelopment and requires social transformation—there are adequate resources (there are problems of social maldevelopment, over-consumption, and overpopulation—the last can be supported by research in psychology as well as carrying capacity and ecosystem productivity)
- Socioeconomic naiveté, that transformation will be benign and politically independent; problems of production are simply from unequal distribution of property (transformation may be violent, but not likely more violent than that caused by current inequities and unbalance)
- Scientific naiveté, that the systems approach can balance society; yet Elkins argues that the systems approach can be appropriated for technocratic management as well (a dynamic balance is the

goal, and a systems approach is only one tool)
- Failure to see the historical domination of nature by man and of women by man; Salleh states Naess's anti-class posture is only superficial (yet this domination of both was one of the starting points of deep ecology)
- The "artificial" limitation of human populations is rationalist and technist and contradicts the life-affirming value of woman as bearer of life (Naess rejects the separation of rational from emotional; both are in gestalt. Men are also bearers of life; furthermore, how many children should a woman bear before becoming only a breeder? What of those women who nurture life without bearing children?)
- The anthropocentric critique ignores androcentrism and gender difference; women would lose their identity in an ecological self (the individual self is required for self-realization; male selves would not have any priority)
- Deep ecology has an anti-feminist bias, as in patriarchy and capitalism (I have never found a quoted source to have actually shown this bias, but it may exist in some writings)
- Its bad name; people have (rightly) pointed out that deep ecology could refer to the feeding patterns of deep-sea fish (deep ecology seemed to have caught on while radical ecology, ecological resistance, ecophilosophy, sacramental ecology, and others seem to have not).

There is no doubt that deep ecology can be improved. It must be consistent with a stereoscopic vision of science, feminist insights, and comprehensive values. Many of the criticisms of deep ecology, however, are based on an Aristotelian logic, that is, a bipolar logic that contrasts shallow/deep, feminine/masculine, or progress/stasis, for example. Deep ecology itself uses a complementary logic, so many of the criticisms may not apply. Other criticisms result from misunderstandings. As a movement deep ecology embraces a wide variety of people, with many visions and ideas. Perhaps some of them do not realize that nature is a social construct, or that there is inequality. Perhaps some are more extreme than others. Theorists have a tendency to distill and synthesize their own philosophies that are contradictory and limited. Naess has offered deep ecology as a generous framework of thought. Like systems theory, by incorporating too much, deep ecology may be too yielding and accepting.

For Deep Ecology as an ecological cosmology, what specific changes would occur in a framework for the human use of other species in self-organizing ecosystems? Deep ecology offers a different way of viewing reality, the possibility of a new cosmology, with a new value system and new logic. These would lead to the following actions: Recognition of individuality in trees and other beings; recognition of the feelings and emotions of animals and the sensitivity of plants; promotion of a noncommodity, ecocentric approach to science; minimization of the devastation of wild forests and wild ecosystems; and, emphasis on habitat loss as a human ethical issue.

Furthermore, in the near and far future, deep ecology could contribute to an ecological approach by: Suggesting ways that biosphere cultures (where resources from everywhere are moved around) can be converted to ecosystem cultures (after Ray Dasmann), characterized by wonder and wildness; promoting ecosystem lifestyles, characterized by frugality and joy; relating the success of microorganisms to ultimate success of living is self-sustaining ecosystems (education); linking ecological sustainability with the richness and diversity of ecosystems and with human pleasure; working for immediate solutions to inequity and destruction under worsening and thankless conditions; educating with confidence and energy for ecological enlightenment over the long-term, despite short-term discouragement and wobble; and, learning to gamble wisely with an uncertain planet. Deep ecology emphasizes a deep relationship with place.

Deep ecology did not spring fully formed from Arne Naess's head, like Athena from Zeus. To some extent it is the most recent flowering of a line of thought that extends from J. W. von Goethe and G. P. Marsh to Maurice Merleau-Ponty, Rachel Carson, Paul Shepard, and Gary Snyder. Merleau-Ponty grounded philosophy generally in the human bodily dimension. The body is the basis for metaphysics, an access to being as well as an expression of it. Philosophy (or ecosophy) is tied to a comprehensive anthropology—everything perceived and expressed is anthropocentric and anthropomorphic. All philosophy becomes human first. Ecosophy can expand the narrow anthropocentric evaluation and see things from the perspective of the whole. Arne Naess offers a biospherical egalitarianism, where all beings have an equal right to life and fulfillment, but without denying necessary human exploitation. Total egalitarianism is impractical, even for Jainists. But ecological egalitarianism considers the beings of different species in context. Complex beings may be more valuable on a one-to-one basis, but have less value on a regional basis.

Anthropomorphism is a necessary human way of knowing; all

knowing is based on it. But the knowledge is not limited to just human experience. Anthropocentrism is the natural centering of human experience. But humans are not the only centers of experience. Anthropometric behavior is the statement that humans are the measure of all things. But humans are not the value of all things. Not everything can be measured. But everything can be put together in a metaphorical language. Metaphor permits language to carry beyond direct reference, to extend meaning. The word 'logic' means putting together. Anthropology is the putting together of diverse human worlds embedded in unique places.

All three concepts dealing with shape, center, and measure are needed for human knowledge. By rejecting anthropomorphism, the experience of others is restricted, and the scope of self-knowledge is reduced. Narrowness of experience is a source of human insecurity. By rejecting humanity as its own center, the experience of selfness is suppressed. The self is the basis for exploration and success. By rejecting measure, perspective is lost. And if humans claim all value for themselves, the term is meaningless. Deep ecology includes the full spectrum of human knowledge and interaction with all. The proper study of humanity is all beings.

Humanity is embedded in an ecological world. Ecosophy attempts to preserve the balance of humanity with other diverse species. Balance is an ecological value, as is flexibility and richness. Placing humanity at the center of the universe makes a cosmology unsustainable. The modern industrial cosmology that dominates most human cultures is creating flatscapes, 'no places.' And that is the true meaning of utopia, no place. With changes in consciousness, with understanding of the ecological relationships of human cultures to wild habitats, and the moral relationships of all beings, real eutopias, good places, can be created. It is the role of ecosophy and other synthetic disciplines to encourage these changes.

Holocosmology

Four evolutionary stages in the history of cosmology can be distinguished: Mythical, Rational, Mechanical, and Ecological. Each stage is characterized by a different set of ideals, morals and tenets.

1. In the mythical stage, the relationship of humans to nature is one of kinship or affinity. All beings fall within moral consideration, except for profane areas and other tribes. (Fox calls this symbiotic.)

2. Rational humans analyze and deduct the operation of nature, but only regard other humans morally, in general. Sometimes moral consideration may be extended beyond all of humanity to other conscious or living beings. Kinship is not a cosmic relationship, but hierarchical and human. Rituals become stylized.

3. Mechanical men try to explain and dominate external processes. Time is linear, and nature is demythologized. Each individual is responsible for moral standards, sometimes leading to self-righteous anarchy.

4. The ecological interacts with nature much like the mythic, but understands the rational and mechanical sides. All things are treated morally, in an 'I-Thou' relationship (M. Buber, *I and Thou*). The human place in nature is not diminished or glorified. (Fox calls this stage spiritual.)

This fourth stage does not reject or judge the other stages, but incorporates practicality and paradox. It makes no distinctions between right and wrong or good and bad; these polarities are more like positive stimuli useful to evolution. Hence, there is no evil, as considered in the previous three stages. Only an evil that results from lack of wisdom.

Many of the cosmologies examined thus far basically belong in the first three stages. Even ecological resistance is not ecological enough to describe human participation in the balance of nature. Process and ecological philosophies take an anthropocentric view of humanity as an endpoint to evolution, as with Teilhard's one consciousness on earth, the Omega Point. The view of a holocosmology is the opposite, if anything. It considers living beings the results of evolution, whose only goal is experience or living-time. Relationships are personal and spiritual. Rene Dubos notes that Julian Huxley, in reformulating Origen's thoughts on man being a second world in miniature, offers two complementary attitudes toward earth: the fact that man incorporates part of universe into being provides a scientific basis for feelings of reverence toward the earth (toward the extended self, in his book, *A God Within*, p. 40). But the fact that man can act on the earth makes him behave as a master and alien. A holocosmology could reconcile these attitudes.

The present ecological crisis is a consequence of the rational, mechanistic world view. Problems are more than matters of policy or management; war, injustice and environmental destruction spring from a common sickness. The problem is cosmological. The issue is not conservation against exploitation, but an experience of the natural world distinct from these two alternatives. An experience that reconciles the antinomies of exploitation and preservation, self and other, human and natural. A sense participatory rather than manipulative, a sense of the world as presence rather than object; a universe moving in vast cycles and rhythmic harmony instead of serial stages of beginning, progression, decay, and end. This cosmos is being rediscovered; its tools are dance and song, and history; it is open to nonvisual communication. Everything is vital. The consequences of this cosmology would alter the character of modern life; make it closer to human and ecological reality, counteracting the tragic consequences of war against ourselves and nature.

A cosmology rarely meshes perfectly with the natural order or the social order. The ambihuman order of nature could exist without humanity. In a sense it is indifferent. Cosmology arises out of the needs of humans. That cosmology includes so much—science, mythology, theology—makes its fitness less. To the degree that it is effective, any of the ideologies mentioned will fit the order of nature; science may manipulate invisible particles; technology may mold metals; beliefs in theology may save human or ambihuman lives. But the total mix of ideologies makes the overall fit very sloppy. As long as nature can be dominated, without catastrophe, the importance of the fit is not critical. But we do not know enough of nature to know when catastrophes occur, nor how to avoid them or minimize them.

All peoples want some power over the natural order for their security. Archaic peoples rely on ritual acts instead of machinery. But as technology supplies power to archaic peoples, rituals decline. Exploitation can become pathological. The intrinsic worth of beings can become supplanted by monetary value. For example, some North American Indians were seduced into the fur trade by the lure of manufactured materials. The spread of power has two other effects. The natural order becomes simplified; the human world becomes increasingly complex. And both orders become unstable.

Unfortunately, the language from a mechanical world view dominates even ecologists and politicians. This world view impoverishes humans by claiming all consciousness for humanity. It claims that nature offers no joy, or love, or peace, or certitude. Emphasis on the evil of nature creates a gap between humans and their universe. In contemporary cosmology, there is no room for the intrinsic worth of nature. But science undermines the scientific cosmology and provides the elements of its alternative: wholeness and relatedness.

Man is still the measure of things in economics. Yet, cosmology needs to be liberated from economics. Cosmological ideas are needed to fit humans into the scheme of things. This is a local-global problem, which occurs everywhere throughout the discussion. Although all affects all, those things farther away (nonlocal) cannot have as much influence. Consider a hologram from the view of one very local patch. Although the whole picture can be reconstructed from that part, it will have very poor resolution, because all of the parts are needed to give better resolution. All the parts are made equal by the laser light source (cf. Holography).

A world view is more than skeleton of theory, it is a view of the relation of the human mind-heart-will to universal factors. Powerful cosmological ideas can influence many cultures over centuries. The principle of plenitude, restated in Christian terms, says that an intelligible creator gave an earth of unlimited bounty to humanity for their use. This principle was confirmed in the Renaissance with the discovery of the richness of heaven, of microscopic life, and unexplored continents. Many modern political ideologies and economics have been shaped by the principle of endless wealth. Adam Smith calculated that the real price of anything was just the toil acquiring it. Inequality in a world of abundance could only exist through human suppression and exploitation of other humans. The invalidity of this principle came with the recognition of limits.

Ultimately, a model of the world—world-view or ideology—implicitly or explicitly guides the processes of social change. The basis of an ecological world view can be found in history, in the experiences of diverse cultures, and created intentionally by defining new values.

Alas, most cosmologies fail, eventually, as all finite, human efforts fail. No descriptions in a cosmology can be expected to be good indefinitely. Deductive conclusions about natural events will be true longer if the events are convergent, but where they are divergent, as with evolution, their accuracy will be short-lived. The special cosmologies of many philosophers are myopic, inconsistent, inadequate, vague, and final. The limitations of a special topic are acceptable in science. A cosmology, however, cannot confine itself to one science or perspective, explaining away everything that does not fit. It expresses the general nature of the world as disclosed to human beings. It must find the most general interpretive system. But it is not a conglomerate of sciences, either. It generalizes beyond any one science.

A holocosmology cannot be limited by the scientific facts of any science, even ecology. The insights of mystics and the wise should be included. Individual world views penetrate each other in a transepistemological process. Each mystic or scientist tells of a way the world is; together, these ways make a holocosmology. It is a framework for all truths. It takes into account the established institutions constituting human society. "It is only in this way that we can appeal to the widespread effective elements in the experience of mankind," states Whitehead (in *The Function of Reason*, p. 85). Further, a cosmology must give multiple descriptions of processes.

Since the origins of the environmental crises are in human traditions, it should be possible to select—and create a new cosmology—from what is valuable in the traditions. If the world becomes as humans imagine it, then a larger frame will make a larger world. A global holocosmology is necessary for a framework of local world-views on earth. Most cosmologies are circumscribed; their views of the whole are of low resolution. A holocosmological framework would provide a higher resolution image of the whole, since it incorporates all human cosmologies. It includes its predecessors, recognizing a scope of validity, that each says something important and true.

Cosmologies once justified the limits of humans in nature. A new holocosmology would justify wide diversity in nature; accommodation to natural laws. It could even allow a deeper understanding of utilitarian. For example, what is the use—or the beauty—of a burned forest, as related to the function of lightening or the planetary carbon cycle? The whole idea of irreversible history sanctifies behavior, making it moral. If a life or species cannot be repeated, then it is special. A holocosmology shows the relationships and our debt to other species. If we continue to consider only ourselves, and inflate ourselves out of proportion, then we diminish other species and ultimately ourselves. Responsibility considers the interests of ambihuman nature. The rightness of human behavior is all they need in terms of special rights. The interests of other beings is the same as for human: to live and experience, to reproduce that similar beings may do so. A new cosmology must recognize the value of total biosphere; respect for all forms of life, present and future; provide equal opportunity for human beings.

When cosmologies and human societies were small, the amount of control and security required was small. Although societies have grown, human security has not. It should be easy to give up control that we never had; giving up trying may be more difficult. A holocosmology can show that we need to fashion our behavior to the cosmos, not the reverse. Since complete security is impossible, since complete power is impossible, why try? We are already participating in the cosmos; our images need to reflect that. We are already in relationships; those are what we need to learn.

Michael W. Fox and others have pointed out that death-awareness motivates much human behavior. Although a cosmology can help people to cope with fear, it cannot offer security against biological fact. Many archaic groups have worked acceptance of death into their myths. Weiss describes the Campa attitude toward death: since the first Campas were made of earth, they return to earth after death; if they had been made of stone, they would have been immortal. According to an Eskimo myth, the first human beings lived on an island, Mitligjuaq, in the Hudson Strait; no one ever left and eventually there were so many that the island began to sink under their weight. An old woman shouted: "Let it be so ordered that human beings can die, for there will no longer be room for us on earth." Her wish came true. Death was seen as the solution to survival. Death is a natural event. But so is the human longing for immortality, it appears. Even Neanderthal Man seemed to evidence that.

Many myths toyed with the idea of the avoidance of death, against the background of necessity. Now that death seems to be capable of being postponed by counteracting biological processes modern myths are promising immortality. But perhaps a mortal limit is necessary to make our lives count. It may be necessary to accept death to preserve the species. Acceptance of death would certainly waste fewer resources. Cosmology will never be able to rid humans of fears. Fear increases as control does; there is more to fear (the loss of control). So reverence will never go out of fashion. Nature will provide much to fear, beyond ourselves.

We create the organization of a cosmology, then see nature work that way. But we create nature by seeing what the brain filters. W. Ong thinks that our hypervisualism may be outmoded; it may hinder understanding of the world as it is organizing itself. It would be productive to cultivate aurally based concepts: harmony or melody or cacophony; on which to analyze a world view. And to move from concept of world sense to that of world-as-presence (as in sense of presence between two persons).

The human desire to refine the focus has neglected the frame of reference. An adaptive holocosmology would place human values within a global framework, attaining a balance of human and ambihuman nature in a field of being. The sciences, humanities and other ideologies could be balanced in a holocosmology.

A holocosmology is an expression of an ecological philosophy, rather than a psychological one (with the limits of abstract, self-knowledge). The ecological is broader than the psychological. A holocosmology would unite contemplation and participation (cf. Heidegger's "concern"), historical and ideal science. It would place humanity and the earth into an ecological cosmos (analytical ecology). It would bind humanity with a theology of the earth (synthetic ecology), where nature is a right order and the proper attitude is geopiety. The conception of a holocosmology draws on the scientific study of ecology (e.g., Fox, Klein, and Evernden) and a religious ecology (e.g., Cobb, Skolimowski, and Naess). It would apply to ethical and political questions, where these issues are given cosmological foundations through myth. It would concern itself with the earth as home for humanity. Perhaps human behavior could be put in tune with nature through a popular literature or poetry. We have never made earth completely home; until we do, no place will ever be home.

Other Beings Other Worlds

The word culture, from the Middle English, meant 'place tilled' (from the Latin colere meaning to 'till, care for, inhabit, worship'). For the Romans and English, to have a culture was to inhabit a place and cultivate it, to be responsible for it. Malinowski tried to show that almost the entire whole of human culture is can be seen as a mechanism to modify and satisfy the sexual needs of an individual. What a filter that was. One could argue that the mechanism of culture is also to channel energy or to distribute material goods. By either of these last two distinctions, it seems likely that other living beings also have cultures.

Most of the recent definitions of culture have been tailored to fit specific human characteristics. A larger definition expands culture as a codification of reality, a symbolic system that transforms physical reality into experienced reality. Culture codifies reality through expressions, which can be preserved and transmitted through generations through language. Different languages program events differently, therefore no culture or belief system can be considered entirely apart from language, or language entirely apart from place.

Human beings are mammals—omnivorous, social, bipedal, featherless, symbol and tool-using, game-playing, neotonous, bilateral-hemispheric, culture-making generalists. We live on a planet whose characteristics are formed by other living beings, with their own worlds or possibly cultures. We humans are unique in many ways, but we are also part of a continuum of complexity. We create worlds and cultures, but so might other beings.

Other animals have their own specific self-worlds. Adolf Portmann shows that every form of life appears as a Gestalt with a specific development in space-time. All living forms develop an image of their environments. Genetics provides the proper image choices for some—frogs, for instance. Others must learn what is valuable using their senses. Animals have their own strange and fascinating universes. When we realize this, we find that reality is immeasurably greater than the human idea of it. Jakob von Uexkull (1957) suggests representing the unfamiliar world of animals with bubbles to denote the self-world or the phenomenal world of an animal. According to von Uexkull, perceptual and effector worlds form a closed unit, the umwelt: "Figuratively speaking, each animal grasps its object with two arms of a forceps: Receptor and effector. With the first it invests the object with perceptual meaning, with the second operational meaning." The world—life-image—is what has meaning for an organism. The umwelt can be considered a region of brightness, or just a focus. The first principle of his self-world theory is that all animals from the simplest to complex are "fitted to their unique worlds with equal completeness," according to Uexkull. Each is optimally, or satisfactorily, fitted to a niche or habitat.

A simple world corresponds to simple animal; a well-articulated world to a complex animal. For example, the rich possibilities around a tick shrink to a scanty framework of three receptor and three effector cues (butyric acid, motion and heat)—her umwelt. But the poverty of this world guarantees the certainty of actions; and security is more important than wealth. Bodenheimer hypothesizes that an animal has an optimal umwelt in a pessimal environment. The environment must be pessimal or a species would gain ascendancy. The umwelt allows the creation of familiar paths that are strange to others, or invisible.

Time is different for each species; the tick can wait 18 years for prey. Human time is made of units of 1/18th of a second; which Uexkull says is utilized effectively by the motion picture technique of film projection. The subject sways to the time of its own world. Since all beings feel, the smallest unit of time is a duration for that being. Larger beings have larger durations. Similarly, space is a unit of place for a being. Uexkull implies that the human world is only one of the many possible. Although this is true perceptually, the use of symbols allow humans to imagine and represent other worlds. Humans can even create virtual worlds by limiting what could be received, for instance, only seeing in the x-ray part of the spectrum. Yet, human imagination is limited, as is human knowledge. Many organisms exist of which we know nothing. Their worlds have little meaning in a human world. E. Hall's space bubble or Lewin's personality field extrapolate the umwelt to humans.

According to Arne Naess, 'Self-realization' is a norm formulation in a metaphysical sense. The conceptual bridge from Self-realization to a positive evaluation of diversity, complexity, and symbiosis, and other ecological principles, is furnished by self-realization potentials; the realization of potentials increases the Self-realization of the earth—life-images, not just man-images. Each species has an equal right to live and develop, free from interference.

Other animals have cultures. We can distinguish certain requirements for a population to have culture: Language (for communication); dexterity (for tool making and using); brain power (for artifact design and making); social skills (for home building and habitat modification), governing or self-regulation); and, external memory (in customs or things, for intergenerational continuity). Many animals have some forms of these requirements. Wolves, for instance, have social skills, language, brainpower, and memory, which they use effectively in pack hunting, raising pups and adapting to environmental changes. Although their dexterity is limited, they can use (but not appear to make) simple tools like sticks; some adult wolves have been observed using twigs or dung to distract or teach pups to cross unstable talus slopes or to enhance their scent. Although wolves do not write books or manufacture data storage devices, they are able to extend external memory through scenting and in learned behavioral habits.

Termites, detritivorous arthropods, also have a complex world (perhaps 'termerld') and forms of culture. In fact their culture seems to parallel human culture in surprising ways. In Tanzania, for instance, termites are fungus 'farmers,' living in high-rise 'cities' with deep basements. Mounds may be 12 feet high, 90 feet deep, and all cover 30 percent of the soil surface. Although wood and root eaters, they consume any kind of organic litter. They vacuum the surface for organic litter in the area, which concentrates it in their mounds. Due to low organic matter in dry tropical forest soil, they digest most of the carbon available. Termites are quite efficient builders. The structures can become as hard as concrete. Some termites (Apicotermes) build entirely out of excrement; others use bits of wood, sand, and dirt glued with excrement and saliva. In C and S America, the mounds stand out after land is cleared and burned. In constructing the mounds, termites bring up clay from lower soil depths. This clay increases water-holding capacity. Farmers frequently plant crops on termite mounds (and use the soils to build human houses). In Uganda, individual humans claim ownership of termite mounds, for food. Termites have high protein and many other nutrients, from B vitamins to Iron and zinc. In Australia, the meridian termite (Amitermes) erects structures in a N-S direction, up to 15 feet high, 60 feet deep, 9 feet long and 1 foot wide.

Termites maintain a dense, 'urban' population in a large 'arcology.' They have solved the problem of air-conditioning to keep the insects cool, during their farming activities, sometimes, with 'domestic' labor. They often build covered 'highways' and tunnels to facilitate getting resources. They have a division of labor that can include royalty and slavery.

The termite colony is a good example of emergent order from simple laws in practice. Despite the simplicity of each member, their social organization enables them to gather enough food to maintain dense populations. Each individual member has to follow only several simple rules of behavior to build and survive, mostly concerned with picking up and depositing building materials (wood, clay or dung), food, or eggs.

Termites create a very complex web of detritivore interactions that can link the entire community. Termites have evolved symbiotic relationships with nitrogen-fixing bacteria. This increases food normally limited by nitrogen. Some termites have an array of microbes that have cellulose-digesting enzymes to decompose wood fibers. The microbes have a favorable environment in termite guts.

Consider a more synthetic definition: Culture is a symbolic system that emerges as a unique, coherent, whole pattern of life, that orders the experiences and meanings of its members and is transmitted through learning to new members, from a complex of ecological, social and historical processes, and helps members adapt to changing environments. This definition acknowledges the different levels of culture in animals and possibly plants.

Self-reference is the basis for all reference. The self expands through itself into other beings. Through human emotion, human identity becomes enlarged, to include other beings and the earth, to include our own posterity and its image of the future, without which we might lose the will and capacity to solve current problems.

Each culture has a different view of the earth. One world is a human image of part of the earth; each culture has one. A culture needs many things and does many things for its participants: Makes a common language; orders experience; personalizes a place; adapts and preserves aspects of a place; justifies human behavior; and, provides identity and security. Still, most cultures are incomplete (as they have to be since places always change), inflexible, and often indifferent to other cultures or individuals. Cultures need not compete or try to be the 'right' or final culture. But, every culture has to recognize how diverse kinds have developed to adapt to places in the planet.

The Gaia Hypothesis

> I shall sing of Gaia, universal mother,
> firmly founded, the oldest of divinities.   Homer

Paul Sears suggests that the whole of nature can be conceived as a self-repairing, constructive process representing a type of equilibrium that approximates an open steady state. Individuals and species do not pursue basic reproduction with full independence, but manifest restraints to keep within the bounds of balance in the integral ecology of nature.

Nature is both an ektropic phenomenon and a series of entropic processes, which result in hierarchies, where the system adapts to its medium and the medium itself becomes ordered. If there is anything in nature truly evolving, it is the largest structure, the total suprasystem, which imposes constraints on entities and subsystems. It is being, stretching into beings. The movement of being is *physis*. Physis refers to the power that emerges, the self-presenting of what is. This includes Logos, as gathering. Beings appear and disappear, reveal and conceal themselves in the self-organizing play of nature.

The whole is alive; this idea can be traced from the pre-Socratic philosophers to Plotinus, Kepler, and modern thinkers. For Plotinus, the material universe is a "living organic whole, the best possible image of the living unity-in-diversity" (in Glacken, Traces on the Rhodian Shore. p. 77). Predator and prey are equally necessary to the diversity and abundance of life. Life weaves variety into being. Without life and death, the earth would be bleak. Kepler considered the Earth as "a great round beast." O. T. Mason (1892) regarded the earth as a "living, thinking, being" (in Dubos, Celebrations of Life, p. 189). Recently, the living earth was put forward as a scientific hypothesis by James Lovelock.

James Lovelock and Lynn Margulis put forward a hypothesis that the planet exerts a living control of the atmospheric and hydrologic processes to maintain minimum conditions for life over long periods of time. The hypothesis notes the phenomenon to be explained: environmental natural regulation, atmospheric and oceanic home- stasis. A hypothesis can sometimes be disproved, but never proved.

Lovelock hypothesizes a collective global mind immanent in the cybernetic structure of the global system. He calls it Gaia, after the Greek earth goddess, as suggested by William Golding. Nature is active, resilient and powerful—as Gaia. When modern ecology strives to think of the planet dynamically and holistically, it returns to personification. Lovelock states: "It appeared to us that the Earth's biosphere was able to control at least the temperature of the Earths surface and the composition of the atmosphere. . . . This led us to the formation of the proposition that living matter, the air, the oceans, the land surfaces were parts of a giant system which was able to control temperature, the composition of the air and sea, the pH of the soil and so on, so as to be optimum for the survival of the biosphere. The system seemed to exhibit the behavior of a single organism, even a living creature."

He continues, "One of the laws of system control is that, if a system is to maintain stability, it must possess adequate variety of response . . . What is to be feared is that man-the-farmer and man-the-engineer are reducing the total variety of response open to Gaia. . . . Let us make peace with Gaia on her own terms and return to peaceful coexistence with our fellow creatures."

Lovelock hypothesizes that every element in the system is related in a feedback network to every other element. This is reminiscent of Whitehead's organic philosophy, where every atomic unit has feeling and influences every other. For example, the biosphere can control the temperature of the surface and the composition of the atmosphere. On the other hand, soil types and the weather can limit vegetation; invasions of vegetation change soil types. Lovelock and Margulis have shown that it is sophisticated enough to maintain a constant temperature and pH for billions of years, in spite of great atmospheric and solar changes.

The hypothesis is:

- The average surface temperature of the earth has been in a relatively constant range for more than 3 billion years, despite an gradual rise in solar energy.

- The concentration of the atmosphere is improbable, compared to the composition of Venus and Mars; it should be mostly Carbon dioxide.
- Each atmospheric gas is optimal proportion for a life supporting function.
- The salinity of the ocean is far lower than it should be from runoff from land; the present percentage could have been achieved after 80 million years.

Lovelock concludes that the chemical and climactic properties of the earth have always been optimal for life. Since this could not have happened by chance, the explanation is Gaia, who he defines as "a complex entity involving the Earth's biosphere, atmosphere, oceans, and soil; the totality constituting a cybernetic system that seeks an optimum physical and chemical environment for life on this planet. The condition of the earth has been actively made fit by life itself." The earth's biomasses, air, oceans, and land form part of a giant system which is a single organism. Life exists as a consequence of the right material conditions. Life defines the material conditions needed for survival and then tries to maintain them. The Earth's biosphere controls the temperature of the surface and the composition of the atmosphere, from major constituents to trace elements. The system has maintained control over instabilities for millions of years through a variety of responses.

At a scientific level of thought, the Gaia hypothesis extends the fundamental ecological doctrine that all things in nature are densely subtly and systematically interrelated until it includes humanity, ethically and mentally, as well as physically. The entire earth is envisioned as a unified entity, actively shaping the material conditions of the planet for the purpose of maximizing the survival and variety of living beings. As a superorganism, however, the planet is nearly blind and dumb. W.F. Doolittle criticizes Lovelock for failing to identify the feedback mechanisms for sensing the deviation of global physical and chemical parameters from an optimum, and the mechanisms for correcting processes (in *Coevolution Quarterly* 29, p. 59).

Lovelock and Margulis do provide some explanation for the balancing of oxygen with methane by anaerobic methanogens in swamp areas. Recent research reveals a surprising amount of methane produced by cattle and termites as part of their digestive processes. They also note that salinity may be controlled by evaporation in shallow bays. Doolittle has difficulty imagining any evolutionary mechanisms arising to maintain feedback loops. Especially by leaving greater numbers of offspring through natural selection. Margulis noted that there are at least three components to evolutionary process, each of which has different facets: Faithful replication; inherited variation (mutations, alterations, fissions, duplications); and natural selection. She states that the whole process explains Gaia as a control system, even though most of the mechanisms are unexplained. Mutation is probably a last resort after others have been used.

Doolittle thinks existing feedback loops are accidental and accidental balances are fragile; their maintenance depends on chance. Life is of a low probability, but only mathematically (which works against Doolittle). He assumes that chance is the only required explanation. But chance is only the shuffling; the sorting is ektropy. Properties emerge from hierarchies in an historical process. At some time, life mutually arose with the conditions necessary for it. As a local phenomenon (life could not come into existence everywhere), life changed the global level. All local levels are intertwined to some extent. Margulis thinks Doolittle overlooked physiological, developmental, populational, and ecological phenomena between the molecular and the biogeological. Life is continuous and all levels are in continuity. Whenever there are too many replicating units for space and resources (genes, organelles, individuals, families, cultures, and species), some persist and some fail. So selection acts on various levels at different time scales. More than one unit is selected. Not one is the unit.

System complexity is a limit for rogue species; since all species have the same building blocks. Lovelock sees mechanisms as well developed and controlled; by contrast, Doolittle leaves a large role for chance. Lovelock thinks Gaia is a manifestation of the tendency for complex systems to be stable and persistent. He also notes that R. Dawkins raised the possibility that natural selection predated life. M. Eigen and associates have demonstrated the kinds of pre-organic selection that could occur. The options open to life as a whole are constrained by its past activities. Life slows water erosion and so mass movement from mountains, thus slowing cycles of mountain wearing. Life ties up some minerals, like phosphorus, and recycles others, like oxygen or carbon, at hundreds of times their natural rates. Although the universe depends on values of a few basic physical constants, life did not manipulate those.

Lovelock regards Gaia as a closed loop, a symbiosis of global dimensions. He questions whether the current level of industrial activities could endanger the life of Gaia. He is worried about disturbances to the tropics and shallow seas, which perform essential metabolic activities. If humans alter systems too much, a new adaptation may take place unfavorable to humans. Catastrophe could come with a reduction of resilience and a large disturbance. Although the Gaia hypothesis renews the idea that the earth is a mother for us all, and reinforces our understanding of interconnectedness of biological processes, it falls short of our responsibility and relies too much on our consciousness. Ecosystems are self-corrective; but there are no sense organs. Gregory Bateson thinks the systems are quantitative and gradual; the quantities whose differences are informational indicators are at the same time quantities of needed supplies (light, food, water). Nevertheless, humans, as a result of consciousness and power, have responsibilities to avoid unnecessary change. That is not to say that ecosystems should be frozen, only that we should not accelerate extinctions and habitat destructions or try to redesign the earth without sufficient knowledge or understanding.

Human Ecology
The Wall of Incomprehension

What has made humans human was that in addition to living in human social groups, human groups lived in communities with other species. Lanteri-Laura believes that we exist spontaneously in the entourage of animals as well as other humans (in P. Diole, *The Errant Ark*. New York: Putnam, 1974). We learn from animals. The experience of the existence of animals is an essential category of human experience.

Many wild animals seem to enjoy human company. Certain Amazonian tribes, the Choroti and the Ashluslay, allow tamed wild animals in their encampments. There are pigs, otters and cranes; wild ducks are playmates of children. Often animals make the first advances. And although the animals may become tamed, they are not domesticated, not modified. This mixed society was probably what led to domestication. Siberian reindeer seem to be attracted to human urine (perhaps by a chemical from digested mushrooms); jackals and antelope evidence curiosity about humans, also. In a real sense humans have coevolved with their plant domesticates. Only a few plants—wheat, rice, corn, barley, bean, peanut, soybean, and potato—are used to provide most sustenance.

Humans are not content with a totally artificial environment. Humans fought to steal niches from animals. Now they try to save a few for them. Once they bred animals for docility and now they breed for wildness (in the almost extinct red wolf which had interbred with other canids). This is the working of enantiodromia, the working of the universe and of tragedy. P. Diole recommends demythologizing animals and desacralizing them.

But we need to resacralize them instead. Nietzsche's tragic view holds earthly life sacred; "existence is considered sacred enough" to justify the suffering involved (in Kaufmann, *The Portable Nietzsche,* p. 459). Animals do not need to be saved from natural death, a great regulator of life, but from suffering, experimentation and premature extinction. A reasonable place needs to be created for animals in human society or left for them outside society. Different forms of life improve the quality of human life. The natural community can be rebuilt; not to what it ever was at any time, but as a self-regulating evolutionary unit.

The ambiguity of the word 'nature' reflects the doubts and uncertainties that humans feel about nature. Nature is alien: other. As we have isolated ourselves in human artifacts, we seem to have lost touch and grown cold-hearted. Nature is separated by a wall of incomprehension. Humans will only be completely humans in the community of living beings on earth. The human spirit needs to be joined with animal and plant spirit. D. H. Lawrence judged that no human being can develop except through prolonged connection with other beings.

The New Dinosaurs

To assume that evolution necessarily progressed to humans ascribes an anthropocentric purpose to nature. But for environmental effects, dinosaurs, birds or whales could be the dominant species. So, humans are not the unique end or goal. In fact, like new dinosaurs, humans are good competitors, suppressing other species and creating their own pseudo-species.

Evolution is usually seen as ascending view of transformism. Humanity sits on top of ladder. There can be a hierarchy of systems where processes are bidirectional, complementing each other in constitution of hierarchy as a unity of reality. The net result of this shuffling is null. There is no blueprint for the universe, with man as chief executive. Nature builds upwards and outwards, as well as inwards and downwards, from the simple to the complex, as well as back again. Once the world was thought to have a direction or purpose. It still is.

Some scientists still believe that energy considerations determine the direction of the evolutionary process. And some ecologists treat natural communities as a superorganism and subordinate species to the ecosystem need for balance. We expect nature's creations to tend to move toward overall harmony, which is felt as beauty in perception and analyzed as coherent and ordered functions. Harmony tends to make for species survival, but is no guarantee. Each type of harmony leads to survival only in limited conditions. Humans cannot do other than to seek to live in harmony and beauty, without which survival has no value. For M. Grene, the end is not survival, but the survival of a type of living. Survival is only the context of life. There is no driving force if the universe is merely the pervasive, and there is arbitrariness in every transition. Why should these generate one another? The universe created us in its natural history. We have come to terms with consciousness by feeling the edges. Our thoughts and ideas are nature, as much as clouds and waves. We confuse our systems of symbols with the natural world, the universe represented with the universe present. Order is the highest ideal of mind; but chaos is necessary to preserve it in its mutual duality. Natural order is dynamic, creative, logical, and temporal. We live in a natural order. To preserve what we are, we must admire the matrix out of which we arose. Marveling at nature includes marveling at oneself, for although there are others, humans are remarkable examples of dynamic order brought forth by the universe in its history. Nature has only the intention to be, to develop.

Panecology & Consciousness

Hegel realized that reality is a living, evolving process. For him, Absolute Universal Reason moved through eternity embodied in the natural world. The universe was rational in all things. It was as high as its highest common denominator, which was at least human rationality. The evolutionary process reached the stage of the human mind. Individual consciousness was thought to be a stage in the development of self-awareness in the absolute mind. Kierkegaard criticized this as the greatest fault of the system—the exaggerated emphasis on abstract reason with the human as the central concern of philosophy. Minds are patterns that have the power of knowing other patterns; the entire universe is patterned, but not equally complex.

Mind is an arrangement of molecules in such complexity that they are aware of themselves in that arrangement. Thus, the evolutionary process is aware of itself to some extent. Ecological theory is at the same time an interactive theory of mind. The rise and development of mind is essentially the story of dim light reflecting on itself and becoming brighter. Reality for an amoeba is less than for a fish and even less than

Mind is an arrangement of molecules in such complexity that they are aware of themselves in that arrangement. Thus, the evolutionary process is aware of itself to some extent. Ecological theory is at the same time an interactive theory of mind. The rise and development of mind is essentially the story of dim light reflecting on itself and becoming brighter. Reality for an amoeba is less than for a fish and even less than for a human. The richness of experience is in proportion to organism's capacity to receive and decipher and influence the proximate environment. But the organism receives from reality what it puts in; it enriches reality. The mystery of the mind in evolution is its capacity to enlarge reality as it grows and transforms itself.

An ecological theory of mind accounts for all stages of the real in its evolutionary unfolding, from amoeba, to grasshopper, to dog, primitive and modern human societies. Bateson concludes that there is a collective global mind immanent in the cybernetic network (in *Mind and Nature*). The global ecosystem, with its marshes, forests, schools and businesses, contains a large number of individual minds, all interconnected in such a way as to constitute a single collective, global mind. Bateson emphasizes that this mind (or god) is immanent in the structure and not transcendent.

Genetic and cultural evolution becomes an identity. This identity could foster the human resacralization of earth. The unit of survival in natural selection was the species. Bateson expanded that to be the organism plus the environment, making it identical with the unit of mind. He localized something called mind immanent in the large biological system, the ecosystem. The individual mind is immanent not only in the body, but in pathways and messages outside the body; there is a larger mind of which the individual mind is only a subsystem. This large mind is personified as God, but it is immanent in the total interconnected social system and planetary ecology. What Bateson called mind is a field of feeling, a net of relationships of nonreflective consciousnesses.

If all patterns are forms of consciousness, then nature becomes conscious (through dynamic feedback processes). There are many definitions of consciousness: The ability to process input (Descartes); the ability to order; ability to give off energy (Bly); the ability to feel (Whitehead). Perhaps, one could add the ability to react, or anticipate, or communicate.

What is consciousness? There is no great unity in natural consciousness. It could be laid out on a spectrum from red to violet. Rocks and chemicals have a red glow; they are simple. Plants give off a green glow. Elephants and dolphins are in the violet range.

The earth is an organized field of activities taking place at various levels, in different spheres of being and realms of consciousness. Consciousness exists at all levels. All these diverse and hierarchical modes of activity and consciousness should be seen "integrated in and perhaps transcended by an all-encompassing and eonic planetary Consciousness," according to Christofer Stone.

Humanity is part of the system. The earth is a loosely formed spherical organism, with all its working parts in symbiosis. Leopold described conservation as an attempt to harmonize civilization with the land towards a "universal symbiosis" (in *A Sand County Almanac*). We are neither owners or operators—we are a part of the nervous system for the whole being, motile tissue for receiving and creating information. Lewis Thomas believes that humanity is the whole nervous system, but animals and plants also are part of the organic network. Humanity is a circuit around the earth, in the words of Thomas, a computer, capable of fusing all thoughts of the world into a syncytium. The circuit implies shimmering networks of beings which may be traced in part but not isolated. A circuit is a complete connection (disease leads to death when it's broken). The cycle is movement through a circuit (pollution leads to stress and death when out of balance).

Mankind is part of a planetary whole. There can be no truly global society as long as humanity will not recognize the fact that it has responsibilities within the planetary organism. Nothing in nature is entirely complete. The motion of circuits spirals through time. The next order of quality is unrealized. For humanity, God is the being towards whose emergence or submergence the evolutionary intent of mind is directed. The heavens and earth create god and are created from god. There is no logical necessity at the beginning. God may be denied in pure atheism. God may be forever in the making. There will always be more than is comprehensible, being and becoming. The basic values of life—truth, goodness, beauty—are always in the making. Nature just produces experience.

Macrocosm
Macrocosm is the largest cosmic level, everything that exists. It seems knowable, in some of its laws and limits, which restrain and shape the cosmos and its embedded levels. We can see that it develops through time. And, we can measure some of the extents of distant influences on our physical environment as well as on our cultures and images.

Part Two: Making Worlds

The Flesh of the Body

In *The Phenomenology of Perception* and other works, Merleau-Ponty criticized the empiricists in biology and psychology for fracturing the unity of the organism in its biosocial situation with destructive analytics. Instead, "Our body is in the world as the heart is in the organism: it keeps the visible spectacle constantly alive, it breathes life into it and sustains it inwardly, and with it forms a system" (p. 203).

The body is the primary unit; it is embodied in the world, embodied in being. From the oldest language we know, the Indo-European tongue, we took the word for earth (*dhghem*) and turned it into humus and human (*dhghem*=earth—>*humanus* in Latin—>human in English). Yet, the word for man was shaped into man-image, world (Indo-European *wiros*=man—>*weorold* in O. English—>world). One word progresses from earth to human, the other from human to earth. We cannot be any closer to the earth and its processes, since the parts are combined in us. We are indissolubly one with nature.

Since objects in the world and the body in the world form a system, there are lived-through correspondences making up experience, and not multiplicities of objective correlations; the unity of the object is correlative, however, with the unity of the body. The body is not a transparent object or a constitutional presentation; since it is not, and since it is an expressive unity that can be known only through its active expression, this same structure will be passed on to the sensible world. "The theory of the body image is, implicitly, a theory of perception" (Ibid., p. 206). Merleau-Ponty stated that we relearn to feel our body, that we are our body, that we are in the world through our body, and that by making contact with our body and the world, rediscover ourselves. The body is a unity, and sensing an object is a unity. The body is the seal of expression. "My body is the fabric into which all objects are woven, and it is, at least in relation to the perceived world, the general instrument of my 'comprehension'" (Ibid., p. 235).

The body gives significance to natural and cultural objects. Before they become symbols of concepts, words or signs are events that grip the body. For instance, in one psychological experiment, words are flashed on a screen below the threshold of recognition nevertheless produce a typical effect on the subject; the word hard may produce a stiffening of the back.

Merleau-Ponty conceived of normal behavior as that which is constituted by an intentional arc, whereby the organism reaches out and grabs the existential situation, and responds to it in a synthesizing fashion. He urges: "Let us therefore say . . . that the life of consciousness . . . is subtended by an 'intentional arc' which projects round about us our past, our future, our human setting, our physical, ideological and moral situation, or rather which results in our being situated in all respects. It is this intentional arc which brings about the unity of the senses, of intelligence, of sensibility and motility" (Ibid., p. 136).

Like a sacrament, the sensible has not only a "motor and vital significance," but it is a way of being in the world, suggested to us and acted upon by us, "so that sensation is literally a form of communion" (Ibid., p. 212). The parts of the body and the actions of the body, the whole body, is a system of systems devoted to the inspection of the world, capable of altering it, piercing the future, outlining relationships, and giving meaning to the "flatness of being."

By its pointing gestures the body flows over into the world and possesses it at a distance. The gesture of expression, by delineating its intention, retrieves the world even more. All perception, all action that presupposes it, every human use of the body, is already primordial expression, for Merleau-Ponty. Perception takes place through the body; the body and the objects constitute a field, but since the body is in the field perception is always ambiguous.

This is true of cosmology, considering incompleteness and self-reference. Perception begins with a sedimentation from the past—the world is already patterned—and opens toward a world that is also in the act of being structured. The body and the world are contingent—this allows their synthesis—and so have openness and temporal thickness. The body perceives space; this perceived space is existential space, it is always oriented toward the perceiving subject. A good example of this is Stratton's inverted vision experiment, where the subject is fitted with lenses that invert the entire visual field; the experiment was repeated by Kohler and others. After a short period of confusion, the subject adjusts to the change; the visual field appears normal.

All the dimensions of space perception—size, height, depth, and width—are abstractions from a being in a situation. Movement can be reversed by alternating figure and ground; after spinning around and falling down, still, the earth spins (Wittbecker, 1970). Space is contracted at night or during sickness; or it can be expanded with mood, consciousness or instruments. Space perception is a structural phenomenon and, as Merleau-Ponty observes, "is comprehensible only within a perceptual field which contributes in its entirety to motivating the spatial perception by suggesting to the subject a possible anchorage" (Ibid., p. 280). Meaning is also anchored in the lived-world. The senses all work together, such that a certain space may be red, warm, and smell sweet. Werner cited instances of sound being 'seen' with colors; there are other experiments linking smell and taste, and still others using Mescaline and LSD.

Merleau-Ponty recognizes that "Synaesthetic perception is the rule, and we are unaware of it only because scientific knowledge shifts the centre of gravity of experience, so that we have unlearned how to see, hear and generally feel, speaking, in order to deduce, from our bodily organization and the world as the physicist conceives it, what we are to see, hear and feel" (Ibid., p. 229). The body is made up of interacting chemical compounds; it is a dialectic of living being in a biological milieu, with subjects and social groups. "The body in general is an ensemble of paths already traced, of powers already constituted; the body is the acquired dialectical soil upon which a higher 'formation' is accomplished, and the soul is the meaning which is then established. The relations of soul and body can indeed be compared to those of concept and word ..." (Idem, *Structure of Behavior*, p. 210). But only as joined in operation, for without the expression of the body the soul is nothing.

Merleau-Ponty confessed that his analysis led to an ideality of the body, but preferred that to Descartes' inability to deal with perception, and subsequent bifurcation of the soul and body. The soul of which he speaks is the mind that comes into the world, and arises from primary consciousness, which is identical, through naive reduction, to perception. Similarly, his ideality of the body is also an incarnation of the soul. In tracing the evolution of mind, in *The Structure of Behavior*, he is mindful that the delivery of the brain function from strict localization is not a delivery at all; although inferior levels are submerged during normal behavior, their disruption for any reason, e.g., injury, disrupts the superior level. Perception as a whole, lived consciousness characterized by the perspective and symbolizing activity that is mind, emerges from the body under certain evolutionary conditions. Mind is the integration of a corporeal schema. The 'cogito' is grounded in human experience and is a corporeal phenomenon.

> Shew'd erring Pride, WHATEVER IS, IS RIGHT;
> That REASON, PASSION, answer one great aim;
> That true SELF-LOVE and SOCIAL are the same;
> That VIRTUE only makes our Bliss below;
> And all our Knowledge is, OURSELVES TO KNOW.
> Alexander Pope, *An Essay on Man*

Andre Malraux recognized the paradox that after sixty years of effort and suffering, of development and maturation, an individual is ready only for death. Human life is short and static. So much of it is private. Even the most self-conscious and engaged individual spends most of her life in private (as a nonpublic and nonhistorical figure). The Russian essayist Vasili Rozanov defined the private life as "picking your nose and looking at the sunset," that is, the enjoyment of physiological and aesthetic reactions. The great deeds of history are not very much noticed. Even the most brutal events do not engage people for very long. Montaigne admits "how little an expense to my peace of mind I have lived half my life in my house, while my country was in ruins" (*Complete Essays*. Stanford: Stanford, 1958, vol. 3, p. 376). Aldous Huxley observes that we "find ourselves living in a strange amphibious world. Man is a multiple amphibian, living in many double worlds and leading many double lives, and one of them" is the life of a private individual embedded in an unfelt, objective history (*The Human Situation*, p. 120).

The individual blends and overlaps the lives of other individuals. The individual is a microscopic opening for the energies of society and the universe. The development of an ecological understanding of the human condition depends on the study of the souls of individuals (through psychology, philosophy and religion). The unique experiences, problems and solutions make each life unique. A number of philosophies study humans in place. Existentialism centers on the human as participant. It stresses the dynamic, concrete, intersubjective, ambiguous consensus, and passionate uniqueness of a participant. Most of the ideas of the self in the world are dependent on the phenomenological movement, beginning with Brentano. Brentano wanted a complementarity of induction and deduction, a totality of ways of knowing the human phenomenon (Wundt and his school of psychology renounced deduction and speculation). Husserl and Stumpf were students of Brentano. Heidegger was a student of Husserl; Wertheimer, Koffka and Kohler, the founders of gestalt psychology, were students of Stumpf, as was Lewin.

Merleau-Ponty existentially interpreted Husserl's transcendental phenomenology, defining description, reduction, essential, intuition, intentionality, and the ideal of rationality according to his own stance: all truths meet in the world. The phenomenological description is concerned with the abduction of the pre-reflective world that forms the background for perception. It depends, not on an "egology" as described by Husserl (in the *Cartesian Meditations*), but on immersion in the world. For Husserl truth dwelt in the consciousness of inner man. With Merleau-Ponty, the subject body is human and consciousness is incarnate. In order to avoid the unavoidable end in solipsism of Husserl's transcendent idealism, Merleau-Ponty recognized the impossibility of a complete reduction, due to the nature of immersion in the world. The world already has meaning, and no one can be completely removed from it. For Merleau-Ponty, the eidetic reduction is for the purpose of exposing the world as it is before reflection. Essence becomes an unthematized fact and not a pure idea, so there can be no absolute knowledge of essences since they are provisional. Thus intentionality is not a constitutive power of the ego, but the incorporative power of a human being for working everything in the world into a pattern of meaning.

Rationality is the human ideal of continuously and progressively clarifying the world. In Husserl it was the basis for the meaning of the world. There is no absoluteness of meaning for Merleau-Ponty; it evolves and changes with the world. Phenomenology is the study of essences, an understanding of which starts from the givenness of existence. It is a transcendental philosophy of the world, characterized by detachment.

The central theme of phenomenology is the lived-world, which is only accessible through a phenomenological method, which is a matter of describing, not analyzing or explaining. The phenomenological world is not pure being, but a sensible place where experiences intersect and overlap—one person's and other people's. Subjectivity and intersubjectivity are unified. Phenomenology is not the bringing to explicit expression of pre-existing being, but "the laying down of being" (in *Phenomenology of Perception*, p. xx). Merleau-Ponty's primacy of perception emphasizes the embodiment of a human mind/body in a temporal, physical world. We start by reflecting on ourselves and what touches our embodied situation and go on. Merleau-Ponty looks for being as it comes into view (a phenomenon is what appears in light). Merleau-Ponty initiates development at the preconceptual level, by trying to discover being from the place of the perceiver, the lived center (flesh and chaisma). Reflection (as perception) reveals self and place. It is a way of looking that reverses clarity and obscurity.

Phenomenology is an approach to understanding through lived experience. It admits value, meaning and involvement in the world. Ecological necessity can be accommodated in phenomenology. But it is opposed to the dictatorship of scientific thinking; knowledge is gained from experience. The phenomenological method is a procedure of description for the life-world. Describing beings from one perspective is like guessing. Heidegger cautioned against depending on guesses, but as absolute knowledge is impossible, guessing is necessary. Guesses form filters like glasses. We cannot shed these entirely, but we can understand what they do by using a real phenomenological method.

Merleau-Ponty was impressed with Whitehead's observation of the fragmentation of nature by philosophy. Only Bergson and Whitehead had taken the idea of nature as a central theme in recent times. Merleau-Ponty attempted a beginning on nature. His mode of operation was a repeated examination and assimilation of the empirical, everyday and scientific. Merleau-Ponty's last, incomplete plan—"1. visible; 2. nature; 3. logos"— was to be presented without any compromise with humanism, naturalism or theology (in *The Visible and the Invisible*, p. 274).

The Geography of the Brain

If, as C. Sherrington says, the brain is an enchanted loom, then experience is the fabric. Bohm and Pribram conclude that the brain constructs reality by interpreting frequencies from another dimension, a realm of meaningful, patterned primary reality that transcends time and space (*Brain/Mind Bulletin*, 4 July 1977). Certainly, their ideas are consistent with W. James, who described the brain as a filter of the larger reality. Seeing with patterns filters out nonessential events. These habits allow the brain to condense familiar experience and be open to new patterns.

Gregory Bateson considered that the brain is cybernetic: The system operates on differences. It consists of networks of paths for differences and transforms to be transmitted. Walsh notes that most brain structures, from whole brain down to synaptic morphology, appear to be plastic. Time-lapse photography of brain tissue cultures suggests that neural tissue may be continuously active and mobile. Ultra-structural remodeling may take place continuously through life; synapses may be formed and dissolved as shifts in demand and patterns of input occur. As without, so within; nothing is permanent. Many events within the system are energized by a respondent part, not the triggering part. The brain shows self-correctiveness in the direction of homeorhesis, implying trial and error. The brain is pieced together from effective strategies. Different parts evidently have different strategies.

Triune Brain

P.D. MacLean identified three distinct evolutionary stages in development of human brain: A basically reptilian brain, encircled by an old mammalian brain, and a neocortex. These are distinct in structure and chemistry. The functions they perform are duplicative and overlap. The two older brains seem involved in ancestral lore of species: dominance, display, ritual, defense, migration, bonding, hunting, grouping, and play. The brain registers mainly frequencies. The limbic brain interprets these.

In MacLean's triune theory, the reptilian brain coordinates behavioral patterns, from territoriality to ritual, migration and hoarding. The paleomammalian contributes to the formation of personal identity, processing information in such a way that it is experienced as feelings and emotions. It is responsible for selection of stimuli essential for self-preservation. The neocortex assumes important visual roles. MacLean compares it to an immense neural screen where symbols can appear. It receives input from outer world and can abstract. The neocortex seems more adept at learning new ways to cope and adapt. The neural chassis beneath all three brains coordinates breathing, circulation, digestion, and motility.

The limbic system is in dialectical balance, operating on cybernetic principles that encompass variables involved in rational/emotional synthesis. But neocortical excess can send the limbic system into an oscillating or runaway mode. MacLean's thesis (supported by Koestler) is that the brain suffers from a lethal design error, a split between reason and emotion, precipitated by inadequate coordination. Anatomically, he has shown that the vertical connections between the limbic (mammalian) and neocortex are relatively few, indirect and slow to react. This dissociation might mean that early humans knew the environment better than themselves (perhaps that has been reversed, now). MacLean thinks that the brains can be bisociated through creativity. But anatomy may only be tendency not destiny. The connections could be enough if there is a logic of emotion.

Dual Hemispheres

The neocortex is divided into two hemispheres. R. Myers and R. Sperry carried out the original experiments (at the University of Chicago) on the split brain, using cats. The commissural system provides each half of the brain with a copy of the sensory world directly observed by the other. This bridge allows an organism to respond to the stimulation of one side. Because the brain seemed to be organized into two spheres, it was concluded that there were two potentially independent mental systems. When the corpus collosum was cut, both halves seemed to function independently.

Although the hemispheres have a functional autonomy and division of labor, they are also tenaciously integrated. M. Gazzaniga suggests that, based on the physiological properties of the pathways, the commissures shuttle sensory messages between the hemispheres. He concluded that the duplication of events in the other half of a brain provides mental unity. Interhemispheric communication "is the mechanism by which the illusion of a single, complete psychological space is created from two separate neural representations of the same information" (*The Integrated Mind*, p. 17).

The hemispheres have different processing functions, which are lateralized by the whole brain. We can process information in two ways, by unifying it or separating it, in right or left brain (cf. Bateson, Goethe). We think of the left hemisphere as verbal, analytic, reductive, rational, and discontinuous; right as nonverbal, holistic, synthetic, intuitive, timeless, and diffuse (see Figure 10).

Left	*Right*
Convergent	Divergent
Vertical	Horizontal thinking
Tree	Net
Positive	Mythic
Linear	Nonlinear

Figure 10. *Hemispheric Functions*

J. Jaynes believes that ancient thinking was different as a consequence of development of brain functions. But thinking functions may have been a result of dominant social confirmation, acquired social values and accepted modes of behavior. These values spoke to the left hemisphere from the right. The right hemisphere (godlike in timeless coherence) binds people together. It was the voice of religion. Religion is from the Latin, *religare*, meaning to bind. E. de Bono contrasts lateral thinking with vertical, in brain. Lateral thinking is a multiphase approach, flexible in attempts. Lateral thinking can allow realization of self-organization and pattern-making (not just recognizing). The left brain is digitally acting; the right operates by analogy. The right half of the brain furthers novelty; the left half confirmation.

Right and left brains may be characterized as a net (cybernetic) image and a tree (hierarchic) image. The net represents brain as a whole, of which the right hemisphere has an intuition. It represents context, being and ecology of environment. The tree image is one of programs that comprise the brain. Conscious purpose makes part its subject and other parts become parts, but the hierarchy is temporary. The left half of the brain seems to function by arborization or hierarchical tree. It seems more likely to dominate in social situations. The right half seems to function as a net. This idea would explain differences in thinking and the preponderance of hierarchies in industrial societies. Fox attributes the splitting of hemispheric functions and higher and lower brain functions to social conditioning that does not inhibit narcissistic impulses and primary process thinking.

Thus, society causes an imbalance and lack of integration. Most people are frozen at a developmental stage where the dualities of emotion and reason are not reconciled. Furthermore, most cultures devalue deep brain processes (emotion) and overemphasize reason. Emotions that are uncomfortable and uncontrollable (fear or death-anxiety) are denied in humans and animals. Left or right brain functions can be emphasized culturally or by choice. A good example of learned hemisphere functions is in the difference between traditional Japanese and European musical perception. Traditional Japanese music, made by koto and shakhuachi flute, seems to be enjoyed by the left hemisphere. European music, with its rhythm and tonality, is perceived as gibberish (as are animal and natural sounds). New generations of Japanese have learned to appreciate European music, and apparently use their right hemispheres (M. W. Fox, personal communication).

One fault with the lateral model of the brain is that it is regarded as a closed system. One side is always regarded as off. The hemispheres operate in unity. Alpha rhythms allow the right half to experience tacitly (through entrainment) what the left half is producing. It expands the search for solutions to "problems" by putting them in context. Emphasis on the left hemisphere could produce imbalance. A central nervous system imbalance, as a result of cultural imbalance, could lead to ecological imbalance. Since earlier structures persist in the brain, humans have access to different modes of consciousness. To think that one brain is higher than others is chauvinistic. To emphasize one hemisphere of the brain forces dichotomies to stay unresolved. The brain is holonomous. In the brain, single things cannot be known. As in ecology, one cannot do single things. Life encodes a network. The brain weaves perceptions and ideas into a cosmos and itself into the universe.

Psychopoesis

William of Occam stated that there can be no abstractive cognition where there is not first a perceptive cognition—*Essentia non sunt multiplicanda praeter necessitatem*—essences are not to be multiplied beyond necessity. This formula is Occam's razor. It is not necessary to explain the mind as a separate essence. The mind is a brain-generated pattern of holistic experience. The mind field emerges from the brain and life fields. Phenomenological description finds normal human behavior, where science finds three orders of events (matter, life, mind) explained extrinsically by cause-effect. Physics, biology and psychology are horizontally related as figure and ground and vertically as matter, body and soul.

Metabolic mind and neural mind meet at the level of organismic mind. The reflexive mind mirrors outer reality which it rebuilds in an inner world. Apperception is characteristic of reflexive mind. It has the capability of forming alternate models of reality. With the self-reflexive mind, anticipation is called into play. With the whole, organismic mind, information transfer can be by imitation or by direct communication with other organisms. Reflexive mentation opens up new levels. Since the closed symmetry of inner and outer world is broken, self and world are opened to new possibilities. Iterative feedback between inner and outer worlds may lead to creative evolution of mental structure. A situation is seen in a new aspect. The composition of facts and the world is understood.

The body and mind are instruments, set in a dynamic reciprocally interpretive relationship to nature. The body and mind build up dynamic structures by which the whole organism relates itself to the universe. The mind is united by its forms with whatever it has perceived. Its relation to its own structure is reflexive. Structures of the mind often take the form of myths, which are used to interpret the universe. Campbell concluded a study of myths with the judgment that mythologies and deities are the productions and projections of the mind. Although each myth is individual, their motifs are similar, probably due to the working of the human mind. The myths of virgin birth, incarnation, death and resurrection, a second coming, and judgment day all refer to the structure and order of the mind, in symbolic terms.

The Primacy of Perception

Perception of the body as landscape and of natural terrain as a body is as fundamental to psychology as it is to mythology. We depend completely on the natural environment, physically and psychologically. D.O. Hebb has conducted experiments that show the effects of a limited environment. Cut off from external stimuli, the mind becomes strange. The external world is needed to keep us alive and sane. This world is composed of remote occurrences, on polar icecaps and distant stars, as well as immediate personal events. The body links exterior to interior. The person (=body-subject) is inextricably woven with the world; the body is a mode of presence to others. This bond of betweenness constitutes the foundation of an intersubjective paradigm for psychology.

The sensory apparatus by which we make contact with the world arose through the process of evolution. Waddington claims that Schrodinger failed to account for this. The faculties by which we arrive at a world view have been selected to be efficient in dealing with existents. Since our sensory apparatus arose through the process of evolution, it has been molded by the things-in-themselves to be competent in coping with them. Evolution operates by the selection of genotypes that endow their possessor with the capacity to react adaptively (or reproductively) to their surroundings.

Heinz's principle of cognitive homeostasis is pertinent here. He proposes that the nervous system is organized to create a stable reality. For example, the eye cannot see small discontinuities. A healthy human eye can perceive an interval of 1/50th of an inch. The eye cannot resolve 1/200th inch intervals between microdots of that size. So printing plates for picture reproductions that are composed of screen dots that far apart appears as continuous to humans. Nor, since the environment is in constant motion, can the eye just be still. As F. Ratliffe and L. Riggs have indicated, the eye is always vibrating; this vibration is termed *nystagmus*. Riggs, Ratliff, Cornsweet, and Cornsweet (1953) devised an experiment to show that this physiological tremor was essential to vision. When a mirrored contact lense and a series of mirrors were adjusted so that eye movements were exactly compensated for, the image was kept still on the retina for several seconds; then it disappeared. Constant change seems to be necessary for sight. The perceptual system cannot grasp the rapid flow; it constructs a solid reality out of the repetitions. Bateson claims that perception operates only on difference; all receipt of information is receipt of difference. All perception of difference is limited by threshold.

This cognitive homeostasis is a veil of attachments to habits that work. Habit is a self-defense and self-limit. Merleau-Ponty concludes, "In the case under consideration, the ambiguity of knowledge amounts to this: Our body comprises as it were two distinct layers, that of the habit body and that of the body at this moment" (in *The Phenomenology of Perception*). The habit body is bound in a certain environment, but the actual body is capable of transcending it. Consciousness can avoid the factual body. Merleau-Ponty implied that the acceptance of scientific prejudices is an avoidance of the responsibility for creating the world. Our senses transform rhythms. The interplay of senses is kept in proper rhythm in the midbrain, beneath the conscious thought in cortex.

Seeing also involves body functions such as position of joints, position in gravity, what is being touched or smelled. Electrical pathways of nerves develop before the tissue itself. The priority of pattern over matter refutes mechanism. *Aesthesis* means perception. True perception grasps wholes and figures (like tribes hunting berries). Truth is a form of *alethia* (unhiddenness)—perceiving reveals. Describing the experience of objects is difficult. As one attends to specific qualities, one brackets out the balance of less relevant experience. This has been shown to be true of aesthetic perception by the Gestaltists, who noted that figure and ground deny, in the act of requiring, each other. Aesthetic understanding amounts to a form of reading the world (informing the world) and receiving inherent meaning (cf. aesthetics). Unfolding permits experience of a different reality.

Wild Experience & the Unconscious
Subjectivity

On every level being feels. There is an incarnate subjectivity in all beings. Perception is ontological, not psychological; the psychological is derivative. The contours of things are the contours of being. Opposition always appears with an intrinsic connection, which cannot be directly observed, and so is not stressed. We study object/subjects as structured histories. In the pursuit of cognitive science, exclusive objectivity can be a stumbling block.

Subjectivity intertwines with the world, behind which is nothing. There is no subject/object difference. The subject and the world are mutually enveloping and inseparable. The mind hides on the other side of the body, invisible. Consciousness brings the invisible over into the visible. The first step of analysis dissects a unity into an experiencing subject and an experiencing object. This dividing line is often artificial and arbitrary; it is a convenience, a necessary, illusory partitioning for perception.

Nietzsche expected that the idea of substance was the outcome of concept of subject. He states, "We distinguish ourselves as agents from action; we misunderstand the feeling of power, already the beginning of action, as the cause." (in R. Pfeffer, *Nietzsche: Disciple of Dionysius*). The thing-in-itself is a concept of the subject-in-itself. If we abandon the acting subject, we abandon the object, substance and materiality.

Wild Experience & Emotion

Ordinary experience, like Goethe's fact, is highly synthetic and made of a complexity of strands: past memories, desires, present perceptions, places, and histories, all hopelessly beyond the power of science to analyze. It is quintessentially wild, irrational, uncontrollable, and unphilosophical. It corresponds to wild nature, despite our efforts to garden both, by inventing social and intellectual disciplines. Almost all the richness of personal existence derives from this synthetic and eternally present confused consciousness of both internal and external reality—we know it is beyond the capacity of science. Being in the wild—just being—means being it. The importance of events is directly proportional to intensity not extensity. One can be inspired by moments in a forest, and remain dull after years of travelling the world. The life field expands into the geofield. The individual is the whole world. As the Brahmins expressed: *Tat tvam asi*. Inner recognition is the ultimate act of knowing—resonance with the true; it is the highest court of appeal, transcending time-bound, pragmatic criteria.

Emotion and experience exhibit field characteristics that can be measured. Much of modern biology treats the moments of consciousness and experience of animals as physical magnitudes. M. Clynes records a precise way of defining emotional states with the product presented graphically by computer as a pulse, a form against time (in G. Leonard, *The Silent Pulse*, p. 57). Each of seven basic feeling states (anger, hate, grief, love, passion, joy, and reverence) has a unique essentic form. But experience cannot be reduced to or exhausted by measurement.

Unconscious Experience

Sigmund Freud demonstrated that the unconscious had effects on conscious processes. The ego can be swamped with id demands. In an experiment with hungry chickens, it was discovered that they were unable to take their eyes off the food on the other side of a wire fence long enough to go around it; moderately hungry chickens could. Similarly, the id can swamp creativity. Curiosity is the mother of invention, necessity never was (according to Aldous Huxley).

Darwin, Freud and Lorenz all saw irrationality as a fundamental part of humans. Ernest Becker pleaded for taking a larger phenomenological field approach, viewing man as an animal who enjoys organismic self-expansion, who needs to feel powerful, and who considers larger phenomenological problems.

J. Lacan believes that the unconscious is structured like language but through associations, not causal links, that are discovered through poetry, word play (Freudian slips) and dreams. Dream is the basis of anticipatory consciousness. Dream deconstructs reality as a psychological metalysis. Dream realizes unconscious desire. Dreams deal with the anxiety of age and death. R.W. Emerson thought that "Dreams and beasts are the two keys by which we are to find out the secrets of our own nature" (in Lewis Mumford, *Interpretations and Forecasts*, p. 421).

Consciousness

Human identity establishes itself more slowly than that of plants and animals, through introspective experiences. The abstracted "I" is an experience of an inner self, a dimensionless and virtual point of view. In fact the word virtual came from the Latin *vir*, for human. Inner and outer converge on the reference point, "I." As the focus enlarges from that point, knowledge grows. At the extreme of total diffusion, the experience of "I" slips away and the experience seems observerless. Religion seems to spring from this mystical dissolution with the "It." Jung offered iconography (image) as a way of objectifying the feel of identity. The mandala can be used as a schema for the cosmos, as well as the self. The schema of the tree expresses a changing identity. Where the mandala is static, the tree is a process that can represent the changes that the self and the cosmos both experience. The mandala could be considered a cross-section of the tree (cf. the evolutionary tree with the great chain of being).

Consciousness is a state of being, not an essence to be found. The enfolded structure of information and matter enters consciousness. When listening to music, a note is heard while a number of previous notes are still reverberating in consciousness. It is the simultaneous presence of reverberations that are responsible for directly felt continuity. The reverberations are active transformations of what came earlier, not holding on in memory.

Husserl addresses the paradox: I am the ego in whose stream of consciousness the world itself—including myself existing in the world—first acquires meaning and reality. The statement 'Man is measure of all things' means that man measures. Things are reflected in man. Humans use consciousness to see world and events as symbols, as meaning. The world entering us must be balanced by us entering world. Thought is a matrix, engendering our reality. Matrix means mother, maw, or void.

Consciousness is wider than verbal thinking, which is only one aspect of it, but characterizes it. Consciousness can be described as a lexical field, whose terms are metaphors or analogues of behavior in world. Even the most basic verbs are metaphorical: 'To be' is from the Sanskrit *bhu*, meaning to grow. 'Am' or 'is' derive from the Sanskrit, *amsi*, meaning to breathe.

Participation

Would a rose be red if there was no one to look at it? No, the whole situation would be different; wavelengths would be reflected, but color would not be evaluated. A world without observers would be impossible. All beings participate. Fortunately, nature contains roses and eyes. There are no lone observers. The autonomy of our social system goes beyond our individual autonomy; the knower is the observer/community. Humanity participates in the natural world, so nature is human history. All beings participate in relationships that make up their worlds.

Through participation, consciousness is released to a thing so that it thinks in the participator. Full participation removes barriers of language; thingness pours through. In self-abandonment the space between self and thing disappears. This is meditative thinking as distinct from rational thinking. Intelligence must be involved with experience. Intelligence may be defined as insight into the relations relevant to compatibility of being with environment.

Self-conscious Experience

The large human body size, with billions of neural circuits, is a prerequisite for self-conscious intelligence. Galileo first discussed the importance of size in determining the form and operation of physical objects. Language is only possible, also, at certain sizes of brain.

Language creates strange loops when it talks about itself. Something in the system jumps out and acts on the system as if it were outside. We are disturbed by topological wrongness, by a blurring of inside/outside distinctions. The mind as an emergent phenomenon may be based on a strange loop. It may be an interaction between levels in which the top level reaches back toward the bottom and influences it, while being simultaneously determined by it. It is a self-reinforcing resonance between levels.

Understanding our own minds does not entail monitoring the brain state in all its detail (as Bateson's analogy with television implies). Self knowledge will always be incomplete and probably indescribable. It depends on a whole logic, *logos*, that no formal systems can have.

In *The Visible and Invisible*, Merleau-Ponty attempted to actualize the process of radical reflection started in the *Phenomenology of Perception*. Radical reflection is the doubling, the intertwining of the perceiver as he comes to himself in the perceptible world. It mirrors existence at its root, at its upsurge out of the anonymous sensible. In that sense the universe is a paradox: beings creating and being created by being.

The human life-world is symbolic. When it fails to create meaning, sickness results. Self-image is considered as a constellation of body images. Individuals have a personal space, that is, a sensitive projection of the body into a nearby area. W. James observed that we feel as if we extend into contiguous material (a car, home, or clothes). The body image may also include an internal concept of the spatial organization of the world.

Creativity

There is a basic need to diversify, to be free to try, after the basic survival needs are met. Maslow thought that humans had a hierarchy of needs, beginning with physiological needs and moving up to safety, love (belonging), esteem, and self-actualization. The higher do not take over until the lower are satisfied. Humans cannot measure everything, so they abstract, creatively. Any describable event is an abstraction from the indefinable totality of flowing movement (savage being). The whole process makes an impression on the inward side of man and this is expressed. By relating expression to new perceptions, relevant features are abstracted. Deep perception demands new, fresh, creative abstraction.

Through abstraction, human beings assimilate the world into consciousness, while participating in it, that is, transforming it. Assimilation and creative participation (=accommodation) are sides of a circular process. Qualities are immanent in the world and they are human objects—abstractions from our level in the process (not transcendent eternals, as Whitehead thought). Qualities are dependent on perspective and relative to position. Fear of complexity drives humans to abstract a consoling fiction. Out of the mysterious immensity of nature, we impose unity, and fundamentally homogenous thought.

Bateson assumes that thought resembles evolution in being a stochastic process. But that is only partly true. Thought patterns are a selection product of patterns of reality. Thought and abstraction is a form of human play. Role playing is a trying on of other consciousness. The reward of Aesthetics is the pleasure resulting from biologically appropriate activity.

A highly creative person deliberately challenges and shakes and disintegrates the self to reassemble the parts better (a good analogy is quantum foam). Virtual consciousness is a way of knowing that provides insight into the way the world works. It also has no effect, good or bad, on real world processes. A thought-world emerges from a real-world as a tree emerges from the earth. In some cases it loses a vital connection and drifts away. Then it can order the real world. Ideas can be expressed through the physical environment. W. Stevens said that each man dwells in the reality of the mind, an incorporeal world, of which paradoxically the corporal world is a dimension shared with others. The greatest poverty is to aspire to transcendence. For Stevens, the unity of being and knowing, word and being, can only be of theoretical significance. The world around us is actual. As soon as we try to account for the presence of the world, we step into the domain of the possible, philosophy, myth or poetry. Imaginative activity takes on meaning only as an event in the world for Stevens. Imagination is a way of seeing and feeling things as they compose an integral whole (after C.S. Peirce). Stevens shows the power of imagination in "The Idea of Order at Key West" (*The Palm at the End of the Mind*. New York: Vintage, 1972), p. 97):

> She was the single artificer of the world
> In which she sang. And when she sang, the sea,
> Whatever self it had, became the self
> That was her song, for she was the maker . . .

Except for her singing, she would be a worldless being, closed to a world and out of time. Stevens uses the image of the rock to stand for the ultimate horizon that is a more fundamental limit than time. It is that in which man must dwell, inclusive world of thing and idea that harbors the self and paradoxically the self harbors. Creators are drawn to paradoxes of one and many, unity and variety, determinism and freedom. Creativity is putting the matrices together. Metaphors can stand in for later connections as heuristic devices. Koestler conceives of knowledge and biological evolution as processes of creative accretion. The human mind, with its creative bisociation and moral judgment can turn targets into values and responses into ethical aims. The complexity of thought must increase to sort out intellectual contradiction. Calvin Taylor showed that creativity was the reconciliation of opposites; diffused attention is brought to sharp synthesis, remote things are associated, richness pruned, flexibility joined to mastery, ordering from chaos.

Figure 11. *World Tree print.*

Living in Place

Life-Space

There does not seem to be a formal relationship between physical and psychological fields; perhaps the relation is like classical and statistical entropy. Field theories in physics provide for continuity, in space-time, for instance. Sherrington had a field theory of subjective space. He distinguished between exteroceptive, interoceptive and proprioceptive fields; the exteroceptive receptive field was coextensive with the body surface and richer in receptors. These elements comprise a biological explanation of subjectivity. The brain evolved upon distance-receptor organs. The distance receptors induce anticipatory reactions, precurrent to consumatory reactions. The subjective field is characterized by a broadening of lived time. This extension includes lengthening of responses.

The field of self is parallel to Lewin's concept. The self is a creature committed to a specific association, a genome plus place; fitting of self to setting is definitive of both. Place/person/act are as indivisible as the STEM field (Space-Time-Energy-Mass). Lewin thought that the psychological fields joining the personality to its life-space (immediate environment) and life-space to larger environment were strong enough to alter objective facts, that is, to make them normative.

Lewin was willing to study the objective factors that are potential determiners of life-space. Psychology has not considered the life-world. The organism's own world is usually left out of consideration. Yet the idea of *umwelten* suggest that "cognitive" representations are very basic and continuous through humanity. L. Binswanger broke the life-world into three interrelated modes for human beings: *umwelt, mitwelt* and *eigenwelt*. The first refers to world of natural objects (environment); it is approximately equal to von Uexkull's idea of umwelt. the second to the human alone, the interrelationships of humans; the third is one's self-world (=thought-world). The same division could be made for animals.

Lewin's life space combines the umwelt and life-world (of Husserl). Topology provided the mathematical model for Lewin's representation of psychological processes. Topology is a geometry in which spatial relationships are represented in a strictly nonmetrical manner. Since topology had no directional concepts, Lewin invented a qualitative geometry (1938) called hodological space, represented by vectors. He used two-dimensional planar maps to represent life spaces (now, recent researchers use a linear graph, on which an indefinite number of points can be mutually interconnected; and asymmetrical relationships).

Lived space requires a three-dimensional representation. It may be Horizontal or vertical (Vertical=warp, horizontal=woof). The vertical aspect includes the high of a drug user or mountain climber; it can mean the loss of horizon and the horizontal. The horizontal dimension requires reciprocity; it is an intersubjective domain. Older cosmologies balanced the horizontal and vertical. That it is out of balance now causes problems. New mathematical treatments of fields tend to be three-dimensional. R. Thom's catastrophe theory and C. Waddington's epigenetic landscape are two such theories. The epigenetic landscape can be used to explain the chicken problem. The chicken's need chreod is deeper than the path of a cognitive chreod around the fence. So the hungry chicken can only go toward the food, pecking futilely at the fence between it and the food. Less hungry chickens could go around.

Field of Person

Our direct intuitions of nature tell us that the earth is infinitely strange; it is alien, even when gentle and beautiful. The earth has innumerable modes of being that are not human modes of being. It seems always mysteriously impersonal, unconscious, immoral, hostile, sinister. Paul Shepard points out that we mistakenly conclude that our skin is the boundary to ourselves. But intuition also senses the interdependence of nature. We extend the boundaries of personality to other things and people. As Whitehead pointed out, everything prehends everything else. The human skin is like a pond surface. The skin's interpenetration ennobles and extends the self—the beauty and complexity of nature are continuous with ourselves. The earth is a living cell. The image of the net or web is too simple.

Our species has been shaped by the earth. The desire to save forests, wetlands—all natural ecosystems is a expression of deep human values (or perhaps a more basic survival instinct). Experience of wildness lets us capture some of our own wildness and authenticity. Our emotional response to the unfathomability of the ocean or luminosity of the desert is an expression of aspects of our fundamental being that are still in resonance with these forces.

Mental health can be related to the quality of the landscape. Rene Dubos, John Passmore, and others argue this. Humans have made landscapes into flatscapes, then concentrated on indulging the individual.

Experiments show that when populations of a number of species are subjected constantly to artificial conditions that appear to favor the growth and survival of individuals, the result is the death of many individuals and eventually extinction of the race. Many humans live piled in cages. During an experiment with overcrowding in rats, John Calhoun recorded that they entered a behavioral sink, with varieties of abnormal behavior (in "Population density and social pathology." *Sci. Am.* (1962) 206: 139-148). The significance of density figures to human health is not known. Hall suggests deep-rooted cultural differences by different people in response to spatial relationships and high densities. The Industrial crusade for mobility has fractured experience. Bombarded by information out of context, our artifactual environment tends to make us more cerebral, and we lose the richness of body sensibility.

What is impaired in the absence of a rich ecology is the individual's knowledge of himself, not only as a person, but as a member of a species. H. Searle's thesis is that the environment constitutes one of the most important ingredients of human psychological existence. There is within the individual a sense of relatedness to total environment. He does not draw the limit, as Schweitzer does regarding the concern of ethics, to include the wider sphere of all that lives; psychoanalysis needs to concern itself with the total human and ambihuman environment, inanimate and animate.

A deep relationship with a place is as necessary as one with other humans. Without it, existence loses much of its significance. A range of experiences can spring from a place, from depression to the peak experiences described by Maslow. Then there is the opposite feeling, the dullness of place, where everything becomes oppressive. Life becomes tedious. Drudgery is part of commitment to place; it is acceptance of restrictions.

The word nostalgia was coined by J. Hofer (1678) to describe an illness characterized by insomnia, palpitations, stupor, fever, and persistent thought of home. The disease could result in death. Thus far, the sense of place cannot be gleaned from an analysis of the nervous system. Yet a place shapes the nervous system, somehow. A place is known through its essential style or physiognomy. Paris, Chicago or Moscow have significant differences. This was so long before Horace: That corner of the world smiles for me more than anywhere else—*Ille terrarum mihi praeter omnis Angulus ridet.*

Spirit of Place

The making of places from undifferentiated wilderness is the human ordering of the world. A place changes qualitatively; it becomes structured. Natural complexity decreases as the human increases, although the two are not mutually exclusive. Places are ecosystems intimately associated with people. Fitness is achieved after slow progressive reciprocal adaptations; it requires a stability of relationships between societies and the place. The overuse of the word environment also conveys the poverty of our relationships with places. Etymologically, it just means whatever is 'around' us. Places, however, are unique.

Human places are complex integrations of nature and culture that develop in particular locations. The feeling of a geography is prior to its study. The place precedes knowledge of it. The knowledge of place is one of the first links in chain of knowledge. Being human is having and knowing a place. This knowing is essential to our existence.

Shepard suggests that for each individual the organization of thinking and meaning is intimately related to specific places. Experience focuses on a place, which acts as the background for specific events. The features of world are experienced meaningfully. The place is a matrix for ordering experience. The essence of place lies in unselfconscious intentionality. Only learning flowing from hospitable presence can promote life and enhance human existence. Lived space is human intention inscribed on earth. Patterns of significance are described. Each difference in the landscape has meaning, as when the aborigines of Northwest Australia perceive physical differences and even a symbolic landscape. In fact they structure space according to myth, where Europeans use buildings and roads.

Lived-space needs to acquire cohesion, to become rich and diverse with experience of living. The world becomes richer with the addition of significant human places to remote wild ones. The specificity of place is important. The earth extrudes itself into particular plants and animals; flexes mountains; and sweats weather. Places animate—from the Latin *anima*, meaning 'inspire'—people. The inspiration of the sentiment of dependence is called impregnation. Animals and humans are imprinted early in life to particular places (philopatry). Spirituality expresses the bond with all living beings in a place. Rene Dubos has eloquently described the spirit of place in France and America, in his book, *A God Within*. The spirit of each place may remain to influence successive generations without being homogenized by mass culture or technological efficiency into a flatscape of little significance. It can be concluded from an MIT study that the delights of waste spaces, odd lots, tangled woods left between housing projects must be preserved (in P. Shepard and D. McKinley, eds., *The Subversive Science*).

Does it take years of research to see that the world needs hiding places and hidden places? People remember most vividly those elements of their childhood which involved landscapes: Lawns, hills, woods, and water. The most popular outdoor activities in America are picnicking (over 80.5 million in 1981) and walking (67.8 million). The spirit of place lies in its landscape. There is a persistence of place that shapes human community. Every place has a unique identity, a persistent sameness as a result of combinations of factors. The spirit of place a constant thread.

At-Homeness

The notion that the earth is a living being is an ancient one. In taoist science, feng-shui or geomancy, subtle forces flow through the earth like blood in a body. To build a city it was necessary to consult the landscape, chart the flow of forces, and place buildings with utmost care to be in harmony with the place. Geomancy is finding the right place. Petitioning the spirit of the place to build a wonderful city.

Gardens and parks have been designed to express an idealized view of natural and agricultural scenes, since Sumerian times, at least, over 5000 years. Many names for the landscape—grove, lawn—are drawn from the imagery of the garden. The complementary aspects of landscape planning are: the invariants of a given area and the artistic imagination of a planner. Conrad Aiken recognized that "The language and the landscape are the same, for we ourselves are the landscape and are the land" (Ibid).

A place is a part of the environment claimed by feeling. Emotion binds together motion and perception. Emotion can transcend distance. Emotion creates an 'in-place.' A place must be found and made; it does not exist before a priori. Neil Evernden asked what it does to a person to see his place, context, destroyed? What does it do? It creates violence, apathy. Modern populations are rootless, moving about from city to city. We are suffering from a placelessness, which arises from our style of efficiency and proclamation of mass values. The environment of few significant places becomes a flatscape. It is turned into uses. John Fowles warns that "We shall never fully understand nature (or ourselves) and certainly never respect it, until we dissociate the wild from the notion of usability—however innocent and harmless the use." (in Seeing Nature Whole, *Harper's* 259: 49-56). This uselessness lies at the root of our hatred and indifference toward it.

We will have to pay attention to the unfashionable mesosphere, where we live as conscious beings: the land forms and vegetation that mining, agriculture and architecture are destroying. The need is basic: heterogenous, textured environments, woodlands, streams, rocky areas—diversity and choice in the natural environment as well as domesticated land, urban places. We need unique and particular places.

Nature is not really seen in the individual present, which no one trusts, but is reported and edited. The created information is emphasized, while the act of creation is ignored. We lack trust in the present, the actual seeing, because culture tells us to trust only the edited, public report. W. Worringer figured that the urge to empathy which follows the natural contours of living things came only after a certain relation of confidence between man and the nonhuman world had developed. Worringer finds the origin of artistic expression in tendency to counter sense of being lost in the universe (in *Abstraction and Empathy*). Empathy is latent in humans, but held in check by dread of space and the urge to abstraction. Trust is necessary for empathetic response to call of distance that bids us move out into the world. When we are claimed and backed up, we feel at home in the world. Life cannot proceed on the terms of mastery and control alone.

One cannot trust using resources, hoarding or spending. Too much control is detrimental to all relationships, especially friendship or marriage. Control and surrender must complement each other. Simplicity and surrender are high values only in a world one trusts, to which one feels attuned at the deepest levels. Word is spiritually alive. Spirituality is a state of mind, of being, in which we experience the world as if it were endowed with grace, a mysterious, wonderful place to be.

There is an ecology of the spirit, which can be trusted like all life support systems, to create balance and compensation. The developing reality may require material simplicity, but can have visionary abundance. We can relearn to trust a place. Home requires rootedness, at-easeness, and regeneration. Von Uexkull describes the importance of rootedness in his concept of lived-world (*umwelt*). Feeling at home is a state of awareness; losing the feeling may cause a crisis of anxiety.

After travelling these problems alone, we can come together toward at-homeness, where we can be ourselves. Ecology relates to at-homeness; a dwelling in neighborhood of its source. Adolf Portmann observed that insects and animals displayed a powerful attachment to places; that it was best understood as home. The attachment to a place is rootedness. What does it mean to be at-home? The fundamental ambiguity of existence is that humans have different capacities for feelings and awareness. Some feel strongly about a place or home; others never do. Humans are present to reality at every moment; the contact is available. We need only to reciprocate and be available; to be and let be; reaching out and being ready to receive the other—any being. We need not feel homeless. But home is also an enclosure, a place for protection and privacy.

Being inside is knowing where; it is safety, cosmos, enclosure. Inside and outside, like a dialectic, can always be reversed. Empathy is willingness to be open to significance, to know and respect symbols of place. A house is a place that provides shelter; it answers social needs; it is a repository of memories, a field of care. For the private self the house is a world; for public selves, the world is a town or civic center. Sitting is a shift from visual to tactile: taste warmth, hunger. The Greek word to eat (*edo*) is similar to that for seat, abode and dwelling (*edos*). In prenatal states to dwell and to live are inseparable.

In English the term for dwelling is to stay. This is the symbolic opposite of moving or changing. It means to withstand against time; existing points to a lasting moment in all changes (from the Latin *ex sistere*, to make to stand out); it resists and persists. Permanence is important element in idea of place. The Greeks valued autochthony and took pride in being natives. The benefits of settlement are economic, ecological and spiritual. Economic because everyone will have to learn to live in the limits of photosynthesis and watersheds. A sense of place, with its beings and features, is necessary for information on how to live, get food, and stay dry.

An ecology is where we live; we need to know about it. Environmental impact statements give people a voice in any proposed changes where they are living. People cultivating a sense of place are people in place. Their work can be appropriate; appropriate growing, logging, mining, or building. The ecological benefits of rootedness are that people will take care of a place if they realize they are going to be there for a thousand years. Having a place means that the inhabitant has stock in it and participates in its unfolding, through planting and caring. Detailed understanding of plants in a locale allow gathering of food and medicine.

People in place—being in place as used here means in a human scale, in unique surroundings—acquire a sense of community, nonhuman and human; shared set of values and concerns; health and spiritual benefit. Caring for a place involves concern and responsibility. This attitude is similar to one described by Martin Heidegger as caring (*Sorge*). Care is presented as the total structure of the person: in the projection of being, in being in a particular situation (with limits), and in absorption in the world by virtue of concern for it (in *Being and Time*, p. 192). Care is the recognition that a human being is a participant in the world. It is tolerance for the essence of a place; the willingness to not change or exploit. A home can only be realized through caring; to have a home is to dwell in earth.

Pangeographies

Terrae Incognitae

Wright suggested that the earth was an immense patchwork of miniature terrae incognitae. The private geographies of individuals. Instead of one world, there are many private geographies. The role of the individual past dominates the milieu. But all this experience comes together in communities to make up a social reality. The learned geography of the world is unified by ideas, art and logic. Each human being inhabits an autonomous, private world; these worlds may be very different, and should inspire respect. We need to recognize the autonomy of consciousness. We construct our normality from information from the senses, which are shaped by culture. We live in a fog of separateness. There is a cultural bias that prevents us from knowing how much we are contributing to the world we take in. Inside the human consciousness is a bit of tree consciousness. Union is recognition. Humans are embedded in places.

Place defines space. Space is created and personalized. In humans space has psychological, social and spiritual meanings. Even neighborhoods share common store of general myths of a larger field or nation, in which their local areas are embedded. Mythical space also functions as a component in a world view that may be better articulated. Mythical space is an intellectual construct, an elaborate response to human needs. It can differ from scientifically conceived space in that it can ignore the logic of exclusion and contradiction; it can have many centers, for example. From a biological perspective, we realize that we and the habitat are one; this is the necessity of a symbiotic and holistic attitude. Reverence for the universe follows from the recognition of the universe as home for humanity.

Biogeographies

A. von Humboldt's *Cosmos* (1842) presented a comprehensive picture of the natural environments of earth and the nature of some human societies adapted to them. Cosmology embraces a knowledge of earth and of dwellings upon it. Cosmology relies on geology and history, as well as on other sciences and humanities. In some sense the planet as a whole can be grasped and understood. But this is unlikely without a finer regional knowledge first, everywhere. The earth can be conceptually divided.

After the entire biosphere, the next highest macrolevel is the biotic or biogeographical province. Ray Dasmann has identified at least 200, determined by climactic and geographical factors. They qualify for separate levels of autopoetic macrostructures; little of the flora and fauna is shared elsewhere. Biogeographic provinces were redrawn by demands of conservation. F. Clements and V. Shelford produced the biome system of classification for North America. Later, L.R. Dice mapped the biotic provinces of North America. And Dasmann applied this classification system to the entire world. In collaboration with M. Udvardy, he proposed the less corrupted term biogeographical province. A region can be defined by species, watershed, landform, or actually cultural. Biotic populations would probably be best, as in place in geographical regions.

Social boundaries would be better aligned to ecological realities. Different cultures could inhabit the same province, e.g., the English and Irish. A. Van Newkirk suggests calling cultural areas 'regional human biogeographies' or bioregions. Inhabitants need to know natural associations because these determine the harmony of growth or development. A natural region supports a great deal of life without human intervention; and, it produces enough life to support a reasonable number of humans.

There should be at least one reserve in each unique province in the world. So it would make more sense to have a national park in the Sahara, Dasmann suggests, than another one in Kenya. There are none in semi-arid provinces or tropical rain forests. A bioregion recognizes the connection between the human mind and nature. Bioregional practice involves resistance and renewal. Resistance is opposition to greed, uncaring and unintelligence. Its focus is against destruction of habitats. Renewal pervades the spirit of planting and caring (in the larger sense). Fundamentally, biogeography relates to knowing land directly, with the body and time, not just intellectually. Gary Snyder explains that maps, histories and lists are just part of the menu. Biogeography is political; it destroys a nation's pretensions; it cuts off exploitation and discourages travel for sensation. It is businesslike and playful; it can nurture or kill, says Snyder.

Mesocosm

Standing in Place

Human beings inhabit many conceptual universes. They move from the universe of discourse on physics to the universe of discourse on Mozart, from ethics to biology. But no one knows how the molecule is related to the canon or mysticism is related to sponges. The universes are combined only in us; we talk about all of them. There are no logical or scientific bridges between them. We can only jump from one to another, intuitively somehow. We know; we have an epistemology. Epistemology means 'standing in a place.'

Scientific epistemology has tried to explain them. But scientific epistemology is a basilisk that kills what it sees, and only sees by killing. Combined with the industrial canon—we should do what we can do—incredible waste in practice and imbalance in theory result. We have built a knowledge killed and devoured by analysis, and while this may be acceptable for understanding certain levels of existence, the knowledge of a whole, living world cannot be obtained this way. Wordsworth accused: 'We murder to dissect.' Scientific explanation lists the contents, but leaves meaning out of the equation. Meaning is a relationship in context. With Democritus, we cut ourselves out of the picture to simplify it, but also cut out ethical and aesthetic values.

A given set of descriptions is conditioned by a world view, and then articulates that view (ontologically bound). In spite of our dexterity at description, we are stupefied by social and ecological problems that do not yield to description. New knowledge is an epistemological imperative for survival. But the increase in knowledge will not necessarily mean an increase in value. Scientific descriptions are often useless for expressing human experience. Not all facts can be expressed in numbers; many require words, or perhaps just gestures.

Bateson recognizes that there is an ecology of bad ideas, just as there are ecologies of weeds or robins. When epistemology is narrowed to personal interests, the larger system is forgotten. Our compulsion to save individual lives has created the possibility of world famine. This massive aggregation of threats to ecological systems rises out of errors of thought at deep and partly unconscious levels, according to Bateson. The ecocrisis is a crisis of ideas, as well as values. The roots of the ecological crisis are epistemological. We need to shift our whole frame of reference and our attitude toward life. This kind of paradigm shift has been described by F. Capra, in *The Turning Point*.

Robert Theobald claimed that the cure for the ecocrisis is a changed way of perceiving reality. Thus the timeliness of a new value system, a new epistemology, and a new world view. A new epistemology can be designed over the years, a subversive metarevolution, resulting from the integration of many ideas. The survival of two antithetical viewpoints— particle-wave theory—provided a stimulating tension for physics that delayed resolution until synthesis was possible. This new epistemology must be structured and unified in a comprehensive framework. It must reconcile the polarities of exploitation and preservation, global and local. Epistemology and ontology are additive truths. Godel stated that any axiomatic system is also a normative system; the goals are built into the structure. But more than one epistemology is required. An epistemology is needed that would allow an investigator to validate or falsify data where samples are small and nonrepeatable, and where uniqueness overrides system parameters. Epistemologies are needed for mystical and practical experiences, for sensory and extrasensory perceptions, for the validation and signification of all types of human experience. There can be no unity of knowledge unless there are epistemologies for every kind of experience, and a framework of sufficient depth and breadth for models to account for experiences. The rational does not need to be pitted against the emotional, intellectual against instinctive, or analytical against inspirational. A new epistemology must be taken from both halves of the brain. Man in the natural world can be known through an epistemology of participation. Knowledge comes into being in autonomous units through an interwoven mesh of frozen histories, pulling up its content from within. Participation is the level above objectivism/subjectivism. Everything we know is our experience, not naive reality. We need to explain how we come to see facts the way we see them (like Goethe). We fit the environment and our personality must be implicit in the scientific world view. We can experience science fact from within, understanding by sharing intentional meaning and personal address of things. A scientist's metaphysical beliefs influence his work. Metaphysics is the transcendence of physics. It signals the beginning of a new epistemology: pluralistic, life-rooted, cosmos-oriented.

Traditional Science

Most human truths are invented. Although it is as real as ideas, mathematical truth is not independent of human thought processes. And that is why it matches the universe so well. It describes the working of thought and nature with great accuracy, although perfect precision is impossible due to the uniqueness of individual events. It is also an element in our way of perceiving phenomena. Piaget states that knowledge is a special case of biological adaptation. He suggests that all human action consists of a balancing of the processes of assimilation and accommodation (in *Logical Thinking in Children*, p. 6). He distinguishes between accommodate and assimilate: the first means to establish a common measure; the second means to digest. Needs first incorporate things and people into the subject's own activity, to assimilate into existing mental structures, then readjust the structures as a function of subtle transformations, to accommodate them to external objects. Knowledge does not begin with knowledge of self or things, but of their interactions. By progressing to both poles, intelligence organizes the world. Science has become stuck in external accommodation.

Monocular Science

Traditional science attempts to control a situation, by thought or experiment. An experiment limits degrees of freedom in a timeless (formal) manner; it screens out quality. The gain from an experiment is an 'if/then' structure. resulting in mathematically specific functions. Portions of the universe are placed behind glass in a laboratory world. As science cuts the connection to direct observation, it becomes blind as mathematics to outer world. The formality of science makes statements about outer world tautological. This is a problem with quanta, species fitness and psychological needs.

J.S. Mill and others have justified the exploitation of nature through scientific technology by holding nature to be brutal and dumb. Mill added that all human action improved the course of nature, that man must strive to make nature conform to high human standards of justice and goodness. Is this the trap of arrogance Schweitzer fell into? The scientific method seems to have assumed both statements. Our culture has been distorted by the modern emphasis on the scientific method, with its devaluation of philosophical concepts. Rational values are exaggerated and spiritual events are ignored or suppressed.

Ecologically, we are deceiving ourselves, not by the objectivity of our facts, but by their triviality and unrelatedness. Parts of problems are identified and analyzed, but the conclusions are trivial and weak. Many studies are too specialized or irrelevant. The analysis of complex problems is as beyond the specialist as is the synthesis. Many scientists, such as Polanyi, Maslow and Koestler, have questioned the adequacy of scientific method and theory, with the intention of eliminating its reductionism and broadening its sensibilities. Science can enlarge its capacity for corrective self-awareness. The blending of scientific objectivity with the sensuous and intuitive capacities of the mind is called hierarchical integration by Maslow (in *The Psychology of Science*). Science should strive for comprehension above clarity.

Modern science does not capture the state of being that experiences symbols. It does not value rare experiences of direct observation or through clear description. Symbolic understanding could improve the quality of human observation. The modern biological view of man is the result of man's loss of a symbolic understanding of nature according to J. Needleman. The symbols are only understood in a different state of consciousness. Pre-20th century teachings are often judged as picturesque or insane. John Ruskin regarded the false perception of smiling fields and somber mountains as a pathetic fallacy. Emotional responses should be tied to the plain facts of nature; but Goethe knew that there were no plain facts. Now our perception is crippled by an apathetic fallacy—we see nature as dead. The pathetic fallacy is a fallacy only to apathetic, who are victims of the apathetic fallacy.

Perhaps big science has too much momentum. Theodore Roszak acknowledges its schizoid attraction and repulsion, with the twin promise of glorious accomplishment and hideous death. Who would escape being torn between yes and no, if even our end would shine with Promethean grandeur. The image of big science is a barrier to a new vision: the scientist as tragic hero, isolated in chaotic nature, but strong in his proud individuality. The scientific cosmology is deficient; it is limited to a certain category of facts. But modern science is undermining the scientific world view. Quantum mechanics has altered the picture of the universe, making it mysterious again.

Binocular Science
Science can never be wholly articulate, by definition. Since the quantum revolution, it has ceased to be mechanical, but it is still impersonal and it cannot afford to be. Roszak noted that there was a humanism of celebration in Pico, Bacon and Newton that once was the pride of science. It needs to be again.

G.G. Simpson made an important distinction between science and other systematic thought; science is self-testing and self-correcting. Perspective can mean enlargement (microscope or telescope), different parts (five blind men on elephant), or angles that can be added up to comprehensive perspective. This can be extrapolated to human diversity; monocular vision is impoverished compared to binocular. James Jeans pointed out that the history of physical science in the twentieth century is one of progressive emancipation from the purely human angle of vision. If we respect ourselves, we must respect other equally purposive, adaptive systems. Science expresses human capacity to surpass present perception and to operate in a realm of possibilities in which the actual experience is only one variant among many virtual experiences. Science is one manifestation of human freedom from fate. Knowledge enlarges the range of options. It generates innovations, but it constantly surprises because new discoveries and applications are so unpredictable. Thus, knowledge makes people receptive to new attitudes and willing to change their ways. Heidegger cautioned humans to wait, rather than guess about their actions. Evernden defines a hypothesis as a guess about part of reality; guesses can be accumulated to build a picture of a way the world may be. And if guesswork is science, then there is no reason not to include insights from Goethe or the Tao Te Ching. Guesses are made by animals or humans in living; it is part of adaptation. When we refuse to guess, for whatever reason, we remain controlled by habit and tradition.

Systems (Differential Science). Erwin Laszlo thinks that the words speciation and complexity should be separated by the concept of differentiation. This differentiation involves more than complexity; it requires high order mechanisms of systemic integration. The word system is used in a vague way. Von Bertalanffy reserves its use to complexes of elements in interaction to which systems laws can be applied. Behavior of similar systems, herds or societies, must be governed by same set of laws, at some level. The term can be applied to any contingent articles, cigarettes, restrooms, paper, water.

A system is a model of general nature, a conceptual analog of certain universal traits of observed entities. Systems have predictive value. Wilson states that systems may operate in three dynamic modes: deterministic, telic (Normative) and probabilistic. First order attributes of these systems are: deterministic— closed, predictable and causal; telic—open, finalistic, irreversible, and forecastable; probabilistic—locally open, generally acausal, reversible, and unpredictable. We would be wise to assume that all three exist and not try to reduce them to one.

The success of general systems theory (von Bertalanffy) can be attributed to the use of telic models, systems of description in which values are admitted implicitly or explicitly as components of the system. A model must be comprehensive, normative and descriptive in the enlarged sense. Bertalanffy distinguishes between open and closed systems. The open system may attain a steady state, as processes go on. This is same as dissipative processes. Analysis of a system cannot begin without acknowledging that the system is a coherent phenomenon; similarly, the holistic view cannot ignore the parts. It is the problem of field and focus in gestalt therapy.

Gregory Bateson lists the essential minimal characteristics of a system:

- The system shall operate with and upon differences •consist of closed loops or networks of pathways along which transforms of differences or differences shall be transmitted
- Many events within system can be energized by respondent part rather than by impact from triggering part (entrainment, sympathetic resonance)
- Show self-correctiveness in direction of homeostasis and/or in direction of runaway, implying trial and error.

These characteristics are generated whenever the appropriate circuit structure of causal loops exist. Feedback is different in general systems than cybernetics. In cybernetics it is regulation by way of linear and unidirectional (and circular) causality; in general, open systems, it is by way of multiple variable interactions. Individuals develop through differentiation. That complexity occurs in human brain, and in mechanical, social and biological cybernetic systems. Social systems develop through differentiation. There is a general trend toward progressive differentiation. The boundary depends on the function of the system. And the boundary cannot be cut any of the pathways of communication relevant to function of the mind.

Cybernetics (Analog Science). Cybernetics refers to the governance of systems; a system is a set of units, any one of which exist in different states, as influenced by states of other units. In all cybernetic systems, such as governor on steam engine, corrective action is brought by difference. A negative feedback loop is stabilizing; a positive one is disruptive. Prigogine indicated that the positive created; negative maintained. Positive feedback concerns the destabilization and development of new forms.

Adaptation is synonymous with cybernetic stability, not structural; this is efficiency in coping with environmental disturbances. Cybernetically stable systems are products of evolutionary process. Boulding likens it to development of chick from egg. Cybernetics assumes that intelligence is a feature of any feedback system that learns. The exact mechanisms do not need to be known. Cybernetics makes reasoning by analogy credible again.

Analog and Digital. Much learning, like acrobatics, is learning by sameness, not differences. Gestalt knowing is knowing through analogy. Differences are used by digital machines. Digital involves a discontinuity. Analog is continuous. Analog is inductive; differences are deductive. Could this be reversed? Genes and blood are examples of digital and analog systems. Complex systems like the body employ both digital and analog.

Two basic ways of doing science, the Aristotelian and the Baconian, can be contrasted. The Aristotelian scientist preferred to observe the behavior of nature, without constraints. Of all the causes of behavior, final cause was most important. Associating Aristotelian science with the Dark Ages in Europe, and with occult forces, Bacon insisted on the exact description of results from controlled experiments. He spoke of putting nature "to the question." Since Galileo, scientists have used ideal models and regarded real happenings as deviations. All events are described objectively, as motions of pure objects without reference to purpose or ends or as the actions of subjects. Aristotelian science saw life and purpose everywhere, and Baconian science responded by becoming atomistic and unconscious. In a sense, they are complementary, but complementarity does not work well in a complex universe. As physicists have found, Baconian science works well with atomic processes. Particles can be controlled. And as ethologists have found, Aristotelian science is very useful in analyzing animal behavior. The nature of an animal that is revealed under cruel and artificial conditions is not of much use in predicting normal behavior. Nor is an ideal model of a dolphin much use. Bees and martins have final causes, although stars and planets may not. An ecological science may combine the best features of both sciences.

Ecological Science

The application of human economics to nature resulted in bioeconomics, or ecology. Competition and cooperation were defined by functions of production and consumption. Tansley's use of the term "ecosystem" was an attempt to remove traces of organismic philosophy from a hardening science; it brought all of nature into an ordered system. Charles Elton transformed the Great Chain of Being into a chain of eating. As ecology has become more mathematical, nature has become a model economic system.

But ecology is an amphibious discipline. Human intention sometimes causes an opposite effect. The result of Elton's food chain was the realization that the bottom link—plants—is the most important. The use of energy flows in ecosystems resembles descriptions of yogic meditations (cf. enantiodromia).

Although economics provided the model for ecology, few ideas on environmental limits and interdependence were taken from ecology. Economists fear that "letting things alone" will lead to stagnation, poverty, and chaos. The technocratic vision is "life under control." The technological imperative is to strive for better efficiency.

Because ecology is amphibious, it has the authority of science and the force of moral knowledge. It is not a division of economics; if anything, economics is a division of ecology (cf. Boulding). Ecological knowledge can explain why nature is not productive in an industrial sense. It can support a "liberation" of life (cf. Cobb).

Ecological principles can be subducted into a cosmology. The relational, total-field image will replace the concept of organism-in-environment, according to Arne Naess (1972). Popular ecological principles are summarized as:

- Everything affects everything else: the holocoenotic environment relatedness is intuitive in reverence for life and leads to practice of caution. Adequate ecological information and infusion of its significance in human affairs will reduce the stress from premature attempts at harmony.
- The earth is covered with a vast array of ecosystems that interact and in which animals create niches.
- There is material cycling and energy flow: things cycle for reuse.
- Limiting factors that may not have a short time scale.
- Prolific nature of biological reproduction
- The carrying capacity can sustain a given amount of life.
- The diversity and stability of ecosystems are necessary; diversity buffers the influence of a single perturbation in the system. During an ice storm in the southeastern United States (1972-73), natural forests sustained breakage proportionate to species with brittle wood; A long-leaf pine plantation sustained great damage, because of brittle wood and long needles.

The critical message of ecology is that if we diminish variety in the natural earth, we debase its unity and wholeness. We destroy forces that create harmony and stability. If we wish to advance the unity of the natural earth, to harmonize on higher levels of development, we must preserve and promote variety. In nature variety emerges spontaneously, as the capacities of new species are tested by the environment. Ethical, aesthetic and utilitarian reasons all support the efforts to conserve the diversity of nature.

Ecology deals with the relationships of organisms to environments. It is not a reductive discipline, and not amenable to easy quantification. Ecology must balance the center from man or beast. Ecology per se cannot be studied, only its components and relations; it is therefore a perspective, a way of seeing. It is a perspective of the human situation in its interconnection. Ecology includes all events.

Adolf Portmann shows that every form of life appears as a Gestalt with a specific development in space-time. All living forms develop an image of their environments. Genetics provides the proper image choices for some—frogs, for instance. Evolution is the production of new codes of information to match a changing environment.

The human mind shares nature's intent—producing experience. The mind fits nature. The whole ecology is related to furthering the greater pattern of the universe itself. The universe is a regenerative system, of which we are a part. No energy is created or lost, according to classical physics. Roszak asked if ecology could approach the sacramental vision of nature. He characterized ecology for its sensibility; it is holistic, receptive, trustful, aesthetic, and intuitive; it is judgmental. This holistic attitude also flows through some professional ecologists, from Clements to Odum. Ecology must be capable of assimilating moral principle and visionary experience to be a science of the whole planet.

Organic Dialectic

Science has its revolutions, too. It does not need to be based on logical positivism and reductionism, though these have allowed great, insensitive changes. Whitehead thought that what had been missing during the formation of science was a sense of relatedness. This lack has been accentuated by conceptual barriers, i.e., scientific fields. As in an organism, the various parts of nature are so interdependent that nothing can be abstracted without altering the identity of it or the whole. Science can be restored to full sight from one-eyed reason only by rediscovering the depth of relatedness. Organismic trends can be seen in science: relativity, gestalt psychology, ecology.

There was a paradigm change in metaphor from machine to organic system that undermined atomism and the old animism alike in developmental biology. The modern notion of organicism goes back to 6th century B.C. China, with the foundation of Taoism. Things are what they are and act upon one another by virtue of their position within a system of patterns. The tao was the great pattern, a field of force in the physical and spiritual world. This organic conception was carried to Europe by the Jesuits in the eighteenth century and had a profound influence on the philosopher Leibnitz. Leibnitz influenced Morgan, Smuts, Whitehead, Needham, and Bertalanffy. For Bertalanffy organicism was necessary to accomplish three specific jobs in biology: appreciation of wholeness (regulation), organization (hierarchy and level laws), and dynamics (process, behavior of open systems).

Certain psychologists (e.g., Maslow) and philosophers (e.g., Merleau-Ponty) have preferred qualitative description to quantitative analysis. Sciences could use synthetic as well as analytic approaches to their subjects. Synthetic branches would be concerned with providing coherent pictures of the realms of study, as exemplified by the application of General Systems Theory to agriculture and farm animal welfare (Fox, 1983).

Ecology could become a unifying science, including the whole of human experience, and permitting science an ethical dimension. Goethe's natural philosophy incorporates a world view described as organic dialectics; its method is described by contemplative nonintervention and the primacy of the qualitative (by T. Roszak, in *Where the Wasteland Ends*, p. 329). Organic Dialectics is a phenomenological science. Goethe was aware of the pervasive pattern of process, of transformation, unity in process. This unity in process was referred to as morphology by Goethe. Evolutionary theory is built on morphology. Goethe's conception of evolution merged selectivity with destiny and external pressure with internal thrust. The two methods are described as follows.

1. *Contemplative Nonintervention*: An observerless and valueless science may be contrasted with the Goethean ideal of contemplative nonintervention. Eddington had asked if advanced equipment does not tell us how nature can be made to behave. Goethe felt that the human being was the best apparatus (perhaps to a foolish extreme). Rejecting analysis, he preferred passive attentiveness: knowledge comes of itself, in wholes (*gestalten*). The unique moment is an open secret (deep down phenomenon). The mind completes natures forms. Maslow recommends an I-Thou relationship as a paradigm for science: fusion knowledge. But what are the limits to these approaches? how deep? Beyond the deep lies "the realm of mothers." Goethe was reluctant to use instruments to study nature, being concerned that they would distort the phenomena or the natural scale. Instruments represented an aggressive desire of science to

stand outside of nature; They were an act of severence, motivated by desire for control. Later Eddington raised the same issue, that experiment might only tell us how nature can be made to behave. And Heisenberg expressed the exasperation that scientific investigation showed us nature exposed to our methods of inquiry. Goethe rejected domineering analysis; his radically different approach was passive attentiveness. An observer tried to get into the flow of phenomena; by observing patiently and receptively, an astonishing insight could cap years of patient watching. This was the attitude of relaxed attention, a receptive state of creation. Knowledge came of itself, in quantum leaps, a gestalt was perceived. The unique moment revealed the deep phenomenon (*Ur-phanomen*). Nature was a friend, beloved.

2. *Primacy of the Qualitative*: An exact sensory imagination is needed to midwife the deep-down phenomenon. Qualities must be evaluated; a script of qualities to be read for meaning. Sensory data were qualities savored, not measurements taken. Starting with qualities, the "exact sensory imagination" could midwife the deep phenomenon (see Northrup in Morris and Fox). Intuitive power transcended the bodily eye by working through it, toward deeper sensory participation. The subordination of qualitative experience to quantitative generalization amounted to death by abstraction: empiricide. Goethe regretted that with Newton, the brilliant meaning of light became merely subjective and uninteresting. But qualities could not be added or subtracted (unless by fuzzy sets); they had to be evaluated. Quantities could be counted. Newton considered colors and light as indirect phenomena from wavelengths; Goethe considered color direct and deduced wavelengths. Color was a presentation, perhaps a message. Neither theory should be mutually exclusive. That Newton was also an alchemist was ignored by traditional histories of science. translated what Goethe read only in the original. Applied systematically, Goethe's method of analogy is equivalent to the comparative method. He sought analogies instead of differences. The analogies were supported by empirical evidence and observation. This approach is not necessarily superior to the method of difference, but complementary.

In Goethe, all being becomes the object of intuition, as poetry is the product of intuition. His biological and physical research was based on artistic intuition. A style of knowledge is inseparable from some bodies of knowledge. How we know as well as what—life enhancingly. All fact is theory: a blend of perception, imagination and needs. Values are diffused through the theories of science as bubbles are diffused through water. We incorporate them through perception as fish breath through gills. These values distort the Euclidean straightness of facts. Facts metamorphose into values. Goethe: "The methodology of forms is the methodology of transformations. The working discipline of metamorphosis is the key to all the signs in nature" (A. Bergestraesser, *Goethe's Image of Man and Society*. Freiberg: Herder, 1962). Goethe attempted to use his method to produce an organic and morphological world-history. This methodology is part of nature. It reflects nature. Rilke wonders whether or not all the dynamics of nature, including those of human society, are hieroglyphics of the methodology of thinking. Early science saw the world as mechanism; modern biology is seeing it as resembling an organism; perhaps it will be seen as spirit or as a composite of all. Consciousness research chooses paradigms of nature that are mental, not mechanical (in the investigations of Tart, LeShan, Pribram, Krippner, White, Kamiya, and others).

Patient Practice

There are ways of dealing with the earth that are not scientific or technological; they are aesthetic or ethical. They are not incompatible with a whole science. In his field theory of being, Heidegger stated that a concern with being implies a patient existence, a willingness to lie in wait for an image to produce itself (without imposing meaning). Heidegger counsels man to watch and wait. Thomas Blackburn argues that we need a sensuous-intellectual complementarity in science. We rely on abstract quantification, but the mind and body process information with staggering sophistication and sensitivity by the direct sensuous experience of their surroundings.

Maslow, in "Towards a Humanistic Biology," saw the good specimen as chooser for the whole species. The organism may be seen as having biological wisdom; it can be trusted as autonomous, self-governing and self-choosing. To examine organisms, and nature in general, we must shift to a taoistic approach, asking rather than telling, observing rather than manipulating; receptive and passive, not active and forceful; "nonintruding," (Ibid, p. 18) and noncontrolling. It stresses noninterfering observation rather than controlling manipulation; it is receptive rather than forceful. This is part of the paradox of duality; it is detached yet concerned; free yet committed; and independent yet responsible. Classical objectivity may be contrasted with taoist, which is another path to objectivity with greater perception. Loving perception provides kinds of knowledge not available to nonlovers; this is especially true in ethological literature. Maslow cites his own work with monkeys. Lorenz, Tinbergen,

Schaller, Van Lowick-Goodall, and Fox have found it to be true. This is the way a good psychotherapist, teacher, scientist, parent, or friend functions.

Soul Science

> In the very earliest time,
> when both people and animals lived on earth,
> a person could become an animal if he wanted to
> and an animal could become a human being.
> Sometimes they were people
> and sometimes animals
> and there was no difference.
> All spoke the same language.
> From the Nalinq (in *America A Prophecy*, p. 258)

Nature is an extremely sensitive nexus of means and ends. Nature is a feeling system. We need a new animism to approach nature. This animism would allow us to behave "as if" nature was intelligent and sensitive.

What is necessary is not a primitive animism or a single-vision science, but a scientific animism, to replace scientific humanism and to understand our animalistic nature and use it as the foundation for a sound human ecology, philosophy and psychology. *Anima* is from the Latin word for soul. An inquiry that would carefully and appreciatively consider the animal aspects of ourselves and how we understand and empathize with other living organisms A scientific animism would consider the relations of humans to vegetation and the human attitudes toward ecotypes, like open plains and dense forests; it would consider the need for sacred places, and open, quiet or wild landscapes; it would consider territoriality, aggression, and the aesthetic reaction to the wonder and beauty of life.

A scientific animism would be concerned with far more than the anatomy and taxonomy of animals; it would be concerned with mutual training between human and nonhuman animals (the emotive bond); it would be concerned with the need for touch and phylogenetic possibilities of animal empathy—dogs, for instance, exhibit strong physiological changes when they are petted and human blood pressure drops. It feels good to be touched.

A scientific animism needs to understand the meaning of being human, to go below cultural or social explanations of love and alienation. And it may, as a genuine science, forget the analysis and lose itself in the ecstasy of the phenomenon that it sought to explain. Science functions best when we understand so perfectly that we no longer need it.

Totemism

Ali Al Amin Mazrui, in *A World Federation of Cultures*, contrasted pantheism, animism and totemism. The pantheist interprets the universe as holistic, but does not necessarily recognize any important duty to it; it is too neutral toward good and evil, destruction and preservation. A. Pope, W. Wordsworth and Spinoza were pantheistic in various degrees. Nor may the animist feel responsible if there is no distinction between life and death, if everything is merely transformed. African animism blurred distinction between living and dead, human and ambihuman; totemism is more selective. The totemist provides a commitment to preserve, through the bond of brotherhood.

A totem, as defined by J.G. Frazer, is a class of material objects regarded with superstitious respect, since it is believed that there is an intimate and special relation between humans and every member of the class. Totemism is an analogy between a social system and the natural world, in religious context. Certainly healthier than machine analogies. People are parts of society; people, animals and plants are parts of ecological system. Empathy is accentuated. Totemism teaches a nonvisual whatness about the self.

The practice of shamanism in itself has at its very center a teaching directly from the ambihuman, without a medicine man or a Buddhist master. It is healing based on naked experience, wild experience.

Paul Shepard (and independently M.W. Fox) proposed a human association devoted to each species of wild animal, so that every creature on earth would have a human constituency. The leagues dedicated to single species will accomplish nothing. It is the ecosystems, habitats, biocoenoses that must be saved. Animals live in communities, are parts of food chains. Emphasis on endangered species does not address habitat; it does not consider wholesale destruction of other species or individuals. A feeling for participation in ecosystems is necessary. A cosmology needs to foster a concern for nature, with a tendency to preserve it. A totemic disposition would increase a "primitive" awareness of the earth. There may be secondary or tertiary totems that overlap with other groups. The lion clan of the Baganda have the eagle as secondary totem. Totemism also occurs in native North America, Melanesia and Polynesia. B. Malinowski realized that primitive religion was nearer to reality and immediate practical life interests than most modern religions or some animism. L. Levy-Bruhl called the primitive awareness of the world the 'participation mystique.' It arises, not from desire for rational explanation of the universe, but as a response to collective needs and sentiments.

A Theology of the Earth

Conrad Bonifazi does not want to assert the sacredness of nature, but to express the personal terms of a human relationship with earth. Bonifazi, like Chardin, believes the rise of evolutionary biology provides a climate for refinement of world soul. The psyche, extending from the biosphere, is principally concentrated in human beings. But we must recognize the quality of sacredness in nature. We do not have to reanimate earth; earth animates. We need only realize it to awaken from a sad history. Magic never died; it was the sacred wholeness of planet, and we live in it.

The experience of the holy, the source of sanctity extended to place, needs to be expressed. Eliade defines heirophany as a manifestation of the sacred on earth. Tuan uses geopiety to describe a subset of sacred space. Some things can be saved by labeling them sacred: The dawn redwood and ginkgo tree were saved this way in China. Michael W. Fox relates an example of the convergence of mysticism and science in India (personal communication, 1981): "An Indian conservationist said to a farmer, "Do you mind if the tigers we are putting back into the jungle kill some of your cattle?" "No," replied the farmer, "You are putting the shakti back into the jungle to make it strong and healthy. We will all benefit." Wilderness should be sacred space because it is wholly other. It puts people in a mood for contact with the sacred and helps them achieve transcendence. Muir believed that wilderness was the most beautiful and moral part of nature.

An ethical attitude in the scientific study of nature readily leads to a theology of earth, according to Dubos. Ecology has opened the path to a theology of earth, short-circuiting institutional religion and pointing the way back to a harmonious mental space of primitive peoples. The hierarchical structure of thought (logical typing of classes) takes place in the hierarchical structure of the great chain of being. Bateson suggested that a sacred unity of the biosphere would have fewer epistemological errors than most religions. Being right means living right, exercising the virtues of prudence, gentleness and mutual aid.

Science is evolving toward the study of relationships as observed in complex systems. Dubos expands: "We may be about to recapture an experience of harmony, an intimation of the divine, from our scientific knowledge of the processes through which the earth became prepared for human life, and of the mechanisms through which man relates to the universe as a whole. A truly ecological view of the world has religious overtones" (in "Theology of the earth," *A God Within*, pp. 29-45). And he concludes that: "an ethical attitude in the scientific study of nature readily leads to a theology of the earth" (Ibid., p. 45). Dubos claims that reverence for nature is compatible with the responsibility for a creative stewardship of the earth.

To this end, he recommends a Benedictine philosophy, which would exercise more control over nature than a Franciscan approach (Idem, "Franciscan Conservation versus Benedictine Stewardship," *A God Within*. p. 153). Yet, St. Benedict cut down sacred groves before establishing monasteries. The concept of a sacred grove, which is very ecological, was regarded as heathenish and contemptible. A Benedictine approach regards the unfamiliar as profane. The quality of sacredness would be limited to gardens and human artifacts. This is similar to primitive cosmologies, where the center is sacred and surrounded with the profane.

Yet that part of the earth which is unfamiliar is most in need of being considered sacred. A new cosmology must regard the whole earth as sacred, for now. White proposes an alternative Christian view, with St. Francis as the patron saint for ecologists. St. Francis' view of nature rested on a unique panpsychism of all things animate and inanimate. If earth is a living being, pervaded by a vital force, we should change our attitude toward it. The Franciscan approach is more appropriate for expressing reverence for nature and for an optimum long-term human existence. We need to admire all of the wonderful combinations of nuclear particles that make up wildlife. We need to appreciate the beauty of their organization. If we were to truly feel the beauty of a river and oneness with water, we would feel its claims on us. Marcus Aurelius stated, "All living things are interwoven each with the other; the tie is sacred, and nothing, or next to nothing, is alien to ought else" (Idem, "Theology of the Earth," p. 44).

Figure 12. *Logo of Ecoforestry Institute.*

Living Together

Mythopoesis

Although ideology and mythology are systems of thought, they differ in at least one important respect. An ideology is a system of thought that aims to justify and preserve the status quo; its emphasis is on the present. A myth is characterized by traditional consciousness. Its emphasis is on the past and the sacred. Yet, it is a timeless understanding of the cosmos. Archaic myth makes all things into living beings, persons having life and movement. Myths sanctify the existence of a culture by underlining the continuity of human experience with recurring elements.

In the simplest human societies, mythology is the text of rites of passage. In Hindu, Chinese and Greek philosophy, it is the picture language of metaphysics. The first function is extended by the second; both harmoniously bind man to his world in its visible and transcendent aspects. von Bertalanffy proposed that myth, magic and language are interconnected near the origin of symbolic activity (e.g., in the stone age drawings at Altamira). Mythology is the womb of man's initiation to life and death.

Myth is usually a cosmological account of the past. Any account of the past that is believed to be true is mythical. Myth does not have to be limited to the sacred. All interpretation and recounting of the past is a form of mythmaking. That is why myths reflect the detail of a culture. The experiences of many lives, in their daily succession, are coded in myths, along with the natural phenomena, features of the culture, supernatural beliefs, and moral values, in a social order in a physical place.

Mythology springs from the psyche (center) and points back. Myths tell of the structure of the psyche; its order and forces in symbolic terms. They cannot properly be interpreted as references to local historical events. The imagery of mythology represents various degrees of opening of ego-consciousness toward the Mind at Large, in Huxley's term. In the *Timaeus*, Plato judged that "the motions that are akin to the divine principle within us are the thoughts and revolutions of the universe" (in *The Collected Dialogues of Plato*). This echoes the sentiments of the earliest of the Upanishads: "This self is the footprint of that All, for by it one knows the All—"

Joseph Campbell distinguishes three functions of mythology. The first function of a living mythology, the religious function, is to waken and maintain in the individual an experience of awe and respect in recognition of the ultimate mystery that transcends words and names, from which words turn back. The second function of mythology is to provide a cosmology, an image of the universe. In fact, the world has to be recognized and assimilated by the mythopoetic imagination. The third mythological function is the validation and maintenance of established order. Social and moral existences are in states of change. The function of myth is to describe the range of behavior that ordinary people are capable of. The spirit is forged only in fire of extreme experience. Levi-Strauss deduced that mind has a rhythm of opposites in which each conscious point has an unconscious counterpoint. Myths are ways of teaching unobservable realities by way of observable symbols. The moral orders of societies have always been founded on myths, writes Campbell (*Myths We Live By*, p. 10).

"All world views, like civilizations, are ultimately rooted in mythologies," asserts Henryk Skolimowski (in *EcoPhilosophy*). A myth is a set of assumptions that form the basis for comprehension of the world. Science is a form of mythology, equally as important as any other. Is it possible to arrive scientifically at an understanding of the life-supporting nature of myths, so as not to disqualify their necessity? But traditional science is too depersonalized and dangerous. It needs new paradigms. M. Polanyi compared a scientific paradigm to the mythology of the Azende tribal society (in T. Merriam, The disenchantment of the world. *The Ecologist*. 7:22-29). Structures of belief provide a means of rationalizing a way of life; and therefore have the same function as mythology. Science is mythical: presuppositions=unproved dogma; method=voodoo; facts=deities; and, neutrality=moral order. As in classical mythology, these characteristics are interconnected and interdependent.

How is it possible to recapture the paradoxical structure of myths? In cybernetic loops, figure is constrained by ground. Contradiction occurs on different language level. When myth is studied in a scientific way, mythopoetic consciousness is left out. The events can be traced, but the matrix does not appear. We have tried to produce a monolithic theory of the nature of myths, by describing them as inadequate attempts to describe nature, or as a protoscience explaining human origins, or as heuristic devices giving the whole vision to be completed by science. Malinowski believed that they were the founding charters for institutions. M. Eliade saw them as evocations of a creative era, to inspire creativity within nature. Radcliffe-Brown held that they were the basis for social rituals.

In a scientific view, ethics and cosmology are separate. But in a good mythology, there is a coherence between areas. The individual feeds back into the cosmology in altered form what was received. It is almost like a closed loop between cosmology, culture and the individual. Archaic peoples translate the natural world into the language of myth. Being a narrative, a myth is aesthetic as well as intellectual. Myths develop in terms of their own internal logic, drawing together observations of the world. C. Levi-Strauss described the process as bricolage, fitting the bits together, identifying impressions of life as sets and forming them into mythical systems; the world picture is a metaphorical puzzle. Bricolage is the mentality of synthesis, a technique for learning, creating, and expressing understanding, using whatever is available from the past and in the present to achieve an integrating form. This is what mythological thinking does, and what scientific thought might. Mythologies are of major importance in the life of society and civilization.

Contemporary thinkers, such as McKinley, see that we need a new mythology of humanity in nature. It is time to commit ourselves to a contemplative study of nature. We are still ignorant of what humans need from a world that has always had vivid mysteries that cannot be dismissed. It is ourselves that lack four-dimensional, transtemporal sight, not nature that lacks balance and precision.

But we need a comprehensive conceptual scheme to accommodate and articulate the variety of new relationships that are necessary for an ecologically healthy and harmonious world view. We will only learn to treat land as part of our community, and not as exploited commodity when we have new myths. Our old myths, that reality is hierarchical, the earth is female, and man is lord over the earth, have proven to be dangerous. They should be retired to the scrolls of dead myths. The eighteenth century held that a golden age would appear if the priests and kings were deposed. In the nineteenth century, a central myth (founded at the 1851 exposition) was that industrialization would bring universal peace. A mythology can affect every element of our social, individual, spiritual, ecological and political life, all at once. To achieve transformations of human culture, we must go beyond the authoritarian conspiracies and technocratic elitism, to create new mythologies.

A new world order is a cultural problem, not a psychological, geographical, economic, or political one. A new, dynamic, organic, flexible mythology is proposed. A mythology must take from and give to all cultures. The integrative ability of myths provides frameworks for decisions and values. When the relevant social unit was the tribe or nation, it was possible for the local mythology to represent others outside the bounds as inferior and its local inflection of the universal heritage of mythical imagery as the one, true, supreme. The young of the group would be trained to love home and hate outsiders. Xenophobia was once adaptive; now it is anachronistic. But there are no outsiders, we are all passengers, inhabitants. All dividing horizons on the planet have been shattered. We cannot hold our loves at home and project hatred outward.

Humans organize their lives in terms of models, metaphors, symbols, and ideals. One function of myth is to weave human knowledge, skills and aspirations together in intersubjective realm of image that blends science and art. Mythic symbols can store and convey vast amounts of information concisely. Myth is of the order of poetry. Campbell states that "Mythology—and therefore civilization—is a poetic, supernormal image, conceived, like all poetry, in depth, but susceptible of interpretation on various levels." (in *The Masks of God: Primitive Mythology*, p. 422). Whitman illustrates the new mythology: "And there is no object so soft but it makes a hub for the wheeled universe," (in *Myths We Live By*, p. 250, from *Leaves of Grass*). Mythologies and religions are great poems; when recognized as such, they point through things and events to the ubiquity of a 'presence' or eternity that is whole in each. All mythologies are alike in this function, according to Campbell. Where inspiring vision remains effective in a civilization, every creature in its range is alive. The first condition for a mythology to be effective is to cleanse the doors of perception to the wonder of ourselves and universe.

The new mythology will be the old perennial mythology, poetically renewed in the present, addressed to waking individuals in knowledge of themselves, as centers of the Mind at Large "each in his own way at one with all . . . with no horizons," as Campbell relates.

Ritual

In tribal or agrarian societies of the past, there was a commonly shared world view; ritual was at once work and play. Ritual is a technique for giving life. Archaic peoples believed that they could control life through ritual practice. A ritualistic view of history extended from millions of years, up to the efflorescence to technology, during the Renaissance.

Becker distinguishes two processes in ritual: (in Becker, *The Denial of Death*):

- macrocosmization: taking a part to be the whole, as in the correspondence of the head to the sky for a Hindu.
- microcosmization: projecting the earth or animals into heavens, as the Greeks did.

Divine kingship summed up the complementary processes; the king represented the humanized sun and the solarized man. The cosmos was set up by primitive man so it could expand symbolically and enjoy organismic pleasures. Archaic games were aimed at controlling nature, for self-perpetuation.

Myths and rituals constitute the mesocosm, through which the individual is brought into relation with the macrocosm. The mesocosm is the context of the social body, a "kind of living poem," in Campbell's words. The fundamental aim of ritual is the harmony and well-being of the community, its coordination with the harmony and nature of the cosmos, of which it is part, and the integration of the individual. The function of myth and ritual is to engage the individual in local organization, by creating intensely shared experiences. Participation is the impossibility of not being a part of a society. Ritual is the means to enforce participation.

In Zen and some Western therapies, initiation into the world of the "IT" (void, creative unconscious) takes place by breakdown and reintegration. The disciple learns from a master; there is transference. The disciple needs messages and techniques. The magic is fetishized, in a shallow ritual. Then creation transcends ritual.

Radcliffe-Brown considered that ritual promoted social solidarity. Pleasure, power and the laws of virtue (dharma)—two primary interests of raw individuals controlled by the mores of a local group—are fields of force composed in every functioning system of mythology. Whatever gives power is considered sacred. Food is sacred because it gives the power of life. If custom is essentially sacred, as Rank taught, why should money be different. Money gives power, and all power is sacred. But money is not sacred because its material power occludes the intrinsic worth of things. Its objectivity reduces uniqueness to the common denominator of economic worth in a closed, limited system. Money has become a modern universal rule of conduct (especially combined with Social Darwinism). Where the new rituals are connected again, there will be the possibility of ascendance, of power, with knowledge and with charity.

Peacock says that the modern, instrumental world view is threatened by inverted symbols. Inverted symbols still have the agrarian quality of cyclic ecosystems and antithetical seasons. Symbolic inversion may break people out of culturally defined roles, making people play opposite roles. It is certainly not the threat that unecological habits are. Ritual inversion may operate in similar way.

Radcliffe-Brown also considered that myth originated from ritual. This may be possibly true in cases, but usually ritual is directed toward an existing being. Ritual is not necessarily directly related to cosmology. Weiss relates that the Campa have a rich cosmology and an impoverished ritual. He concludes that ritual does not provide the basis of a cosmology. He quotes Kluckhohn, the anthropologist, as citing the cases of classical Greece, the Mohave, Bushmen, and Navahos, as having myths without associated rituals.

The real gods in tribal societies are nature gods, whose identity is as a member of the community; they are interested in communal affairs, and they maintain the traditional tribal culture pattern. But when the societies collapse, emphasis shifts to the supreme gods that were creators, but not active participants. The modern religions worship these gods exclusively; but the gods are asocial and have left the ecosystem.

Religion & Ideology
A.F.C. Wallace defines religion as a set of rituals, rationalized by myth, to mobilize supernatural powers to achieve or prevent transformations of state in man and nature. Religion arises from the desire to influence change, by appeal to super human or supernatural power. As a component of cosmology myths identify the nature of the supernatural entities. Rituals are stereotyped sequences, cultural mechanisms, for influencing the entities. They are also closely related to material culture. Ritual has instrumental priority over myth according to Wallace. Ritual behavior must function for the good of society; it must have survival value.

Religion is so complex, even in primitive tribes, that labeling by types seems impossible. Instead, Malinowski identified what religions do. Religion explains why things exist; it supports basic social institutions; it reinforces individual experience; and it integrates that experience into an order. Clifford Geertz defined religion as a system of symbols that establishes motivations in people by formulating a general order of existence. Religion bridges the thought-world and the real.

Religion has a specific set of features in every culture that performs basic functions. It may have its own cosmology, separate from secular culture; it has its own organization and attitudes. A religious attitude is directed toward understanding the invisible part of the world. Ritual is an activity directed toward the hidden properties of the cosmos. In a sense religion penetrates other sections of a culture, economic and political. It explains the world in terms of a necessarily hidden reality; that is, by definition. It makes the universe meaningful by reducing it to human terms; through anthropomorphization. It provides individual solace and hope during catastrophe, and security during danger. It enhances and maintains social order, through participation in ritual.

D.T. Campbell presumed that religion was the factor in changing competition into social cooperation. And there is a good argument that war was a factor. Religion transmits values and motivation for altruism to adhering populations. Moral norms must have had adaptive functions, e.g., curbing selfishness. Abstract inhibitory codes are more effective in urban settings than with face-to-face admonitions. Those selfish tendencies that were kept in check and identified as sins were those related to biological optimization of the self and children (selfishness, envy, rage, dishonesty, and promiscuity). Religious beliefs prompt optimal social behavior, with mutual benefits for the person and system.

Many religions promised long-term salvations, perhaps as a reward for limiting selfishness in life. Perhaps to keep its power. According to N. Brown, the basic enemy of mankind is repression, the denial of a full life. Religions defend their adherents from this enemy. The denial of death is a belief of many societies from primitive to technological. N.O. Brown and A. Harrington treat death as an enemy to be abolished. Becker's last book, *Escape From Evil*, reveals the lethal consequences of immortality systems. Humans expect a final fix: To survive death. In art or corporation, in heaven or children. Rank and Becker represent the general opinion that humans are alone consciously aware of death. But elephants and dolphins have demonstrated death awareness. The literal meaning of Jesus rising from the dead, for them, is that we shall too; and the moral is to turn toward the eternal.

But the mystical reading would refer to the transcendence of time; nowhere, but everywhere, in all; in this world of death is eternal life. In our body is our eternal life, here on earth and now. In India, the object of religion is to be born from the womb of myth, not to remain in it. Whoever has attained this second birth is free from the pedalogical devices of society. In Christian church, by contrast, the second birth is into the church—even for a saint. God is still the father. The poet and mystic regard the imagery of a revelation as a fiction through which an insight into the depths of being—in general and personal—is conveyed anagogically. Thomas Merton pronounced that "One cannot apprehend a symbol unless one is able to awaken, in one's own being, the spiritual resonances which correspond to the symbol not only as a sign but as 'sacrament' and 'presence'" (*Contemplation in a World of Action*, p. 257).

St. Francis found presences throughout. He adumbrated idea of equality of natural objects. The spiritual autonomy of all parts of nature is substituted for their unlimited exploitation. Spirituality and creativity

135

are biological features that connect us more deeply with the earth. A new religion needs to be sensitive to the claims of nature for protection and preservation. Any effort to understand the world is worship in a true sense. Ancient man revered the earth; scientific man has even more reason to do so. Ancient mystical techniques—Yoga, Sufism, Buddhism, Gnosticism—are needed to surround electronic technology with a web of human consciousness.

The primary function of religious structures is to provide a framework for ideals to inspire and sustain life. The adaptiveness of religious belief is related indirectly to ecology. Religion is responsive to ecological and economic conditions. Rappaport interpreted the ritual cycle of the Tsembaga as a regulating mechanism to maintain limits on fighting and using resources. Their rituals also facilitated trade and distributed local food surpluses.

New ethical principles may develop out of the convergence between ecology and theology. The principle of reciprocity in ecology is that no entity can exist by and for itself; everything is connected to everything else. In religious terms, this is the golden rule (see Perennial Philosophy). Reciprocity is the recognition of mutual obligation. All things are bound in bonds of mutual dependency. Ecology has become a philosophic viewpoint as well as a systematic discipline. The counsel of ecology is caution. Caution is an expression of love. Love is treated as the basis of religious feeling.

The Perennial Philosophy

Aldous Huxley, in his study of *The Perennial Philosophy*, began in the middle, at the focal point where mind and matter, action and thought, met in a human psychology. This *philosophia perrenis* has its source in metaphysics and issues from a way of life and "system of ethics." Its goal is the realization of the eternal self in the depth of the divine ground, to reach toward the absolute principle of all existence: That art Thou, *Tat tvam asi*.

Huxley noted a common assumption of a divine ground in all religions. The most useful way of reaching the divine ground is the middle way, the Majihima Pati pada, middle path, of Buddha. This middle path that Buddha found after trying other ways to excess was the first rational code in religion. In his book, *Religion*, A. Wallace asserted that codes are necessary categories of all religious behavior, being the vehicle that asserts the truth of each religion. The code became the religion and not the reverse. Upon inspection, there seems to be a fundamental code underlying all religions. Its single most important tenet is that the middle course is the one virtue, that excess of even a good thing is bad. Too much religion kills god in humans, enslaving them to the order of a church; too much church kills peace of mind, enslaving it in little rituals. The Greeks paralleled the code with injunctions to: "Strive to acquire proper balance—courage without rashness; caution without timidity; mercy without weakness . . . courtesy without fawning . . . patience without carelessness . . . ambition without selfishness." The two inscriptions on the Delphic Temple—"Nothing in Excess" and "Know Thyself"—are forms of the middle way. Indeed, having to much of anything prohibits knowing one's self.

Different religions emphasized the code in varying degrees:

- The essence of Confucian culture was a moral effort to aspire to achieve the commonplace, by holding to the Golden Mean, or middle way.

- Inazo Nitobe described how Shintoism reconciled the peoples of Japan: "Shinto is the source and root of the Way, and shot up with the sky and the earth, teaches man the primal Way; Confucianism is the branch and foliage of the Way, and, bursting forth with man, it teaches him the Middle Way; Buddhism is the flower and fruit of the Way, and, appearing after man's mental powers matured, teaches him the final Way."

- Buddhism: "These extremes, O Kaccana, have been avoided by the Tathagatha, and it is a middle doctrine he teaches . . . " 7,9.14 "He who recognizes the existence of suffering, it cause, its remedy, and its cessation has fathomed the four noble truths. He will walk in the right path. Right views will be the torch to light his way. Right aspirations will be his guide. Right speech will be his dwelling place on the road. His gait will be straight, for it is right behavior. His refreshments will be the right way of earning his livelihood. Right efforts will be his steps; right thoughts his breath; and right contemplation will give him the peace that follows in his footprints." The Buddha.

The same middle way is evident in other major religions:

In Christianity: "Let your moderation be known unto all men." Phillippians 4.5

And in Sanskrit: "Follow the middle course; avoid extremes."

The Bhagavad Gita: "He who avoids extremes . . . wins . . . balance peace and joy."

In Islam: "All acts are good but in the mid degree." Hadis

In Shintoism: " . . . to keep within the limits set by instinct and
    reason . . . This is the fundamental conception of Due Measure."
    Inazo Nitobe
The Tao: "To rule people and to serve Heaven there is nothing better
    than to be moderate." 81
In Zoroastrianism: "Thou shouldst be diligent and moderate . . . "
    Menog i Khrad 2,42

Traditional Ethics

Jonas related that all previous ethics had certain tacit premises in common:
- That the human condition and the nature of things was given for
  all time
- That human good was determinable on that basis
- And that the range of human action and responsibility was
  narrowly limited.

For many cosmologies, the immutability and immunity of nature
was assumed as the background for human existence. But human
actions in nature have changed qualitatively, with technology. The
whole biosphere has been affected and changed. Nature is vulnerable to
human intervention; the scale of modern technology exceeds the limits
of traditional ethics. Jonas considered that technology assumed ethical
significance by the central place it occupied in human purpose (*homo
faber=homo poetica?*).

The city was the model for the cosmos. The cosmos that contained
the human order, that was once home, is gone. The physical cosmos has
replaced it. The remoteness of our cell in nature terrified smaller minds
than Pascal's. The universe without a hierarchy of being has no ontological
support for values. The chain of being had its ethics based on the principle
of fullness. One of the dictates of that ethics was prudent mediocrity.
The human duty was to keep the human place in nature and not try to
transcend it. The moral temper was expressed well by Pope: "The bliss
of man . . . /Is not to act or think beyond mankind." Rousseau added
his own warning: "confine thy existence within thyself" (A. Lovejoy, *The
Great Chain of Being*, p. 201). The idea of a way up was abandoned, along
with the idealism of Plato and the otherworldliness of Christianity. The
best idea that can be drawn from this ethic is the concept of proper place.
Humanity has a proper place on earth and need not usurp the places of
other creatures, each of which has an independent reason for being, and
not simply as an instrument for higher orders. The flaw with this ethic is

that it can be used to keep people in low "stations."

The history of ethics since then, has wavered with cultural emphases, at least in Western civilization. American ethics has spiraled from an individual ethics, with the Puritan ideals of individualism under God, through the technocratic ethics (from 1800) of teamwork, back to an individualism defined by a commitment to the self first. Traditional ethics has become foundationless.

William Frankena illustrates the dilemma of foundationless ethics: there is ethical egoism, where individual determines right; humanism, where moral matters hold for humans; a third type that includes all conscious sentient beings; a fourth type of ethics that extends moral relevancy to whatever is alive; and a final that considers everything to be morally relevant. Frankena thinks the last two are unreasonable. But these positions are not unreasonable, as will be argued later.

The rules of traditional ethics, even the golden rule, were confined to immediate action; you and other shared a time and place. The actors were contemporaries, whose longest horizon was a lifetime, whose farthest horizon was their place. No ethics prepared humanity for a role as stewards of the planet. No ethics had to deal with the fate of humanity and the earth. Traditional ethics are irrelevant for directing human behavior toward the ambihuman world. Traditional ethics was limited to the good and bad in human relationships. Traditional ethics is anthropocentric.

Albert Schweitzer's Reverence for Life
Most philosophies are not adequate to deal with nature and ecological relationships. Many religions are too narrow to consider nature as more than a dominion. Albert Schweitzer examined many religions and assimilated some of their thought. Schweitzer had talents as a musician, musical historian, theologian, and philosopher. He chose to live in Africa, putting his Christian ethic into practice as a medical doctor. Under those circumstances, he formulated a new principle. Ethical thought had been developing since prehuman history and it culminated in the principle of reverence for life. Schweitzer began by examining Brahmanism in India. Within its very character, Brahmanism is world-denying. While its adherents praised ahimsa as the highest virtue, Schweitzer held that their compassion was not natural. It was only a derivative of egotistical metaphysical theories, causing adherents only to refrain from doing evil and not act toward the good. The reaction of the Bhagavad-Gita, in the Mahabharata, was to reconcile that severe nonactivity with human activity. But Schweitzer noted that since the Gita accepted the same world view,

it also failed to meet the requirements of ethics, not doing more than providing a "phantom place for activist ethics within the philosophy of world-negation" (Ibid). Buddha was also swept aside, for setting limits to compassionate activity.

The Chinese sages, and Zarathustra, formed philosophies that were inclined toward affirmation of the world. Lao Tse and Confucius concluded that the fundamental virtue and common aim of all ethical conduct was good will toward men. Jesus, although misled into promulgating an attitude of renunciation of the world, nevertheless, in his ethical code, permitted unlimited action on the behalf of good. Men were free to seek to achieve all that they regarded as requisite. Love became the supreme commandment, including all others in itself.

Unfortunately, people in the Middle Ages were concerned with the perfection of the world through renunciation. During the Renaissance, Christianity became affected by the spirit of affirmation, especially with the discovery and popularization of the teachings of the Stoic and Epicurean schools: Love of man was the virtue above all virtues.

In the philosophies of the 18th century, where reason supported the commandment of love, a natural ethics was constructed. Bentham argued for the utility of love of neighbor; altruism was presented as a function of social welfare. Kant found a moral law immanent in human beings, so that good and evil were discernible by conscience. In Hume's analysis, ethical conduct flowed from the fount of natural sympathy—nature endowed man with the ability to share experientially the joys and sorrows of others.

While admitting the profundity of natural ethics, Schweitzer exposed its quandary: How are its responsibilities determined? How will concern for our own well-being be properly related to concern for the well-being of others? He felt that the questions were too imposing, that the answers were too individual and subjective for the clear formulation of commandments and prohibitions (That is the function of science, to make common answers, and the function of rights, to ensure that all participate). Apparently, what led these thinkers into such a dilemma was the attempt to fit ethics into their world view according to the revealed nature of the universal will to life and describing it in terms of human feeling and judging. Schweitzer considered this an error. Any thoughtful person, reflecting on the quality of altruism, could not help but enlarge the scope of ethical activity until it included all nonhuman life. "We perceive that ethics deals not only with people, but also with creatures" (Ibid).

Schweitzer noted that during the evolution of humanity, the circle of responsibilities gradually widened, beginning with family, then tribe, nation, and humanity—working toward all of life (See Figure 13). Similarly, the circle of knowledge widened, increasing the understanding of the laws of phenomena. He felt that the streams were divergent, that ethics could gain nothing from understanding the universe, that there was no hope of finding meaning in natural phenomena. "A philosophy that proceeds from truth has to confess that no spirit of loving-kindness is at work in the phenomenal world." (Ibid). For him, nature had no reverence for life. It produced life a thousand-fold in the most meaningful way and then destroyed it a thousand-fold in the most meaningless way. Spiders sucked the blood of their victims; wasps laid eggs in live caterpillars; wolves ran down young caribou. "Nature is horrible . . . cruelty is so senseless . . ." (Ibid).

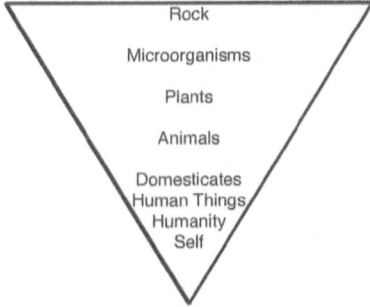

Figure 13. *The Scope of Ethics Through Time.*

Creatures had the will to live, but no compassion, they suffered, but had no compassion. The most precious form could be sacrificed to the lowest. In the struggle for survival, nature was maintained only by being in contradiction with itself. This was a contradiction of the will to live, for Schweitzer; there was life against life, suffering and death. Nature was a dreary spectacle of the manifestations of the wills to live in opposition to each other; each preserved itself by fighting and destroying the other. Nature taught only cruel egotism, briefly interrupted by the urge to love one's offspring. A terrible ignorance lay over each creature, as in a dark valley whose floors were perpetually covered by the fog of ignorance and egotism. But man, using his intelligence, was able to climb some of the peaks and catch glimpses of light; truth and goodness appeared.

It was obvious to Schweitzer that the deduction of principles of conduct from the world led, at best to a naive optimism, and at worst to skepticism and pessimism. Pessimism was intolerable, and optimism was incomplete, being concerned only with human relationships. When humanity extends its concern to relationships with all life, when intelligence operates on the will to live within an affirmative philosophy of life and the universe, then the "Reverence of Life" arises. We already possess understanding of the conduct our own natures require. It is our duty to share and maintain life. It does not matter that we have imperfect knowledge of insoluble contradictions, there is an elemental fact present in every consciousness that guides the spirit in harmonious philosophy: "I am life that wills to live, in the midst of life that wills to live" (Ibid). Sympathetic concern toward all the wills to live is the basis of ethics, for Schweitzer. Reverence for life is the greatest commandment in its most elementary form. The negative statement of this occurs in the *Bible*, Exodus 20:13: "Thou shalt not kill." Recent translations say "Thou shall not murder." Other parts of the Bible, Joshua, for instance, display killing as an effective way of conversion.

Schweitzer stated that we must struggle to wipe out antihuman traditions and inhuman emotions, that we must struggle against our own insensitivity. It is inevitable that we kill some things, unknowingly or to survive, but we must never come to take killing lightly—plucking flowers and squishing ants indiscriminately, we must not become thoughtless and blind, because all this killing weighs against us; "everything takes its revenge." The very saving of lives often calls for the sacrifice of others, but even this action is sometimes arbitrary, since we impose our own values on situations. True reverence for life makes no distinction between higher and lower forms. If we were to act so, distinguishing between pests and pets, we must do so in the sorrow of the recognition that we are killing.

Schweitzer warned not to "let your hearts grow numb." Compassionate awareness would maintain the soul on the way to real goodness. One should do good in gratitude for all the benefits received, in order to balance the "books inside." There is a secret to gratitude, which being more than a virtue, is a mysterious law of existence: its kindness spreads like the roots of a plant, but "whenever we penetrate the heart of things, we always find a mystery. Life and all with it is unfathomable." (Ibid). Our knowledge of life is the admission of mystery. To act justly, then, we must obey the laws that follow from recognition of the mysterious.

But why, after we have discovered the good, are we still at odds? Why is there cleavage instead of harmony? How can a force like God rationally create life and irrationally destroy it at the same time? How is the God of nature to be reconciled with the God of love? In all respects the universe remains mysterious to humans. Schweitzer believed that even if we despaired of comprehending the phenomenal world or the plans of God, we would not need to confront the problem of life with utter perplexity, because the ethics of Jesus, reinforced by reason, lead to the reverence for life, whose edict is the rule of universal love. This same reason would find the bridge between love for God, love for man and love for all creatures, and express reverence for all being, however dissimilar to our own, reverence and compassion for all that is called life. Such a foundation for morality forces the realization that when we establish gradations of values between lives, we only judge them in relation to ourselves and that is wholly subjective. How are we to know the importance of each? The principle of reverence for life rejects relativism— "it recognizes as good only the preserving and benefiting of life: any injury to, and destruction of, life, unless it is imposed on us by fate, is regarded as evil" (Ibid).

Most men are educated with a set of superficial principles, which evaporate when tested; most are brutal, ignorant and heartless without being aware of it. Previously, there was no absolute scale of value, because there was no reverence for life. Schweitzer urged a new renaissance to liberate us from "the poverty-stricken pragmatism" with which we limp along. We need such a spiritual renewal that everyone will reflect on the nature of goodness; our own thought must lead us from naive optimism toward a profounder affirmation of life, helping us progress from ethical impulses toward a rational system of ethics. "In the universe, the will to live is in conflict with itself; in us, it seeks to be at peace with itself" (Ibid). This is an act of spiritual independence on our part, but it carries an element of responsibility to which we must submit: acting toward the good. "The essence of goodness is: Preserve life, promote life, help life to achieve its highest destiny. The essence of evil is: Destroy life, harm life, hamper the development of life." (Ibid).

Individuals must transform themselves from blind men into seeing ones by following the new commandment: Revere life. The quality of personal existence depends more on it than on laws and prophets; it comprises the whole ethic of love in the deepest sense; it is the source of constant renewal for humanity. Those who do not help others by profession must help them as an avocation, seeking out others in need and helping to alleviate their suffering, and in so doing paying off one's debt for happiness already received. "The secret hour does not require of us that we should be happy— to obey the call is the only thing that satisfies deeply" (Ibid).

Humans are to prove themselves in doing and suffering. We are headed right when we trust subjective thinking to yield the insights and truths we need. Kindness does much to make the world better, but sometimes that must be accepted on faith. "Where there is energy it will have effects. No ray of sunlight is lost; but the green growth that sunlight awakens needs time to sprout" (Ibid). Nor may the sower always witness the harvest. Schweitzer thought that the quest for ethics was a hard fight, but that right thinking would leave "room for the heart to add its word." Schweitzer challenges: "Ethics must plunge into the adventure of making its adjustment with nature philosophy . . . . Let it dare, then, to accept the thought that self-devotion must stretch out not simply to mankind but to all creation, and especially to all life in the world within reach of humanity. Let it rise to the conception that the relation of man to man is only an expression of the relation in which he stands to all being and to the world in general."

The Limits of Learning
In spite of a catholic learning, Schweitzer was never quite able to escape many of the limits of 19th century European culture. He showed disdain for other religions. He was limited by the utilitarian ethics and by the social Darwinism inflicted on nature. Schweitzer was very selective in his philosophy. He read Goethe, but did not incorporate any organicism into his own work. Although deeply indebted to the German romantic tradition, he owed some of his arrogance about nature to the utilitarianism of J.S. Mill. These limitations are discussed.

How well did Schweitzer understand meanings in Asian schools of thought? In the dialogue between Krishna and Arjuna, Krishna proclaims the truths of reverence and the indwelling of God in all beings and things in the world process. The *Upanishads* depicted universal joy flowing through the air, earth and water to animals, trees and grasses. This is most evident in the *Bhagavata* (III,2934): "Bow to all beings with great reverence in the thought and knowledge that God enters into them through fractionalizing Himself as living creatures."

Mahayana Buddhism realized the same universal principle that allowed everything to harmonize with everything else. "Without turning towards anything, always unobstructed in his wisdom / He goes along in the world of living beings boundless in space, acting for the weal of beings." In the Mahayana school of Buddhism, compassion ranks with wisdom, the heart is as valuable as the head: "The ideal man is the Bodhisattva, who, caring nothing for his own salvation is vowed to dedicate his being and his every act to the salvation of each form of life, until the last blade of grass shall enter into Buddhahood." Lao Tse and Confucius taught universal reverence and nonviolence as well. These ideas have been stressed in modern times by Vivekananda, Tagore and Ghandi; by St. Francis and St. Thomas, Emerson, Maritain and Tillich. In *Religion in the Making*, A.N. Whitehead said: "The love in the world passes into the love in heaven, and floods back again into the world. God is the great companion—the fellow sufferer who understands. God gives to suffering its swift insight into values which can issue from it. He has in his nature the knowledge of evil, of pain and of degradation but it is there as overcome with good."

Primitive religion and animism do not seem to fit in Schweitzer's evolutionary scheme of consciousness. E.B. Taylor traces the evolution of primitive religion, noting that foremost is the belief in souls and spiritual beings of trees and animals. A. Wallace cites numerous examples of animal sacrifice, ritual worship and animal burial in the Upper Paleolithic era. Various songs of the Native American peoples also serve to indicate the sacredness of the relationships of human and animal, human and plant (from W. Brandon, *The Magic World*).

> Nahuatl: "the people assumed the forms or characters of various
>   birds and animals"
> Pueblo: " —to take the place of a spirit   with my mother the bear"
> Pawnee: "I killed an eagle   I consecrate the eagle"
>   "Listen   the song of the aged buffalo   my aged father"

Is this not reverence for life? To be one with the animal you hunt or corn you grow, to realize that it becomes part of you, living through you? Schweitzer's manifests a disinterested love of life, unlike the primitive attitude.

Schweitzer echoes a profound horror of nature, seeing it, perhaps, as Tennyson did, "red with tooth and claw." He believed the world of phenomena to be a Darwinian battleground where the fittest survived the murderous struggle. Yet there were a number of studies available to Schweitzer at that time that emphasized the cooperation of nature. In 1910, Herman Reinheimer published *Evolution By Cooperation: A Study in Bioeconomics*, in which he characterized organisms as bioeconomic traders, who put cooperation before competition. P.A. Kropotkin, in his work, *Mutual Aid: A Factor in Evolution*, concluded that the element of cooperation in animal life, even between different species, was more impressive than instances of competition. He recounted instances of lapwings protecting other birds from a preying eagle; porpoises or elephants not abandoning a wounded companion; Impalas standing by while a troop of Baboons drove off a cheetah; cats and rats collaborating in a psychology laboratory experiment.

Many more recent studies stress the primary use of cooperation as opposed to struggle: Konrad Lorenz, in *King Solomon's Ring*, studied intraspecial social rituals in animals; V. C. Wynne-Edwards studied self-regulating systems in populations of animals; A. Tinbergen documented the sharing of space by birds; L. Schaller, living among mountain gorillas, observed instances of play, compassion and "altruism;" L.L. Whyte, in his book, *Internal Factors in Evolution*, considered even genetic inheritance to occur by rules of cooperation. Schweitzer was never aware of the spectrum of niche-finding, dominance rites, symbolism, sociability, and sacrifices (usually of leaders and lookouts) in animals.

As Schweitzer blamed Hume and others for the unwarranted anthropomorphization of nature, so he himself readily assigned cruelty to animals, as well as egotistical motives and terrible ignorance. These terms are applicable to human beings only. Man he had already placed above nature rather than in it.

For Schweitzer, nature was a cruel drama of the will-to-live divided against itself. He did not love nature. The enormous mortality in nature was an embodiment of evil, against which the will-to-live struggled. His omissions are the by-products of the pursuit of an abstract harmony with nature. Schweitzer was most concerned with the protection of animals useful to humanity, not the preservation of all animals. He killed wild predators to save domestic goats. The imposition of rational ethics on nature leaves one only in the same paradoxical situation that one attempted to solve. Schweitzer's view of the world as a consequence of evil was a denial of the world, not an affirmation. He was limited by his knowledge of the evil in humanity, by the bias of Social Darwinism and by the ignorance of his European culture. His ethic was a matter of faith.

He referred to life in nature as meaningful and death in nature as meaningless. Death means life in nature. Life is not so much destroyed as used to further more life. There is no waste; most of every being is recycled. Death is only the renewal of life. Certainly what Jesus meant by giving up life to live in him again could be applied metaphorically to the natural world.

Schweitzer realized that life and its joys were subject to death: "Death reigns outside—it reigns over you—" but its rule ended where men inwardly overcame it. He believed that the contemplation of death could be comforting and produce true love for life; what a dreadful and intolerable burden if life continued forever. The death that Schweitzer confronted was Christian, from Corinthians 15:25-26: "The last enemy that shall be destroyed is death." The concept of death that he embraced was as the difficult passage to the Kingdom of Christ. Schweitzer believes that "Something within us shall not pass away . . . goes on working and living where the kingdom of the spirit is present . . . it is working because we are able to reach life by overcoming death" (from *The Philosophy of Civilization*).

He does not describe whether the soul is saved or perhaps only a pattern, as related by the Buddha. Nor does he conclude that something from each form of life, human and ambihuman, will go on. Referring only to humans, he said that a man who lives with death in his eyes, who accepts life as a gift, believes in eternal life, because it is already his. Yet, there is a contradiction: if death is not a limit, as he intimated, then killing should not be evil. Schweitzer hinted that without death, there would be no life as we know it—no happiness, beauty or renewal.

The fact of life entails death. The living dying process in integral in nature for the continuity and renewal of life. If life and death were considered absolute limits, and not the relative continuity preached by Schweitzer, life would be no less sacred or meaningful.

There seem to be a number of instances where Schweitzer could have drawn alternate conclusions from his premises. He called the action arbitrary when we kill worms to save a baby bird; but it is not arbitrary, it is value oriented by human reason, the same reason employed by him when he bemoaned a man sacrificed to the lowliest of germs. It is true that we cannot be sure of the actual importance of each, but neither can we be sure of God's plan for both. Schweitzer stated that any injury or destruction of life was evil, unless it was imposed by fate. But fate is either a deistic plan or a course of events before which we are helpless or ignorant. Then death through ignorance or necessity is excusable, and if that is so, then the commandment for reverence is a very restricted one.

Although he believed that to the truly ethical, all life was sacred, he was forced to kill to save lives. When forced to decide which would be sacrificed to the other, Schweitzer made distinctions, from case to case, under the pressure of necessity, and held himself accountable for the lives sacrificed. But this was pragmatism of the kind he rejected. The more logical behavior following the principle of reverence might be the Jainist attempt to avoid injury to all living things, by sweeping a path through life and eating only dead plant matter. The most extreme and altruistic action would be suicide, since very life causes some unavoidable suffering in others. Schweitzer could not have helped anyone without assigning a hierarchy of values to the phenomena. For him, thoughtlessly picking a flower was sinning against life, or worse for not being under the compulsion of necessity. But what kind of existence is dictated only by necessity? Necessities are limits for play. And we are not even aware of all the limits.

Schweitzer did not describe the extent of responsibility for the ethical being. In the case of one person curing the dread and painful disease of another and thereby saving a life, how is the good calculated if the person is only saved for forty more years of suffering, sickness and hunger? Is the greater good to extend and complicate a life of suffering or to give meaning and dignity to a short life of suffering? If one is responsible for a life saved then one is responsible for how it is lived afterwards. Perhaps reverence is best reserved for personal meetings. It is difficult to relate personally to the fate of over four billion people and billions more ambihuman lives. The principle of reverence for life could be applied to the mistreating and killing of animals for amusement and nonessential learning. It could lead to the realization that all life has much in common and should be approached thoughtfully.

Part of Schweitzer's dilemma came from the prevailing myth of the opposition of life and death, strife and love. But we know that life and death are necessary conditions for each other. Hinduism presumed that the animate preceded the inanimate; Freud based his theory of the evolution of culture on the assumption that the inanimate existed before the animate. Whichever is ultimately true, the two principles are mutually interwoven now. M. W. Fox judged that Schweitzer's ethic was flawed by having no ecological ethic.

True reverence for life entails reverence for death, since life and death are inseparable. No pattern can survive death, when death is the destruction of individual patterns. No one would mourn the content, which is even more evanescent. All life is sacred, but this can never be a reason for not killing, because that is how lives are sustained. Since life is of the utmost importance to the living, it should only be taken in sorrow, used and shaped with respect, and experienced with awe, for underneath it is still unfathomable mystery. Life is its own meaning. Human thought is all that we have to guide decisions about lives. It is impossible to avoid some killing, no matter how conscientious. Even Jainists kill intestinal bacteria, cells, virus, and some plants or insects.

We may fool ourselves into thinking that animals, in a pantheistic communion, allow their life force to be transubstantiated upward into a creature self-advertised as capable of grasping God on behalf of himself and all other beings. Eating is inevitable. But what is inevitable may be spiritually unendurable. It may be justifiable. But what is justifiable may be atrocious. We do not do the best that we can, even if that best may be only organized butchery. Society, as well as nature, is an organization of deaths as well as lives. Realizing this, we should at least be more aware and gentle, with reverence for all lives. Spiritual maturity depends on this awareness. If the world would ever be a garden again, as it once was written to be, nonlife and ambihuman life will have to be shaped reverently, from the values humans have created from the experience of living.

Our attitudes are grounded in a belief system that constitutes a particular world view. The system constitutes a coherent whole. With Schweitzer, the system began to shift toward a biocentric outlook. The concept of reverence, meaning honor-fear in German (*Ehrfurcht*), offered some respectability for nature through a proper attitude. He judges that "The great error of earlier ethics is that it concerned itself only with the relations of man to man. The real question is, however, one concerning man's relations to the world and to all life which comes within his reach . . . Only the universal ethics of an ever-expanding sense of responsibility for all life can be grounded in thought" (*Out of My Life and Thought*, p. 126). So, it seems that man is only ethical when all life is holy to him. Schweitzer proposed an ethics derived from Christian ethics (but really larger) that affirmed the world. But reverence for life sometimes conflicts with the Christian paradigm, which is just a particular manifestation. And it can lead to an instrumental ethic (take care of earth because it takes care of us—this is a problem with the Gaia hypothesis, also.) Man is not the ultimate reference. To preserve the human we must refer to the universe.

As the circle of ethics was enlarged to include the realm of all living things, it could be stretched to include all things—at worst, this is only a pantheistic Monadism. The religious argument for this extension would be that God created everything. A scientific argument would begin with the difficulty of defining life. A genuine affirmation of instinctive patterns is necessary for survival. Adaptive modes should conform to ecological patterns. An ecological ethics is based on attributes of ecosystems and human compliance with ecological laws. The concepts of rights for nature will be examined etymologically. Science could demand an ethic directed to the preservation of life in its mosaic setting. But only a religiously conceived ethic has done so. And Schweitzer's reverence for life is the only one visible in Western world. His reverence for life principle acquires a new aspect when it is restored to ontologically firm ground. Arguments against killing and the consideration of only human values become untenable. The world becomes a synthesis of a philosophy of values with the mysticism of religion, characterized by love, compassion and the reverence for all things.

Ethical Consciousness

Buckminster Fuller is furious with animals; they have failed us, he believes (personal communication 1982). Machines are more reliable. Animals are kept today as objects of leisure, toys, companions, workers, or fellow researchers (for sacrifice). There is an unconscious need for animals. Ritual use of animal art provided a shared image; the form had a dynamic relationship to human experiencing. We are deluded by the idea that what is owned cannot have a soul. Animals cannot be owned in the manner that we try; they disappear when owned that way. Religious conscience emancipated human slaves, not reason; We have not emancipated mere animals from slavery, yet. It is religious conscience again that has so far allowed emancipations, not scientific or philosophic reason.

A new ethic can keep animals free from human intervention, prejudice or overuse. Animals should be preserved because they are as they are; their existence is moral justification. Their intrinsic worth is independent of the instrumental values imposed on them by humanity. Consciousness of the ways of nature, especially life and death, may greatly change the patterns of human behavior.

The spirit and survival of society now depends on an expanded ecological consciousness, an awareness of the global system, of its synergetic behavior, its complexity, connectedness and the role of man in its multidimensional web. An ethical consciousness enlarges the relevant universe of established ethical principles to embrace the entire biosphere.

Waddington argues that ethical beliefs necessarily develop with this new evolutionary mechanism (conscious learning). Jantsch proposes that the next learning mode, superconscious learning, will provide guidance for those ethical beliefs. Superconscious learning is central to noogenesis, the becoming of the human cultural/mental world. Teilhard de Chardin used noogenesis to mean the consciousness of consciousness of the universe. Superconscious learning is present in moral organization and basic archetypes. But this consciousness emerges from individuals, if at all. And the individual must start from knowledge of self, as Pico della Mirandola realized: "'Know thyself' arouses and urges us towards the knowledge of all nature; who knows himself knows all things in himself" (from *Of Being and Unity*).

Millions of people without food or homes may not develop ecological consciences until they have been fed and housed. The uneducated may not care about the future until they learn that they can affect it. The creation of an ecological conscience through panethics can contribute to survival in a number of ways:

- It can expose the foolishness of desire for military machines for protection.
- It can place technology in perspective before we are destroyed by unseen side effects.
- It can permit some cultures to equalize gross material inequities without wreaking havoc on irreplaceable cultural values.
- It can permit all beings and things to be valued.

An ethical consciousness can only be instilled by experience, and only when the respondents are healthy. Methods of altering consciousness are difficult to understand and to use. But precedents exist. Eastern tradition arrived at the same counterintuitive model as particle physics. Mystics and physicists seem to agree that nature is a series of arrays on which human perception and thought impose structure. Phenomena are appearances where structure has been imposed. Eastern philosophies cultivated nonsubjective experiences for the purpose of reordering experience. Indeed, speculative mental models, from the NeoPlatonists and Gnostics to Whitehead actually affected the lives of their adherents.

Therefore, the ethics of a holocosmology could be brought into ordinary experience by making it felt as well as inferred. The question is how to make it felt.

In his study of the bonds of social relationships, Ferdinand Tonnies made a dichotomy between *Gemeinschaft* and *Gesellschaft*. Gemeinschaft seems to be an embryonic model for I-Thou relationships. Martin Buber was apparently inspired by this typology to distinguish between his moral categories: I-Thou and I-It. Reference to nature as 'it' implies an instrumental relationship, not bound by conscience. With the use of 'thou' instrumentality is not present. Thou implies a share of mutuality as Buber states (in "Education," *Between Man and Man*. p. 87), "Only if someone grasps his hand . . . to be his comrade or friend . . . does he have an awareness and share of mutuality." For Buber true dialectic is the dialogue between I and Thou. In *I and Thou* Buber presented the concept of relation as the key to understanding human life. Two attitudes are expressed by 'I-It' and 'I-Thou.' Whenever one interacts with the world one stands in one attitude or the other. The I-Thou experience of place is of total involvement where the two are not dissociable. This relationship involves a genuine response to meanings and qualities. The I-Thou is the basis of spiritual life; I-It of economic life. Buber admitted that one cannot exist in the 'I-Thou' mode for very long.

Searles compares a mature relationship to the nonhuman to Buber's I-Thou type. Harvey Cox modified Buber's term 'I-Thou' to 'I-You'; though it is less formal, it still means being open to experience as well as respect. Relatedness is kinship. Reciprocity is the relation of ethical equality. Animals and trees reciprocate by their existence and difference. Their existence has an instrumentality in human existence that Fox designates 'reciprocal maintenance.' They are part of the biogeochemical cycles that humanity depends on. As long as we are unable to recognize our reliance on the ambihuman, we will be incapable of a panethic.

The limit of Buber's ethical dialogue, I-Thou, is that it is concerned only with the present; posterity is ignored. Human duration is too short. The systems and processes that we deal with are intergenerational. Economic rationality is even more limited. Future values are discounted at current rates. Planting a tree that takes 30-2000 years to mature is calculated to be uneconomical. Who benefits from it? If our ancestors had planted trees for our benefit, it would be easier to justify continuation. E. Burke recognized that "People do not look forward to posterity who never look backward to their ancestors." But identification through time is related to that with place, locational stability. People not living in place have no vested interests. Although mobility improves productivity (in the short-run), it may be purchased by the ruination of resources. No ethical conversation can be complete without consideration of the future, as well as place. Where industrial civilization is willing to collapse the dialogue to "I-It," Buber collapsed it to "I-Thou" by ignoring the necessity of "I-It." The instrumental is as necessary to existence as the sentimental. In order to make another being a means to an end, as when steers are slaughtered for beef products, one must enter an "I-It" relationship.

Both categories are necessary for ethical consciousness. The existence of a "Thou" pole allows for the possibility of loving use of the "It." Perhaps Buber recognized the futility of a perfect solution when he wrote: "What is greater for us than all enigmatic webs at the margins of being is the central actuality of an everyday hour on earth, with a streak of sunshine on a maple twig." (Ibid., p. 135.)

Scientific Ethics

Ethics is based on human experience. Scientific knowledge is part of that experience. Therefore science can change some ethical presumptions. And as there is a rational component to ethical judgments, so there is an intuitive and emotional one, also. Perhaps ethics has not progressed much because human experience has not. A scientific ethics provides the basis for judging ethical positions, through the evidence of many sources. It can expand the duration of humanity to include concern and responsibility for the future. And it can include the ambihuman world in its considerations.

E. Wilson and others believe that scientific findings are relevant to ethics. J. Bronowski has shown that science itself must be a code of ethics. Consequences follow from the intrinsic worth of truth. Science may produce new knowledge about the consequences of our actions. Possibly it can undermine existing beliefs on what is ethical, for example, birth control. Or it may provide humanity with a new set of ethical premises. And an ethical theory that pays attention to the consequences of science may require different actions than previously thought.

Biological processes are no more moral than physical processes; but humans are part of both, and morals are just rules for living together. There are no ethical principles to be derived from evolution. But the evolutionary perspective offers a basis for principles: for instance, it is good to be adapted; it is bad to destroy the environment. Any ethical system must be consistent with the evolutionary and ecological context.

T.H. Huxley declared that humanity and nature were at strife: "Let us understand, once for all, that the ethical progress of society depends, not on imitating the cosmic process, still less in running away from it, but in combating it . . . to pit the microcosm against the macrocosm and to set man to subdue nature to his higher ends" (in *Touchstone of Ethics*). In fact, he worked to strengthen a wall between humanity and nature (compare with Whitehead). Julian Huxley took the opposite view, that evolution moves in an ethically desirable way. That may be true in a limited way. Perhaps it would be better to say that understanding evolution leads to a more comprehensive understanding of ethics. For an ethic to be based on ecological concepts like cooperation among and between species and stability, those concepts must be understood. Scientific knowledge is a start.

Our needs interpret the world. Humans have similar biological, psychological and social needs; many values are acceptable cross-culturally. The right to a livable environment is entailed by natural rights recognized by political tradition. Human values are part of the natural spectrum in which we participate. Nietzsche held that value was the highest quantum of power that a man was able to incorporate—a man, not mankind; mankind is merely experimental material, a field of ruins. Human values are unique human attributes. Value judging is grounded on observable evidence, such as basic human drives. Value judgments are formed according to the observable needs of individuals as they live in the company of others. Judgments are formed regarding murder, suicide, euthanasia, birth control, freedom, property, and learning. The value of certain qualities, such as greed, prudence, utility, and symbol-making, is maximized.

The fundamental image of nature before the 18th century was as a mirror and evoker of knowledge. But Victorian science demanded purposive, increasing knowledge. Science teaches a value-free universe known through reason. (Where once the cosmos was sacramental.) But consciousness generates value in the scientific vision, which results in enantiodromia. If a subject's consciousness in the brain is an objectively knowable phenomenon, then the subject is objective; but since the knower is subjective, knowledge is also. If liberalism tries to retain mind, it must abandon distinction between facts and values. This is a fatal self-contradiction. The distinction is abandoned in a holocosmology.

Value judgments need not be scientific, but knowledge can help form good judgments. Knowledge enlarges the range of options. It generates innovations, but it constantly surprises because new discoveries and applications are so unpredictable. Thus knowledge makes people receptive to new attitudes and willing to change their ways.

But knowledge cannot be the sole basis of decision making. It is always incomplete and therefore cannot describe all aspects of the earth that bear on human life and environmental quality. We have too much faith in the knowledge of certainty and too little faith. Knowledge is a more effective as a generator of possibilities than as a guide to choice and as a source of ethics. Science can also describe the source of values.

We get our values from knowing what is valuable in nature. Although the theory of evolution, for instance, is not a good basis for an ethics, its perspective also supplies principles on which to base values. In the larger view, evolution is value free. Creation and destruction, beauty and ugliness are expressed in one complex pathway.

Values usually encode information having survival or prestige importance. Perhaps the most valuable thing is living time. Then experience of life—aesthetics—is also valuable. Aesthetics is from the Greek meaning perception. This may be why humans value walking in the woods or observing the production of art. Natural processes are their own purpose and constitute their own value. A growing tree is; it does not have to demonstrate or prove.

Ambihuman forms have intrinsic as well as instrumental values that we are ethically obligated to safeguard. An ethics can appeal to religious, philosophical or scientific reasoning; or to all three to form a coherent whole. The good (well being) of individual organisms, as beings with inherent worth, determines our moral relations with wild communities. We have responsibilities with regard to natural ecosystems, at least contingent on furthering human values. Rejecting human superiority entails an egalitarian doctrine of species impartiality. Other species fit in places that humans cannot. Why not place the same value on living nature that is placed on money or children?

Shepard offer four arguments to value animals: economic, ecological, ethical and educational. The economic is based on the fact that animals are self sustaining factories, that is converters. Nature has economic values, as evidenced by price of petroleum. Nature has a rich pliability that we can recombine elements for computers and telescopes. Resource preserves the word source. Economic value is a function of our state of knowledge; penicillium was just mold before Flemming amplified antibiotics from it; wheat was a natural before hybridized with a weed, goat grass. We should preserve much of nature for its undiscovered wealth, that is yet to be know. The technocratic vision treats all interests as human interests; but even so, this cannot be used to reduce all to instrumental value. Not all human values can be quantified and assigned common dollar values. Even if human values (=all) have objective meaning, not all of them will have dollar values; therefore not all natural processes can have dollar values, but all have some kind of values. R.F. Dasmann notes that birds or dolphins have values to observer that do not fit any yardstick. Wildlife has a commercial value; fish can be caught and eaten without being produced. Part of the harvesting can support a game value.

The ecological is based on nature as an interlocking system. The ethical is caste thinking extending membership in human society to animals. Both ecological and ethical arguments are given attention elsewhere. Shepard's educational argument he calls "minding animals;" it is not dependent on changing technology or idealistic ethics. Animals present us with related otherness and further human knowledge of human beings. The presence of many species is linked to others. We can value all species aesthetically, from a belief in their sanctity, and for their potential contribution to human understanding. Unless the educational includes the spiritual, aesthetic and sacramental, it is too limited. Being is value.

There will always be conflicts between forms of life. So we will have to value lives differently. Complexity will be related to value; this is why we can kill millions of mosquitoes to protect humans. A healthy biotic pyramid could be used as a basis for calculating the relative value of living organisms (although, life is immeasurable). For example: 1 human = 7 wolves = 48 deer = 2000 willow shoots = 91000 root bacteria. Living organisms cannot all have absolute values—even humans. Although this scale may be marginally accurate for the value of beings in a living system, it would cause problems at the human end. How could ideas be assessed, or buildings (as new environments)? How much more valuable is a whole ecosystem, like the Amazon jungle, than the few humans it supports? But since the habitat is more complex than any one species, it is more valuable. The calculus of life may always be intuitive.

We cannot see woods economically, scientifically, or only aesthetically. Their greatest utility lies not in scientific facts, timber, or charm. It is in being. From the total of all points of view, all nature is valuable.

Beauty
Hegel prophesied that art would come to deal only with truth and beauty would be forgotten. Certainly science seems to be concerned only with truth. But beauty may have a function in nature: to enhance perception and the biological aspects of life. Perhaps beauty is the playful revelation of truth, the way or style in which truth in unconcealed. Whitehead said that "truth without beauty is trivial," referring to a truth of correspondence and not revelation.

The definition of beauty has important consequences for the conservation movement, since aesthetics is often the basis for saving wildlife and habitats. Perhaps because painters have created the understanding that certain landscapes are beautiful. Perhaps all landscapes need that interpretation. Many landscapes and ecosystems are too impersonal or "ugly" to be valued. J. Meeker judged a burned forest as ugly because it was truncated; but it is as beautiful as a baby is, for the same reasons, potential, development and being in the process of renewal.

According to Grene, Peirce's insight was that, while logic is subordinate to ethics, in the sense of practical knowledge, ethics as engineering is subordinate to aesthetics. Our sense of beauty, of what is intrinsically meaningful, dominates our grasp of what is real. Paul Weiss defined beauty as order in nature. That order includes everything on earth.

> Tyger! Tyger! burning bright
> In the forests of the night,
> What immortal hand or eye
> Could frame thy fearful symmetry?
>   William Blake, "The Tyger"

Inversion of Values

Is value contingent on human interest or preference? There are beings other than human. Ecology can expand the narrow human-centered evaluation and see things from viewpoint of nature. Lovejoy's Great Chain of Being traces the deductive order in classical nature from Greeks to German idealism. But Lamarck inverted the chain in his theory of transformism; mind is immanent and can determine transformations (See Figure 14).

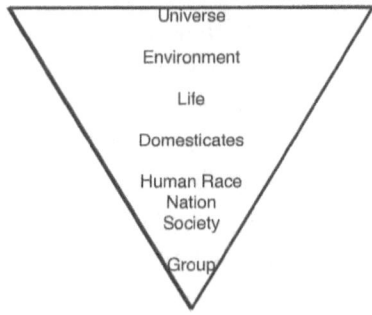

Figure 14. *The Pyramid of Values Inverted.*

Although the hypothesis of inherited characteristics was rejected by Darwin, who shared that hypothesis but denied mind as an explanatory principle, both Lamarck and Darwin inverted the value of life. By inverting the great chain of being, Lamarck escaped the direction directive that the perfect must precede the imperfect. Lamarck's idea of mind, which he thought immanent in living beings, was Bateson's.

The hierarchy of taxa—individual, family, species—becomes gene-in-organism, organism-in-environment, and environment-in-system. Ecology turns out to be the study of interaction and survival of ideas and programs in circuits. Survival of the fittest (Spencer's phrase was survival of the fitter) must be replaced by survival of the ecosystem. The rank order for survival is: biosphere, autotrophs, species (including human), culture, community, family, individual.

Max Scheler described Francis of Assisi as "one of the greatest artificers of the spirit in European History" (Max Scheler, *The Nature of Sympathy*. London: Routledge & Kegan Paul, 1954). He was the exception to the general attitude of Christianity: compassion to man only. He tried to unite the compassion of Christianity and the animistic sense of union with the natural world. Natural processes take on an expression of significance of their own without reference to man. All things have an inhuman value of their own. St. Francis tried to depose man from his monarchy and set up a democracy of all Gods creatures.

Furthermore, the Taoists saw that we were indistinguishable from other creatures; if we seemed distinguishable, it was through our feelings of self importance with our souls and reason. Lao Tse turned pyramid of human values upside down. As there are more commoners than aristocrats, there is a net gain to the success of the community. People are wise to be obscure. The tao is a standard of success; Sisyphus can put down the stone. Production and wages do not have to be higher. Success does not have to be fought for, nor vanity satisfied. They are not important.

By valuing humans alone, we make value subjective and end up without value. Sacred ecology reclaims value by placing it at the center of life. Whitehead has stated that existence is the upholding of value intensity; for itself and shared with the universe, from which it cannot be separate. Everything that exists has two sides: its individual self and its signification for the universe. Each aspect is a factor in the other. Whitehead said, "Remembering the poetic rendering of our concrete experience, we see at once that the element of value, of being valuable, of having value, of being an end in itself, of being something which is for its own sake, must not be omitted in any account of an event as the most concrete actual something" (in *Science in the Modern World*, p. 136). Value is part of the meaning of actuality. Value experience is the essence of the universe. The value (intrinsic worth) each being has for itself is shared by others. Each exists for itself and for others; a value in itself and for others. This is intrinsic and instrumental value.

It has been said that man is the measure of things because he IS all things; but if all things are all things, then they determine their own value. Humans have stripped the world of qualities and significance and claimed them for themselves. Distance allows objectivity and denies interrelatedness, and sight allows distance. Anthropos may be the measure of all things, by default, but it is not the value of all things. Each living being is a perspective and valuing of being.

Evolutionary Ethics

E. O. Wilson argues against evolutionary ethics. "The biologist, who is concerned with questions of physiology and evolutionary history, realizes that self-knowledge is constrained and shaped by the emotional control centers in the hypothalamus and limbic system of the brain . . . What, we are then compelled to ask, made the hypothalamus and limbic system? They evolved by natural selection. That simple biological statement must be pursued to explain ethics and ethical philosophers, if not epistemology and epistemologists, at all depths." But Wilson does not want to say that what is, is good, or that it ought to be, or even that it can justify what will be. That would be to fall into the trap of the naturalistic fallacy of ethics, "which uncritically concludes that what is, should be. The 'what is' in human nature is to a large extent the heritage of a Pleistocene hunter-gatherer existence. When any genetic bias is demonstrated, it cannot be used to justify a continuing practice in present and future society."

So Wilson concludes with Moore and others that evolutionary ethics violates the is/ought barrier, as distinguished by Hume. But in doing so, they commit an "unnatural fallacy." A fallacy entails the belief that an argument is misleading. Their argument contains both semantic and logical fallacies. First, the equivocation of terms used results in an ambiguous conclusion and the invalidity of the argument, i.e., amphiboly. The term ought means obligation, being bound in a necessary means/end argument. "Is" means that which is factual, with no element of choice. Although the seed of "ought" is contained in "is," what is obligated is existence, not the same existence or ideal continuity. Second, the unnaturalistic fallacy is characterized by ignoranti elenchi, ignorance of purpose. Wilson uses evolution to argue against an ethics. But the purpose of evolution was not to produce humanity, or ethics for humans; evolution has no purpose other than being. The solution to the fallacy is a metaethics grounded in psychological experience as well as logic.

The value of evolution lies in providing adapted forms for changing environments. Evolution may have promoted a moral sense. Kindness to relatives, without hope of return benefits, follows from a kin selection hypothesis in evolution. Belief in personal actions fosters more efficient performance than raw calculation for personal gain. Even aggression must have had value to tribal groups. Thinking ethically seems to be selected for. Ethics may be adaptive for humans like instincts are for wolves. The

159

effectiveness of ethics, however, depends on a scientific knowledge of the way the world works. The Aztecs based an ethic on imperfect knowledge of the sun, and suffered disastrously. Ethical codes are common heritages. In the sense that evolution applies to all peoples, it means equality.

An evolutionary ethic would suggest that humans avoid tampering with complex evolved systems, not because they are good, but because they are the basis of life at this stage of development. The human species was shaped by its diseases, smallpox and sickle-cell anemia, as much as by climate and animals. Although not everything that evolves is necessarily valuable, due to chance, many things have functions. Variations in populations allow adaptations to different conditions. Sickle-cell anemia reduced the possibility of malaria; its elimination might condemn more people to suffer and die from malaria. Change and mutation are always leading to new forms of disease. It is silly to think that disease organisms ought to be eliminated for all time; they coevolved with humanity.

Otto Frankel proposed an "evolutionary ethic" as a philosophical background to the concept of biosphere reserves, the hard-headed scientific planning and management of examples of natural ecosystems for study and enjoyment. Natural biomes, unique communities of exceptional interest, harmonious traditional landscapes, and degraded ecosystems capable of restoration would be categorized and an appropriate treatment for each defined. Ethics needs to be extended, to harmonize humanity with nature and take account of all facts. There are other examples in other traditions. Reverence for nature is compatible with the willingness to accept responsibility for the consequences of human action.

Human ethics includes the ethics of whole systems (Churchman, 1968). Jantsch states that ultimately we have to develop an evolutionary ethics, transcending individuals and all of mankind, to embrace the main principles of evolution: openness, nonequilibrium, nonattachment. But his proposal is too abstract. The futures we invent are possible only if they are compatible with constraints imposed by evolutionary past. An ecological ethic will recognize all human endeavors as part of nature. Essential elements of ecological ethics stem from synergy, symbiosis, and ektropy, which are basic attributes of the ecosystem and its evolution. Where symbiosis means "living together," synergy means "working together" (from the Greek word synergos). Dubos sees: "humankind and Earth as constituting a diversity of systems of symbiosis that constantly undergo adaptive changes and thus contribute to a continuous evolutionary process of creation" (*The Wooing of Earth*. New York: Scribners, 1980, p. 148.)

Conservation Ethics

A new morality requires an expansion of the conception of human rights to embrace the global system. Leopold has proposed a conservation ethic, dealing the mans relationships to land, plants and animals. The land ethic Leopold had in mind was a sense of ecological community between man and other species. When we see land as community to which we belong, we will use it with love and respect. Such an ethic would change the human role from master of earth to plain member of it. Predators are members of the community; no special interest has the right to exterminate them for the sake of benefit for itself. This attitude is important for habitat protection. Leopold describes the extension of ethics as "actually a process in ecological evolution. Its sequences may be described in ecological as well as in philosophical terms. An ethic, ecologically, is a limitation on freedom of action in the struggle for existence. An ethic, philosophically, is a differentiation of social from anti-social conduct. These are two different definitions of one thing. The thing has its origin in the tendency of interdependent individuals or groups to evolve modes of cooperation" (A. Leopold, *A Sand County Almanac*. New York: Oxford University Press, 1949).

Bertrand de Jouvenel (1968) proposed a Stewardship of the Earth that emphasized harmony with nature, a balanced ecosystem, and a peaceful environment. We must have public policies for the creation of beautiful cities and control of pollution; education must breath into our conscience reverence for earths bounty. Beauty can be a lasting achievement. Walter Taylor pointed out that American Secretary of Agriculture Henry Wallace had suggested the need for a Declaration of Interdependence similar to the Declaration of Independence in 1776. Communities and species do have the right to survival. We commonly speak of corporate entities, churches and institutions as having rights and duties; this is not that different from species, which have equivalent of constitution and rules.

The aim of an ethic must be harmonious to the total ideas of the world's population of living beings. Fox proposes a biospiritual ethic as a unifying set of principles, ethics and values that will bring about a nonconflicting state of one earth, one mind. The ethic is based on the biological fact that all humans and living beings are kin and that life is spiritual—love is stronger than violence. It arises from seeing humanity in an ecological perspective (from knowledge of evolution).

Reverence for Natural Systems

The world would not be a better place without sharks, silverfish, cockroaches, rats, hyenas, or whales. Humanity has upset the balance of nature in favor of itself. Civilization will have to correct future activities to reduce the margin between bare survival and social development, by reason. We can express the recovery of implicit natural values as a reverence for natural systems. An ethic is needed to say what is at stake and what can be done, and that it is worth doing. Such an ethic can be keynoted by a reverence for natural systems.

In "Reverence for Natural Systems," Erwin Laszlo proposes a social ethic for the age of humanity. Laszlo calls for reverence for level-structure of the microhierarchy, including all systems on all its levels, from atoms to an emerging planetary culture and ecology. "We can express the recovery of our implicit natural values in requesting a reverence for natural systems," he says (Ibid). This reverence expresses the insight that humanity is in nature, a part of an embracing network of dynamic, self-regulating and self-creating processes. Marveling at humanity is marveling at nature. Nature is the matrix from which we arose. Religion, myth, fantasy, and science can show that. Systems science offers a concept of an interdetermined, multidimensional universe.

Reverence for the Universe

All this is not enough; reverence must include all natural and artificial beings and things and fields, from atoms to weeds, computers to galaxies. Atoms, molecules, and organic cycles are parts of humanity. We must revere all the arrangements of earth stuff. The greatest human dignity follows from respectfulness of everything as meaningful as ourselves. Such a reverence would treat all substances of the earth as precious, to be used carefully, if at all. It would include all human artifacts, manufactures and societies. It would promote a society where individuals would live in close contact with natural support systems. It would provide each with the aesthetic necessities of life, to develop all capacities. One aspect of an ecological ethic is to live in ecstasy, to help others to see, feel and understand the world and themselves, to feel, touch, smell, savor, and immerse themselves in the world.

Right Action

Humanity has taken its own opportunities. These opportunities have been codified for centuries as rights. Now, we must allow animals equal opportunities. The interrelatedness of life dictates the interrelatedness of rights. And these rights are necessary to the integrity of the whole planet. Humanity developed in a community of animals and plants, as part of a clade on the same tree of life. The quality of human life has always depended on the quality of animal life. Animals have sensations and feelings, as important to them as ours are to us. The extension of rights to animals and plants does not deny any traditional human rights. Animals should be accorded higher moral regard and legal standing to reflect the intrinsic worth afforded by their existence and sentience. Welfare laws to conserve species and to guarantee humane treatment in research, transportation and slaughter indicate a growing concern.

The extension of ethics to animals and land is an ecological necessity. Extended ethics defines a social conduct that is a mode of cooperation and, ultimately, symbiosis. Ethics are voluntary limitations of freedom, necessary in a complex world of which we remain incredibly ignorant. Ethics are developed in response to problems that arise from increasing knowledge. Science has phenomenally increased our knowledge of physical and biological processes. It has now become the basis of our moral code, but it cannot very long be a science divorced from feeling and art if that code is to help us survive. Science needs to touch the mutuality among the categories of thought. To do this it requires aesthetic perception as well as disciplined thinking and feeling. The magic of a world view needs to be regained. Science is a way for the visionary intellect to contemplate nature. This is what Roszak means by the sacramental vision of nature (in *Where the Wasteland Ends*). Reality is ambiguous and open-ended. Humanity creates its own earth.

Unity & Durational Ethics

The Orphic movement introduced the idea of brotherhood, as well as pantheism and individual responsibility. It inspired the conviction that philosophy is a way of life; there was a communal organization associated with it. The unity of mankind has not been adequately described. Religion has tried. Christianity accepted all of humanity as one, if they accepted Jesus. During the Renaissance, this idea became secularized, such that Donne could write that "No man is an island." As William of Occam showed, the name of unity itself is of the mind and may not be attributed to a substance, full or empty void, or to the ground of being. Being and nonbeing are names. But they can be talked about, in the sense of pointed beyond. Popular philosophers are desirous of attaining an all-embracing unity. Philosophers search for "the" meaning and purpose of the universe. But there is no "one" meaning or unity. Meanings are in individuals.

The unity of the universe is in individuals. Individuals are embedded in a STEM field and there is their unity with other matter and energies in space and time; there is the unity with all beings and past and future generations.

Biological arguments have replaced the religious and poetic ones to support the family of man. Human biological unity with earth is one basis for regarding all things positively. Despite its inhuman treatment of individuals or communities, the universe is the enveloping tissue of human life; it nurtures.

Ethics is a part of the philosophy of nature. All organisms, including human ones, are continuous with nature. In ancient philosophies, being was the ground of ethics. Modern philosophy divorced the two. But a revised image of nature reunites them. Ethics is ultimately grounded in the order of things, the ordo creationis. Being is universal; everything has value in itself by virtue of its existence. Therefore every human action that affects the ambihuman world has significance. There is nothing that does not have value. *In Plato, knowledge and value were combined. Therefore, every human action has ethical consequences. Hans Jonas proposed an ethical guideline (1974): "Act so that the effects of your actions are compatible with the permanence of genuine human life." Being compatible with permanence implies future lives. We have a moral obligation to leave the world habitable for future generations of humans. An ethics that requires a long-range responsibility also requires a new humility. Our technological power exceeds our ability to foresee its consequences. This is the power of a sorcerer's apprentice, who calls up what he cannot put down.

Evil in Ethics

Humans usually distinguish unambiguously between good and bad; their ethics means to further the good and suppress evil. We search for essential difference between good and evil in vain, the constituents are the same. The distinction lies in the way the pieces are assembled, the structure. The universe is comprised of good and evil (agathokakological). Everything seems to work by complementary opposites. Not all good things go together (in same category). The attempt to isolate them accelerates enantiodromia.

Enantiodromia is the process by which a movement turns into its exact opposite; romanticism rejected industrialization, but became mechanized. The German attempt to unite Europe left it divided. The line curves upon itself. Enantiodromia is the rise of ecological consciousness as an offshoot of the space program's view of the planet. Values too strenuously proclaimed go to their opposite. It is necessary to reject the determinism of behaviorists and upward freedom of the humanists. There is no freedom in trying to conquer the life-patterns of ecological connectedness (only self-destruction). Whenever conscious purpose makes a tree out of a net, we have to deal with net as context. Rightness is accessible to beings in context.

Evil is a disintegration, a juxtaposition of opposites, with some parts striving to suppress others. Good is the synthesis and reconciliation of the same parts. We are aware of values as conflicts tear us; we can reconcile values in just proportions to resurrect the whole body, Lucifer reconciled. Disintegration is necessary to the process. There is no evil in nature. In ancient Hebrew, good and evil is a single word meaning everything.

Humans have the power to alter vast processing in nature, and not enough care to refrain from trying. Power without charity is a satanic theme. Freud wrote that Satan desired to be father for himself, agency without community. Many governments have the same desire. Demons, from Greek word for knowledge, have knowledge without charity. A holocosmology should offer knowledge and power with charity.

Silencing the Voices of Existence

Hegel claimed that man was needed so that the universe could be aware of itself. Teilhard de Chardin claimed that the central idea of the Christian Gospel was that the universe was a creative process carried on by the operative power of human imagination. The universe was capable of becoming more fully animate. Teilhard wrote that in human evolution the planet is covered by a web of ideas—the noosphere. He also postulated that evolution proceeded in the direction of increased complexity and that complexity is accompanied by a corresponding rise in consciousness, which is a specific effect of complexity. Teilhard explored the culmination of life; he saw the end as an inward folding combining living and nonliving matter into a reciprocal relationship toward the Omega point: one mind in perfect understanding. The Omega point is an abstraction of intellectual dominance. God becomes a lure as Whitehead would have it. Attention is turned from the eternal now to the eternal future. The passion for unity blanks out the material. *justification of science as functionally identical to religion.

Eric Jantsch identifies humanity with the universe and concludes that the self-organizing universe and human-directed evolution are not contradictory. But this is done by desanctifying nature and assigning a supernatural quality to human consciousness. But consciousness is not the highest state of evolution; it is just a way of expanding experience; the whole universe cannot be identified with consciousness as in Teilhard's vision. Jantsch and Prigogine see their message as ecological; self-organization leads to a new alliance between man and nature. But humanity and nature are allied already by existence. Prigogine thinks that the new nonlinear thermodynamics brings man into contact with nature. And this gives new meaning, through connectedness. But we are connected by more than thermodynamics. We are already connected by existence and feeling, even if we are no longer aware of it.

Conrad Bonifazi, like Chardin, believes the rise of evolutionary biology provides a climate for the refinement of the world soul. Bonifazi calls earth a psycho-somatic entity. Its psyche, extending from the biosphere, is principally concentrated in human beings. Animals and plants seem to be peripheral. By planetization he envisions man coming to form one single, hypercomplex and conscious arch-molecule, coextensive with the planet itself. But, this vision neglects life itself.

Teilhard, Bonifazi and Dubos use the Gaia hypothesis to argue that humans are the eyes, ears and intelligence of Gaia, that they have the right and responsibility to seize the tiller of "an aimlessly drifting planet," to manage and control ecosystems, to direct evolution, to remodel the planet to human specifications. Would their noosphere be a super personality?

The value of wild nature is its independence and wildness. Our astonishment constitutes some of its value. If we can admit the independence of nature, that things continue in their own complex way, we may feel more respect for them. We can contemplate with admiration, sense them as well as manipulate them. But as long as nature is strange, we will be egoistic and disinterested. The emergence of new moral attitudes depends on a more realistic philosophy of nature. The remedy lies in the admission of the debits of science to nature, and in conservation.

We will never understand nature unless we dissociate wild from utility. This human utility can be traced to Aristotle. Our indifference toward nature comes from our judgment of its uselessness. Even ecologists cannot think of uses for large birds and mammals. This makes a coldness in the heart of our coexistence with ambihumanity, other species. Nature is feared as unfathomable and uncontrollable. Natural processes entail death; we fear death. Nature was desacralized by the simple filter of science, the false promise of control. That which we know, as well as that which we do not, is wrongly regarded as profane. The lack of reverence for nature is mistaken for maturity. Reverence (as honor-fear) is reserved for technology and humanity. Nature has been disenchanted.

The disenchantment of the world is only another name for the hushing of mediating voices between nature and human. Without these resonances—partial words—Levy-Bruhl's mystical participation in nature is impossible. Science accepts the sentience of plant life, but does not adjust its methods. Human knowledge grants emotions to animals, but uses them badly anyway. We turn inward from the earth, for human purposes. We distance ourselves from what is uncontrolled or unowned. This detachment is the greatest threat to the welfare of nature. The attitude of distance toward beings excludes consideration of necessary information. The vivisection of the world depletes our ability to feel compassion for it. We are destroying the voices of existence.

Panethics
Linking Beings Together

Some philosophers think that there are no ethical principles to be derived from a theory of evolution. It is difficult for them to speak of the right to life of a sandhill crane without overextending their ethical system. Rawls, Harmon and other philosophers exclude animals from consideration in the sphere of ethics because of the conception of lawful justice as mutual restraint—the golden rule. The futures we invent are viable only if compatible with constraints imposed by evolutionary past. An ecological ethic will recognize all human endeavors as part of nature. Synergy and symbiosis are basic attributes of the whole earth ecosystem. Symbiosis means "living together;" its lesson that we must live harmoniously. Politics and economics are advanced symbioses in which the original free-for-all competition has been replaced, in part, by co-operative mechanisms with an ethical content. An animal not in symbiotic relation is a parasite, according to S.P.R. Charter. There is an etymological argument for ethics.

The word ethics is derived from the Greek (*ethos*) meaning 'custom,' which itself came from the Sanskrit (*SVADHA*) for one's 'own doing.' Since it was used in the plural, it meant 'doing together;' it also meant 'abode.' The word 'morality' comes from mores, the plural of *mos*, meaning the 'will' of a person (self-will, humor, caprice); (*mos* probably comes from the verb *meare*, 'to measure,' as to measure ones way, to go ones way). Mores means the way of going together. After the etymological derivations, morality will be applied to individuals and ethics to groups.

We need a moral order considerate of all beings before we progress to power and control. For Buddha the ethical takes precedence over the acquisition of power. The first step of yoga (yama) is moral duty—

rejection of violence, theft, covetousness, lying, and incontinence. The second must be the intuitive recognition that all beings must be joined in a human ethical code.

Rights & Being

The Dickey-Lincoln hydroelectric project on the St. John river in Maine was questioned because it would drown a recently discovered colony of furbish louseworts, a relative of the snapdragon thought to be extinct for thirty years. Even the discoverer was quoted in the news as saying that the plants had no commercial value and were not beautiful. Economic and biological arguments are fragmented. The controversy continues. There are no good reasons put forward for saving species and habitats, although there is the larger issue of the biological impoverishment of the earth.

A general theory of rights is needed. Then, ascription of rights to all living beings would provide the necessary rationale. Some philosophers have maintained that a right is a claim to something (Feinberg, Richie); others that it is an entitlement. Regan divides rights into special rights, under which the above fall, and natural rights, which exist because of the type of being a being is. R.A. Watson takes reciprocity as central to the general concepts of rights and duties; few animals and no natural objects have rights intrinsically. He mentions that some primates and mammals (dolphins, dogs) are moral entities because they are self conscious, have free will, understand principles, and intend to act accordingly. But the assumption of self-consciousness would rule out children and feeble-minded adults, also.

So, a larger definition of reciprocity is needed. The strongest argument for rights is interrelatedness in communities. It is a basis for assigning rights to nonhuman nature. Existence implies intrinsic worth. Hardin considers interrelatedness, but interprets it narrowly. He considers rights as rules of competition. Every right is a ploy in the struggle for existence; and every right implies an obligation to furnish it. This is good as far as it goes. Life is more than competition; it involves cooperation, play and violence. Rights are simply rules for living together.

Peter Singer rejects speciesism and extends the principle of equality beyond the human species. His argument amounts to a clear understanding of the principle of equal consideration of interests. The reverence for all beings is concerned with the right functioning and right numbers in the right places, according to standards of health and quality of life. Size and quantity are not always values in nature— too much calcium kills a gull; too many lemmings drives them all over the cliff.

When mankind was divided into citizens and slaves, there was no freedom; when divided into governors and governed, freedom was advanced by providing the governed with protection against tyranny of governors; when people became self-governing, protection was needed against majority opinion—this by distinguishing between individual and society; now, new contraries—public and private—are needed to provide clarification. These "natural rights" were used by minorities to legitimate their claims against controlling powers.

Rights and obligations were first thought of in a political context consisting of customs and practices within and between states. In the seventeenth century they were thought of in a constitutional context, where forms of government were established to protect natural rights. Now they are thought of in a human context. Freedoms of—speech, worship—depend on institutional protection and are political rights. Freedoms from—want, fear—are extensions of economic rights. Freedoms for—pleasure, reproduction—are biological rights. Dansereau lists the rights of individuals as:

- Physiological: light, air, water, food, shelter, procreation
- Psychological: minimum space, form attachments, free from shocks
- Social: choice, work, association
- Economic: income, dispose of property, use resources
- Political: education, information, participation in decision
- Religious: adhere to creed, join in groups.

These rights are only very analogous to those of other beings. Socrates argued in the Republic against the conception of justice as giving every man his due, and proposed a definition of justice as every man performing his proper function. This proportion of reward to function in the community was named distributive justice by Aristotle. It describes the right to participate in the benefits of science and culture. If justice is a proportion set up in the community between men and goods, justice is also the restoration of the relation of men and goods, when disturbed. Aristotle called this justice, rectificatory. This has constituted the business of laws and courts.

During the stage of universal rights, world order transfers the criterion from the nature of man to the community of men; both law and justice, obligations and rights are reduced to equity. Thus new nations demand to participate in a common justice, as opposed to the extension of natural rights. How can the idea of equity be given determinate content and political force? Society should be organized on the basis of functions, not rights. Ecological rights (customs) could be based on functions. It is foolish not to assign rights to animals, plants and earth because of contractural formalities. Morality means living together; symbiosis means living together. We are living together with everything on the planet, and in the universe. Therefore we ought to extend rights to all beings. Human life depends on a matrix of life. The matrix is historical. It has duration; it extends from the past into a future of following lives. This allows the past and future to have formal rights. They are part of the continuity of relationships.

Knowledge & Understanding

Knowledge gives freedom; and we pay for freedom with the risks of mistakes. Knowledge is power and we pay for power with possession. Mental constructs (knowledge) become the primary resource of the earth. Knowledge is conceptual and can be passed on by symbols. Understanding is not conceptual and cannot be passed on. Pascal metaphorically described knowledge as being like a sphere is space: the larger the sphere the greater our contact with the unknown. But as Gould points out, the greater the sphere, the greater the ratio of known (volume) to unknown (surface). Consider another analogy: The sphere of knowledge could heat up from the activity of knowing.

Of the vast sum of human misery, Huxley estimates that one third is unavoidable; the remaining springs from human stupidity and malice, and their great justifiers, idealism and dogmatism, which exist through our intellectual sins of laziness and pride. We are too lazy to think in terms of multiple causes; instead we oversimplify and abstract. We attribute significance to meaningless pseudoknowledge; we cherish the false notion that knowledge is the same as understanding.

Artificial piety can be fabricated by ritual and symbolic acts and organized into religious or cultural traditions. Those who are imprisoned by words, mistake the pointing finger for the moon. But the conditioned reflexes, when the prison is shed, can lead to understanding. We cannot make ourselves understand. But we can foster a state of mind that understanding may visit. Conception unfolds through the inclusion of new experience. But conceptualization is open, that is, fuzzy and indeterminate. So misunderstandings can occur, even if the gap is closed by trust or confidence.

Environmental, cultural and psychological processes operate as a unified system. Understanding requires a multidisciplinary style, dialectical. Humans only understand selves by understanding environment. An experienced present emerges from living and relates to the past and future; this is history. Consciousness becomes time consciousness and links backwards; through the process of religio.

Humans create the world as an image of themselves; and create themselves by creating a world. The essence of humanity is something we make and grow into. But learning to be human interferes with self-realization and understanding. We imitate, but are bound in words and imitations. In order to understand, we must subtract some of the learning. This is what is meant as the practice of tao: subtracting. This challenges the social order. Both self-realization and socialization are necessary. If truth is defined as understanding then it must be lived; there is no argument. The saving of truth was never preached by Buddha or Christ.

Knowledge by Participation
Other modes of knowledge must be accommodated along side science. Roszak proposed to define true knowledge as "gnosis,"—Gnosis is used in a generic way here, not the way the Gnostics used it—of which scientific rationality is only a small part. It is gnosis that is needed to perfect the universe and soul, mutually, with the spirit of love. Gnosis is the whole spectrum: the hard, bright lines of science, the hues of art, the dark voids of religion. Gnosis is augmentative knowledge (intuition and revelation), in contrast to the reductivity of science. Tillich calls gnosis "knowledge by participation." And that is what humans need to do—recognize that they automatically participate in everything, and that we cannot unparticipate by choice. Many experiments in physics and psychology recognize this in experimental design.

Education could enlarge or alter the perceptions of all human beings on earth with the selection and presentation of relevant information. Ecological consciousness could be fostered almost immediately. The basis of an effective participant education must include the development of gestalt psychology, the application of perception research to ecological concerns, and generally the promulgation of ecological wisdom in a large world view.

Education now simply trains people for functions in industry, but it could foster the growth of culture. The way to effect a cultural transformation is by surrounding society with a new field of consciousness, not by attacking institutions or society. On a sailing ship in crisis (after Fuller), everyone cooperates spontaneously because they all know how to sail and what their functions are. Humanity will only cooperate spontaneously when all humanity knows what it is all about. That is the purpose of education. Society must comprehensively become aware of what it is all about.

Letting Be

One role of ecology could be to urge the toleration of fluctuation, irregularity, uncertainty, and diversity. Its basic premise is interrelatedness. Like quantum theory, ecology can deny the subject-object relationship. Interpenetration of boundaries makes the human less discrete. But the study of man is still properly man, as a focus of the universe, for understanding it.

We do need a new metaphysics, that is genuinely nonanthropocentric; it would be the best foundation for ecological concern. Spinoza and St. Francis call for a radical rejection of anthropocentrism. This implies a rejection of technological domination and fosters an attitude of letting beings be. Humanity does not stand over the environment as manager or steward, but as cocreator (in M. W. Fox's term).

Heidegger's attitude of "letting be" *lassen*, while similar to the use here, was a call for reverence for what is behind appearances, "Being." But "Being" is an abstract "It" that makes no moral difference. If it exists, it does so only in appearances. Although Heidegger expresses repugnance at the idea that humans are masters of all beings, he shows little concern for the nonhuman beings; in fact, he does not emphasize the dignity of the ambihuman as much as stress the nonanthropocentrism of nature. Some of Heidegger's expressive phrases are used in a different context here; his general outlook is considered too passive, placing beings in an instrumental hierarchy in a strange, impersonal universe. The interpretation of letting be presented here is more active and taoistic.

Living Images

Know then thyself, presume not God to scan;
The proper study of Mankind is Man.
Plac'd on this isthmus of a middle state,
A being darkly wise, and rudely great . . .
Alexander Pope, *An Essay on Man*

There is a gulf between ideal conceptual models in a thought-world and living with the pressure, variability and chance of the lived-world. A way of life consists of accommodation between a thought-world and a lived-world. The world—man image—is a construct of human arts, sciences and associations. Human knowledge reflects the stages of human awareness of and reaction to the world. Heidegger described the world as a unity of paths and relations in which birth and death, disasters and blessings, secure the shape of human beings. The world is shaped out of the massive earth by human groups. The world is called into the openness of being, but the earth remains an undisclosed field, resisting attempts to penetrate it, a receding horizon. Each group has a unique world, that interacts with others. Each world measures itself from a group; the world is the field of experience. There are a number of ways that groups can interact in a heterogenous society of beings.

E. O. Wilson also talks about the extreme plasticity of human behavior, the ability to adapt to live in almost any social environment. Dubos warns of overadaptation. Perhaps humans are hyperadaptive. Goldsmith thinks we are capable of adaptive behavior because our biosocial structure is highly specific; our associated behavior is governed by specific laws. We are more aware than our ancestors but also less; we are aware of our separateness, but blind to connectedness. Self-consciousness is not awareness, but trades one aspect of reality at expense of another. Human society acts from ignorance. Ignorance of the bonds of living and nonliving beings. Yet we may be unconscious of the metaphors used to control mind through habit. Campbell said that a social myth must be able to encompass individual values. An individual making sense is synonym for being congruent with social assumptions. In communities, humans live in rich cultural matrix where all feelings are interwoven, and presented and represented in symbols.

Language

Merleau-Ponty locates the beginnings of symbolic behavior in the figure/ground structure of human perception. Logos, the ultimate coherence in and behind language, possesses us, but never definitely. Gestalt systems are individuals related through homology. Lorenz stated that Gestalt perception is capable of discovering unsuspected laws that the rational function of abstraction is unable to. He offers the example of a child inventing a noun, bowwow, for all dogs, thus extracting as essential configuration, the gestalt of dog.

Language plays a dominant part in shaping a world view. But language is possible only with certain brain structures. Primates can master some language, but do not seem to originate it. Other animals, like apes, do not babble as babies; and they do not have the spontaneous acoustical utterances out of which language can be formed. They are poorer at socializing and seem to have less to say. But we know that some capability is there. It emerges in humans, not completely explicable in terms of just mental activities. Brain functions only give hints. Language leaps to a new level of communication, a radical discontinuity between beings and signs.

Taken singly, signs do not signify anything and each expresses only a divergence of meaning from the others. Taken together, Merleau-Ponty concludes that language is made up of differences that appear among terms. Since language is learned, one is obligated to go from a part to the whole; if one began with the whole one would need to know the language to learn it. Besides, the part implies the whole, holonomically. Merleau-Ponty charges that language is something like a universe capable of lodging things themselves in it after changing their meaning. Language does not represent an inner text. It is not complete; there is no such thing as a complete expression. Although words and expressions are not complete, the language itself is a whole. In learning a language, meaning is expressed when it is embodied in available terms. Words are "haunted" by thought at a distance. For things, words deliver the "captive" meaning.

Before humans named it, the whole earth was wild. It moved gracefully to constraints; life flowed into available space. Nature is beyond words; using them makes one a namer. All words are tools that disturb and rearrange primordial nature. Fowles holds that tools addict us to purpose. Words (or film) cannot capture the sounds, scents, temperatures, moods, ambiance of a woods, the levels of beings in vertical ascent, the subtlety of relationships. The woods defeat paper and frame. We transform energy into words and release it as a different kind of expression.

Words should be regarded as arbitrary symbols for events or things.

This relationship was reversed once in the European Middle Ages, where the idea was held to be more real than the event. And since the ideas were of human origin, everything was given human meaning. Nature was humanized; every being took on the "stink" of humanity. Misguided politics arise from the wrong relationship of words and symbols. Things are regarded as symbols for words in totalitarian states, which has the advantage of reducing individuals to stereotypes, which then can be tortured or disposed of without involvement. Such semantic prisons confine and warp thought. People become prisoners of an order that rejects new knowledge and solutions. Science promises to keep the bounds of order open and symbols in a right relationship, although scientists sometimes act like prisoners (as when medicine rejected the use of hypnotism). The desire for order without a scientific search for the real nature of order can have disastrous political consequences. The Aztecs used the wrong symbols to interpret their universe; they believed that the sun needed human blood to survive and sacrificed great numbers of lives to ensure the sun's life. Their political policy was based on continual raids for victims, and this policy contributed to their overthrow and decline with the arrival of the Spanish.

Technical languages have been analyzed for their role in specialized thinking, but normal and literary languages, in which persons do their thinking about politics and religion, have been neglected. Yet our conduct and character is largely determined by the nature of words used to describe the world and ourselves. Jesus and Buddha both insisted upon the importance of words. Jesus warned that we shall be judged by our words. The Buddha warned his followers against becoming entangled in the chains of metaphysical argument and insisted on Right Speech, one of the branches of the Eightfold Path. Words and their meanings are more than amusements and delights; they are matters of the most profound ethical significance to every human being. Language is an orchestration whose theme is the exchange of personal identities; without its symbolic power, it is impersonal to incomprehensibility. The words are human, but the voice is nature.

Thinking & Being

The study of the origin of words is a sort of archaeology of thought processes. It is important to know how thinking has developed. By giving attention to the older meanings of words along with the current ones, insight is obtained into the full significance of general notions not provided by only specialized meanings.

Language is a treasure house of fossil observations. But language use ('An idea occurred to me, I see it clearly') implies that thoughts have their origin in an external world. Thoughts seem to be mental, external facts. For Heidegger, man is preeminently a being-in-the-world for whom existence takes on meaning only as he opens himself to the being of his finite situation. Heidegger writes that if we walk through a forest, we are already passing through the word 'forest,' even without speaking or thinking. But what of places with no name, trees or flowers with no names? Part of nature is hidden; part will always be hidden by enfoldment. This is the invisible that will never be named.

Bohm proposes a rheomode for communicating, that should reveal a certain wholeness without specificity. The world view is currently reflected in the subject-object-verb structure of language. But language is really an undivided field of movement, involving sound, meaning and emotion. The rheomode is compatible with the notion of process and more capable of presenting a world view. Heidegger writes that the true function of language is conversation, a "turning with," not the transmission of information. For Heidegger language is an event as wondrous and purposeless as the blooming (Heidegger refers to the tao as "a great hidden stream" and thinks that is analogous to logos—tao=physis=logos=being?) of a flower, but it becomes aware of self. Heidegger calls language the House of Being. ("Letter on humanism," In: *Philosophy in the Twentieth Century*. W. Barrett and H. Aiken, eds. New York: Random House, 1962, p. 271). Grene reverses this to say being may be the house of language.

Bohm calls thought a dance of the mind. Thought is an art form, like poetry, that may dispose us toward order and harmony. The process by which thought and environment are linked is a cycle—a spiral movement. Emerson says that "Nature is the incarnation of a thought, and turns to a thought again, as ice becomes water and gas" ("Nature," *Selected Writings*. New York: Modern Library, 1950, p. 421). At no stage in the process does thought actually begin or end. So reality is not independent of thought. For James Jeans, the entire "universe begins to look more like a great thought than like a great machine. Mind no longer appears as an accidental intruder ..." (in *The Mysterious Universe*, p. 158).

Thought & Culture

In all thought, there is a transformation, a coding, between the report and what is reported. The map and territory, or word and thing, relationship is of similar structure but not an identity. Korzybski noted that the map is not the territory, the name is not the thing named. But there is a direct relationship. Different territories produce different maps; different places different languages.

E. Sapir (1931) and B.L. Whorf (1936) questioned to what extent and in what way language is related to the world view of those who speak it. Sapir viewed language as defining experience "for us by reason of its formal completeness and our unconscious projection of implicit expectations into experience." This means that reality is not the same for different languages or different beings. Whorf also thought that the forms of thought were controlled by laws of pattern. Thought was in a language. This is a world-view problem. R. Brown modified the Whorfian position into linguistic relativity, which holds that where there are differences of language there will be differences of thought; they covary. A perceptual category that is used more is more available and may be shorter.

Some psychologists tend to think that reality is the same for all people, but that they segment it differently. But thought and consciousness are being confused. The relationship of meaning to thought is not considered. Nor is nonverbal behavior to thought. Many language differences deal with relationship of language elements to cultural elements, but not to thought. According to M. Polanyi a theory of the universe is implied in language itself, as we expect to apply it to the future of our experience. We test the theory as we continuously talk about things. This is the equivalent of saying that language is cosmological by nature and in intention, and that it is a specific mode of behavior for managing space/time. As Bohr expressed it, we are participants, as well as spectators on the stage of life. Physicists and poets employ similar metaphorical logic to describe the human functional need to explore a common world image.

Culture

Our minds are not only nature dependent, but culture dependent as well. The wind, trees, birds are sources of signals and symbols. So are gestures and words. A community implies that the experiencers share ways of experiencing or the same experiences. This enables an individual to go beyond a finite view, to see the embedded culture as one of many ways of relating self to universe. Culture evolves from the interactions of humans with nature; both are in a constant state of flux. Cultures may be thought of as parallel to other species [mnemes (ideas)=genes]. The study of human adaptation to nature is cultural ecology.

Culture is a codification of reality, a symbolic system that transforms physical reality into experienced reality. Culture codifies reality through expressions, which can be preserved and transmitted through generations through language. But language is more than a medium to express thought. It is a major element in the formation of thought. Language is the means used to program our perception of the world. Different languages program events differently, therefore no culture or belief system can be considered entirely apart from language, or language entirely apart from place.

Culture is everything created as a group, tribe or nation, physical or ideal, in the past or present. This embraces cookware, arrows, steam engines; artworks, books, legal codes; symbols, values, social structures. A cultural system surrounds the network of human interactions with raw materials, forms of life and other humans. Culture may be represented in the new hermetic manner as:

$$* = components/ideas$$

Culture stretches vertically to include the physical, economic and political. It stretches horizontally to include society as a whole. In fact, culture is concerned with all things and beings and wholeness. It is organic, like Aristotle considered a work of art, and whole. So everything in it is interrelated in some degree. Four relationships are encompassed by the holistic perspective of culture: relation of people to themselves, to each other, to objects they create, to natural environment. These bear on psychological well-being, social bonds, material legacy, and on the association with other forms of life.

Culture has at least four constitutive elements that add up to the coherent whole. These four most fundamental dimensions of any sociocultural system are:

- kinship culture, concerned with succession and obligations (loyalties or entitlements);
- intellectual culture, providing the framework of reasoning, the presuppositions of inference and deduction, basic ideas of discourse, and boundaries of abstract and analytic capability;
- economic culture defines the means of production and liveli- hood, techniques of distribution, and values and norms underlying economic behavior (can be more closely related to kinship);
- political culture holds the values, prejudices, inhibitions, and ideas that condition political behavior and determine nature of institutions and change.

Kinship culture can be more rigidly localized than other dimensions. which can be more rapidly disseminated and assimilated. The transition from kinship to citizenship is slow. Kinship loyalty sometimes clashes with global perspectives.

Culture distills the greatest of human achievements in art, science, politics, poetry, architecture, and philosophy. In a UNESCO study, all nations considered art in their definitions of culture. The arts were considered essential because of the relationship between creativity and excellence, the soul of a culture. In most, arts are considered to be the most essential ingredient in culture. Culture is a wholistic perspective concerned with the unity of things. This is a perspective of art. In a work of art the whole is never sacrificed to the parts. Excesses and imbalances are permitted only in relation to the whole. A lesson from the holistic perspective is that the solution to one global problem may cause another.

Most cultures are multiracial and multilingual. Nations are even more diverse in peoples, customs and life styles. Culture forms an integrated design. Elements are fit into the design and related. A traditional culture integrates these relationships in a coherent whole, according to cultural values. By virtue of its integrative potential, culture provides an ideal framework for public and private decision making. Order is a cultural problem. Order provides stability and security. Cultural order is necessary to deal with the redistribution of wealth and power. Furthermore, justice, ethics, freedom, and truth are based in culture. The study of cultural ecology—human adaptation to nature—has been neglected. The dilemma of the world reveals the extent of this neglect.

Mary Douglas measures the order between cultures with a grid/group classification, where types of social organizations are mapped with types of symbolic patterns. Intercultural order will not be elaborated on, yet.

Ideology & Evolution
The myth of ideology is that humans are engaged in a life process of choosing sides, opinions and belief through selective preference; that elements constituting the self and group are equally detachable: politics, role, style, gender, natural relationships. Things can have no enduring relation with the environment if reality depends only on a contingent mind (as in quantum mechanics). So modern art has no communicative function, architecture is unrelated to surroundings, history is a collage of extraneous acts. All fields of study are trying to confirm that man makes himself, according to Shepard, no matter how the world is made. Geography endorses economic determinism; history studies the rise of

Promethean civilization; the arts separate abstract qualities from content; socio-anthropology encourages the theme that everything is possible; the sciences posture with value-free facts. Ideas are no longer connected. All aspects of life have become interchangeable, including soil, water and land. All concepts of natural seem to turn on the definition of human. If human beings are part of ecosystems, then evolution should illuminate that; but most anthropological theories cling to comparative ethnology, where humans are defined by intraspecies comparisons, by human difference, without due consideration of likeness.

The past is no longer a primary element in our identity. Darwin's theory of evolution has had little impact on modern consciousness, according to Shepard. Evolution was interpreted as supporting the theory of progress. And the corollaries were derived of normalcy, of perpetual change and the idea of adaptability, which appear to justify change for its own sake, permutation and pursuit of fashion. Further, Shepard argues that the reintrojection of the ideal of transient forms and values into evolutionary settings allowed the argument that human biological evolution has ended and cultural evolution taken over. This allowed society to disengage itself from Darwin's determinism without refuting it. Our humanity and ecology becomes an ideological choice. So all views on use of nature are regarded as valid in their own way. The biological, historical perspective is ignored.

Does culture evolve? Shepard thinks not; Thompson and others claim so. There are many differences between biological and cultural evolution: in rate and frequency of transmission, serial nature, and nonphyletic transmission. In the cultural inheritance of acquired characteristics, behavioral evolution resembles Lamarck's idea of organic evolution and draws on Darwinian evolution, also. Some think that it is too plastic, but many values, habits and traditions are concrete and stable. Culture is not coded genetically. It is more like a species. Evolution within a species is slow, in theories of microevolution, and dictated by chance. Cultural evolution may be compared to macroevolution, as the selection of sets in a changing matrix. Cultures that are not flexible, die out. The idea of colonization has vanished as silently as the idea of the Holy Roman Empire. There is no biological/cultural dichotomy. Studies of cultures, the intellectual dimensions of primitive thought, and research on primates demonstrate that. Culture is embedded in biology.

Culture is tethered to the biosphere, part of the evolutionary process. It is part of a natural history that exemplifies stability and diversity. Cultural evolution may slowly bring about better ways of using technology for a benign effect on individuals, families, communities and the environment. But we cannot destroy the environment first.

J. Peacock plots an evolutionary trend of cultural types from the primitive through archaic, historic, modernizing, and modern. He speculates that the later developments are more adaptive than the earlier and replace them. Certainly, each culture dominated a place on earth. But their relative adaptations have yet to be contrasted. Social science realizes that the world's ethnic groups are not evolutionary stages culminating in Europe, but are equally valid ways of life.

Value & Identity

The concepts by which personal experience is organized are imposed by language and culture. Culture provides a larger identity. Identity is basic to human existence. The ideal types of many cultures—the hero, the saint, the artists, the adventurer, the lover—maintained their virtues for an entire lifetime. People were fixed in permanent roles and personalities. They were identified by their roles. One was an incarnation of his trade and national group. In human ecology, niches are called institutions. A value system is held in the womb of cultural institutions. Humans and institutions both live out mentally conceived values.

Meaning and value arise from the assessment of the consequences of an action. Meaning arises when significant experience pumps blood and air into the corpse of culture. There is then an effort to match new experience to the existing categories of culture. Culturally-derived values are continually tested against experience. Personal systems of values are created and associated with the ambihuman environment. Freud thought that humans strove for biological satisfaction, but Becker corrected that it was for meaning. By using Maslow's hierarchy of needs, it can be seen that both are true. As an illustration, F. Mowat relates a tale of an eskimo woman separated from her group by a storm. She was forced to live by herself for years. After taking care of food and shelter and making tools, she began engraving them. The symbols were as important as the tools, or considered part of them. They were found after she died.

With Husserl, the question of the reality of the world was shifted to the question of its meaning. The meaning of existence is to be found in how thoroughly one understands that existence, taking full responsibility for self, comprehension and relation to the entire world. Humans need to reach for meanings to fulfill; happiness is a side effect to meaning fulfillment.

There is meaning in the world before the perceiver initiates it, but the meaning discloses the connaturality of the perceiver. Merleau-Ponty calls this the idea of 'thrownness.' Nature is as much naturing as natured. Objects are not discrete because every one is embedded in irremovable background and tightly interwoven with every other entity in field. We create meaning by trying to ascend through the givens. The universe is in process of continuous ascendance.

The modern role of a competent technician, impersonal, limited and incurious, dominates industrial society, as Max Weber predicted it would. Mumford judges that he who belongs exclusively to a single nation or religion or vocation without any touch from the world is not yet fully human. Perfection in any single field must be renounced for the sake of balanced and continued growth. As the wider circle is embraced, the masks of singleness are cast aside, until the complete person is naked, without the clothing of culture and ideology.

Sometimes the widening of a culture results in a creative, explosive radiation, as when medieval Christian culture made contact with the ideas of Greece and Rome and with the achievements of China and India. Then people have more opportunities. The ideal images intensified human experience and widened its potential. But an open society will not limit everyone to one role. Perhaps everyone will be educated by Hegel's definition: One can do what any other can do. There is a need for order as well. The real challenge in life is to lead a good life, in the Aristotelian sense of life of moral, material, intellectual, and spiritual integrity. Economic growth needs to be placed in a proper perspective with other areas of life; economic values have a place with other equally important values.

Leopold's ecological conscience does not engender social expediency or blind economic growth. he rejected the tenets of his own profession and admitted being one who cannot live without wild things. The wild, community of species, is prior to the big questions: peace, race, poverty, economics, and politics. With order comes stability, and security, without which nothing can survive. Order must emanate from a new set of ideological principles and pragmatic reality. The development of mature identity reaches out to all things, to the growth of organic relationships, through its own history and rootedness and is not limited by the traditional attitudes toward nature.

There have been three general attitudes toward nature:
- As victim: The Ik have had a string of misfortunes after their hunting ground was turned into a national park. The difficulty of farming and worsened social conditions makes life hard and unfair

(as questionably described by C. Turnbull). This attitude may be characterized by a cluster of attitudes: Nature as alien, unjust, violent, or vengeful; things were better in the past; humans are out of place.

- As conqueror: The English treated tropical lands as enemies to be defeated; then made them into plantations. Biogeochemical cycles and soil requirements are temporary obstacles in world where everything has its price. This is the prevailing mode in institutions dealing with land use today. The Western attitude is that nature is a beast to be tamed controlled and exploited. Although Passmore mentioned other models of relationship, such as stewardship, mastery is the most dominant trend. Even the notion of stewardship suggests that humanity is superior.

- As part: The Pygmies of the Ituri Forest of Zaire see themselves as a part of the forest, an abundant provider; they regard the forest as mother and father, conceive of themselves as children of the forest and live in harmony with it. The Peublo Indians consider the sun to be their father and earth to be their mother (Ortiz, 1972). Earth and sun create an endless series of cycles that govern life. People and animals and seasons were part of nature.

The Ik have a pathological attitude, partly forced on them by an unsympathetic government, of being almost totally controlled. At the other adolescent extreme, the Western attitude is one of total noncontrol. Although the Pygmies are well adapted, their attitude seems inapplicable on an earth where thirty million humans starve to death every year.

Yet this last attitude may be the most appropriate for humanity. Humanity is part of nature, as valuable and unique as cranes or louseworts, but not more valuable or unique. This attitude would entail using what is necessary, exploiting some ecosystems completely, changing a place to fit human aspirations, and killing plants and animals for sustenance. All animals and plants alter their environments to fit to some extent. But it would also mean limiting humanity and its technological effects, limiting human use to local impacts, and letting other beings live without interference. It is not necessary to dominate or terraform the earth completely. Humanity could contain itself to five percent of the earth's surface and ecosystems and only visit or ignore the remainder. This ideal requires change.

Cultural Change

W.I. Thompson distinguishes six great cultural transformations (1981):
The hominization of primates, symbolization and origins of notation
and art in Upper Paleolithic, agriculturalization in 9000 BC, civilization
in 3500 BC, industrialization in 1800, and planetization in 1960. The
first one he calls the feminization of primates; females abandoned estrus
and became open sexually. In observing synchronicity between bodies
and nature, women established system of symbols and notation. Then
women discovered that they could collect enough cereals in three weeks
to last the entire year, more than a hunter could kill; but it required
storage. Agriculture gave a surplus; that and property lead to excitement
of war. Civilization became the domestication of women. This started
the patriarchal structure. Industrialization is really an intensification of
civilization (still an ektropic process). In each case of cultural absorption,
there was an attendant process of miniaturization. The forest was
miniaturized in clumps of trees; animals were miniaturized in artistic
image; time on a lunar tally stick; plants in a garden; women in a
household; nature by culture in 1800 (under the glass roof of the Crystal
Palace); and now by the new consciousness surrounding the old. Ratio
becomes logos. Measuring becomes pulling in, and perhaps shaping
(morphos).

How does this happen? Culture does not fit together into a perfectly
integrated whole. A culture is a loose-fitting patchwork of ideas,
relationships and things. In that sense it is parallel to species adaptation to
an environment. There are discontinuities and contradictions. Humans can
tolerate inconsistency and operate with contradictory beliefs: soldiers fight
for peace; ministers save the unborn for starvation. If the contradictions
become too great and maladaptive, then the culture disappears.

The mode of operation of nature consists of a rhythm of dissolution
and reformation. Often the elements of a culture will simply be rearranged
by a succeeding culture. A new culture can only be made from the heritage
of the old. The International Workers of the World urged its members to
make the new world in shell of old one. *(cf. genetic recombination) Our
survival depends on the capacity to remake the image of the world from
within, phoenixlike.

There are pictures called anamorphoses, which are fragmentary
deformities to the naked eye, but reveal perfect forms in a conic mirror.
Like the mirror, culture organizes the fragments of life. The life of
an individual, often won at great cost, receives its complement from
culture. But the conic mirror is lost to modern cosmologies; the world

is fragmented. The pieces of experience can be reconstituted by a gestalt, a perception of the total pattern. Nature, myth or love can bestow the mirror again. Nature has an inherent order. Myth creates an order. Love combines orders.

Unlike classic cultural change, revitalization requires the explicit intent of the members of society; and it can take place in one generation. Changing the image requires changing the gestalt of images of self, nature and society. That effort is revitalization. Secular or religious revitalization depends on restructuring existing elements or subsystems already in use (or known to a leader). The recombination into consistent structure is from the inspiration of a person or group. It can occur in a moment of insight. The moment of transformation can be mystic and scientific (metanoia is a fundamental transformation of mind, from the Greek for religious conversion). The original vision is applied through steps of communication, organization, adaptation, and transformation, which feeds back through culture. Where the movement remains responsible for performance of ritual or preservation of doctrine, idealism is preserved. Images held by a culture influence the fate of the culture. When images are anticipatory, they lead to development and social change. Attractiveness reinforces the movement towards them.

Bateson and Odum debate whether a Confucian (social) or Taoist (ecological) model should be the basis for a new culture. In the Confucian, everything would be based on ecological balance; the property of Li, and maintained by a global elite. The elite are the flaw in this scheme. Elitists tend to be out of place everywhere; they have no local knowledge. And elitism is usually based on some kind of superiority. It assumes that nature is a resource that can be managed with knowledge. In general, elitists have power without knowledge or knowledge without charity. Where Confucius recommended the qualities of goodness and duty, Lao Tse suggested that men should keep their natural qualities by studying the course of heaven, by guiding one's steps by the inward power, by following the course that the way of nature sets. Then goodness and duty do not need to be advertised. Confucius complained that he had mastered the scriptures and faced seventy two rulers expounding knowledge, but none of them made use of his teachings. Lao Tse was relieved that none of the rulers was anxious to reform the world; the scriptures were no better than footprints in the dust, telling nothing of the force that guided the steps.

The taoist does not hide from the world; what he hides are only his inborn powers. He practices the art of living in the world. In the taoist model, authority would be separated from power. Tao would flow as ultimate moral order beyond human ideologies. The cries for world order represent a misunderstanding of true order, the tao. We must understand that no ideology can contain the truth; enemies will not be hated, but cherished as opponent who brings us closer to realization of being. Rabindranath Tagore recognized that "We must prepare the field for the cooperation of all the cultures of the world where all will give and take from each other." (in *A Tagore Reader*). But that can only happen if the integrity of each culture is maintained, by strong myths, images and rituals.

The Tao of Images
Revitalization can be accomplished through education in words, numbers, links and images. An effective education need not be bound by the conceptual and economic limits assumed by most institutions. A minimum education may train students for an economic role in society, but a good education teaches them how to enjoy living among other human beings in an ultrahuman nature and to perpetuate a good society. Poets like Wordsworth and Auden recommended that broad training in science and technology was necessary for poetic knowledge, which is part of a good education. Novalis considered that the study of the external world, through science, was only the first, half-way, step to full human consciousness. The second step was introspection, the contemplation of the self.

In his educational theory, Plotinus went still further and laid down a triple organization of education, requiring a social education, a personal and self-revealing education, and a synergetic one that would permit a perspective of the whole of human existence. Only institutions that integrate education within a balanced society can achieve this triple objective. By encouraging students who are already working outside academic walls, ecological institutions can foster this necessary kind of synergetic education.

The most valuable qualities of an ecological education are personal contact, which allows noncompetitive constructive criticism, and flexibility, which allows the educational process to fit an established and meaningful life-style. Ecological education lets one learn how to feel and live, as well as to think. As Aristotle recognized long ago, experience is necessary for thinking. Formal institutions fail to teach communal responsibility, self-reliance, and physical work—those qualities most dear to R. W. Emerson. Education must embrace three concepts, according to Schiller: liberation, play, and community. Liberation is freedom from the limits of identity; play is imaginative experience; and community is the supporting matrix of life. This ideal is most closely approached in already established communities (not the artificial, involuted, temporary university dormitories) and when play and freedom are not limited by arbitrary rules and economic goals.

Ecological institutions provide for education within the larger community, in the larger context of work and recreation. All human beings need a life that is protected and ordered, loving companions and contact with the wild universe. But, one cannot pretend that this little world is not part of a larger one riddled with hunger and fear—one which everyone's actions affect. The beliefs people hold are worthwhile only if they enact them in a larger world, ethically (which comes from the Sanskrit word meaning 'doing together'). Very few institutions concern themselves with the scope of ethics; that is left to the employee or student.

Everyone needs the courage to question society and express their beliefs and findings without worrying about the cost. For only through sincere, studied expression or example can anyone hope to influence the consciousness of others. And only by surrounding society with a new field of consciousness—not by attacking it—can any transformation occur. When human beings cooperate spontaneously, because they understand what it means to be human, because they understand how to treat their places on earth, only then can education be considered successful and, perhaps, lead to a more peaceful and humane world.

Garret Hardin points out that education is not just literacy, and that literacy, the ability to understand what words really mean, is not enough anyway. It needs to be supplemented by "numeracy," the ability to quantify information and interpret it intelligently— computers, remember, use numbers for everything—and, on another level, by "ecolacy," the ability to take into account the effects of complex interactions of systems over time, for understanding of the complexity of the world, that things are interconnected and affect one another. Together, these are three major filters against folly that citizens can use against the blindness, short sightedness, and sheer idiocy that experts disguise as eloquence or expertise. The filters are literacy, numeracy, and ecolacy.

Literacy (Words). Literacy is the quality of being literate. Specifically, it is the ability to read a short passage and answer questions about what was read. The word comes from the Latin word meaning letter or later 'writing.' Being literate is being characterized by learning. A person who is educated has been "lead" from ignorance, out of the self in other words, by fostering the growth and expansion of knowledge through a course of formal study. Knowledge is a condition of knowing, an acquaintance with theoretical or practical understanding. There are no limits on what can be known. But, most knowledge is concerned with survival first. It is important to know what plants to eat, where to find shelter, how to make clothing. This was, and still is, the most basic level of literacy. But, literacy occurs on more than one level. Gandhi put literacy in a similar perspective, "Literacy is not the end of education, not even the beginning, it is only one of the means." Education should include a core of mathematics. Poetry and narratives should still be memorized. Literacy, as the skill in the written and spoken language, enables readers to draw on the wisdom (and foolishness) of human beings distant in space and time. Hardin notes, in a discussion of the sins of the literate, that language has two functions beyond communication: "To promote thought and to prevent it." The second function is why literacy has to be accompanied by the ability to think critically.

Numeracy (Numbers). Numeracy involves the ability to measure and to interpret quantities, proportions and rates. Hardin warns that human beings have learned how to use literacy to hide numbers and the need for numerate analysis. He draws attention to the problems created by always thinking solely in terms of dichotomies, e.g., safe vs. unsafe or pure vs. impure, rather than in terms of relative risks and benefits. James Lovelock has also noted our inability to assess risks mathematically. The quantitative analysis that is so important in science, technology, business, and government is dismissed with indifference. In a complex, rapidly changing society, understanding quantities, ratios, rates and duration of time is crucial. Numeracy has limitations, also—the conclusions of an accurate mathematical analysis are only as good as its premises.

Ecolacy (Links). Ecolacy was once achieved by studying natural history, the plants and animals that surrounded every human group. Ecolacy is the ability to ask and answer the question: 'And then what?' This would allow the effects of the interactions of systems to be taken into account. Scientists have been extremely successful using reductionistic methodology on every problem, breaking problems down into their components and studying the properties of these components and their interactions. This has led to the ascendancy of mechanical science—thinking that one can do just one thing. Garrett Hardin stated the important ecological understanding of ecolacy as: 'We can never do merely one thing." This statement is now known as Hardin's Law, and it means that there are always wanted and unwanted effects, products and wastes.

Reality is composed of causal chains of events rather than single effects. Events are embedded in causal networks and are produced by multiple causes and have multiple effects, each of which triggers a causal chain of future events. Hardin contends that since we cannot do just one thing we must always ask and answer that question: "And then what?" We have to try to ascertain the benefits and costs of proposed courses of action on both the individual, social, and ecological levels. The ecological systems way of thinking employs scientific theories and knowledge to study the interlocking processes characterized by many reciprocal cause effect pathways. The ecological systems way of thinking must become an integral part of the thinking of the well educated person if we are to adequately control technology and human actions.

Discussion of Filters (Plus One). The world is too complex for our minds, suggested G. P. Marsh and many later thinkers. So, our minds have to filter out what is less important. We filter data, arguments, emotions, and information. The filter allows a total picture of the whole with relatively little information. Of course that picture might be wrong. But, it is clear, as a result of filtering and thinking. Other human activities act as filters, also, especially culture.

In education and communication, noise is a problem. We are flooded with information, and much of that noise. We have to filter out as much noise as possible and much of the information. But, many cultural filtering systems are collapsing.

The industrial system developed like a jigsaw puzzle with an unknown design. With only a few pieces the pattern is unknown, notes Charles Taylor. Partly, however, that is because we are making the pattern, generating it, as we go along, with bricolage. Our efforts at aggregation and filtering result in a form. As we generate it, more of the pieces fill in and a pattern emerges. But, if the pattern does not fit the environment, it has to change.

Garrett Hardin contends that most of the major controversies of our time can be understood as the result of the participants relying too much on any single one of these three filters. No one filter by itself is adequate for understanding reality and predicting the consequences of our actions. There is, however, a filter that has gone unmentioned, in its ability to concentrate or distort human perception. That filter is the image.

Imagacy (Images). When a hierarchical order cannot adapt its function
to an actual situation, then there is a synchronous change in the vertical
order. The change in order is discontinuous, although the function is
continuous. Since the details are not abstracted to a higher level, one
cannot predict when the revolutionary change will take place. In general,
revolution is discontinuous and synchronous, whereas evolution first
appears to be continuous and diachronous. In the synchronic mode, form
is complete as soon as it appears; in the diachronic, the form is slowly
elaborated. It would appear that complex processes, like evolution, actually
use both modes.

Hierarchical thinking is limited in cybernetics. The concept of
control might better be stated as kind of reciprocity or mutual causality.
Furthermore, in an open system, the environment, structure, program,
and feedback all govern the system in concert. Hazel Henderson states that
only the system can model or manage the system, but this is not entirely
true. Images can model the system in miniature.

An image is an imitation or representation of something. It can also
be a symbol or type, a metaphor or concept. An image can stand for
something else, for instance the image of a dove is often used as a symbol
for peace. In the etymological sense a symbol is something 'thrown
together,' as a problem is something 'thrown forward.' Unlike an image, a
symbol often represents some other thing, process or quality. Symbols can
be processed by 'Analytical Engines' or computers. These machines have
been used as metaphors of the brain, which also processes symbols, that
is, the operation of both parts of the metaphor, brain=computer, can be
described in terms of algorithms, or mathematical rules for manipulating
symbols.

An image of course can be used in a variety of ways. It can reference
similarity, correlation or a formal linkage, according to the categories
of association developed by C.S. Peirce: Icon, index, or symbol. Icons
have a similarity with an object, as when a landscape painting depicts a
landscape. An index is when an image is causally linked with something
else, as when a wolf's howl is related to location or emotion. A symbol
has a social convention that establishes the relationship linking an image
and a thing. Physical connection is not necessary for any of these modes.
Peirce suggested that the difference between the modes of reference could
be understood in terms of hierarchical levels of interpretation. Symbolic
relationships are composed of relationships between sets of indices,
and indices are composed of iconic relationships between sets of icons.
Understanding a higher level means decomposing it to a lower-order form.

Understanding the logic of images, as well as their power, is important to their use in communicating and design.

An image, especially a cosmology or an image of the world, models the system in miniature. From the image, which can be a paradigm or mind-set, a whole system can arise, with unique goals, rules, parameters, and structures. A cosmology includes a mythology constructed as a poetic system. Joseph Campbell states "Mythology—and therefore civilization—is a poetic, supernormal image." Mythologies and religions can be understood as great poems. When recognized as such, they point through individual things and events to the ubiquity of a presence that is whole in each. This is what P.B. Shelley meant when he wrote that poets are the 'unacknowledged legislators of the world'—not that they pass laws or prophesize the future, but that they generate images for the future, and these images can be articulated into goals to influence our actions. Bad images can relate to severe cultural problems. For instance, the mechanistic images of science, from Shelley to the Fascists, determined much of the violent conquest of nature.

Kenneth Bounding notes that the image as a cognitive construct of the world has several aspects: Spatial, temporal, personal, relational, value, and affection (emotional) for each individual. The total sum of individual images is a world of interrelated constructs. This parallels the experiences of other living beings, which use their senses to create life-images, or umwelts.

In fact, human beings design complex images for a variety of purposes, including to make a profit or to persuade others to join a group. In this, design reflects the economic and political bents of humans. In a hyperactive marketplace, design responds with sophisticated images and crass intentions. In the city, design responds with an architectural icon, the skyscraper, for expressing power, status, success, and victory over limits and the environment—however temporarily. Images have importances and weaknesses, but they contribute to a complex ecology of people and processes, languages and cultures, in a partially-designed, open, living system.

Part Three: One Earth

All things are connected . . . Whatever befalls the Earth befalls the
sons of the Earth . . . This we know—the Earth does not belong to
man, man belongs to the Earth . . . Man did not weave the web
of life, he is merely a strand in it. Whatever he does to the web, he
does to himself.

  Chief Sealth

If Plato was the first to attempt to define the role and function of the artist
in society and the first to ask about the relation between life as lived and
art as an imitation of life, it was Aristotle who treated the problem as a
theoretical study by investigating the uniqueness of the artistic experience
and the objects of art as a separate field. Although, in the *Poetics*, he
analyzed the important issues as narrowly relevant to his theory of tragedy,
he still formed notions that significantly altered Plato's and expanded
them. The artist is no longer an inspired madman, but a maker of things.
Art is not so much a dangerous pastime, as a means of deepening the
understanding of life. Artifacts as imitations of real things are more
appropriately works structured like living organisms. For Aristotle, art
is a mimesis of nature: as nature produces living organisms, so works of
art are structured in a similar fashion without copying those things or
producing living things itself. This is order, with a beginning, middle and
end; combined with size as a condition for observation, order and size in a
unified whole create beauty, which is a characteristic of nature and art.

Expressing the Earth: Aesthetics

In the 1700s, Baumgarten used the Greek word for sense awareness,
aesthesis, as the name for a new discipline, aesthetics. Previously, Plato had
sense and reason as mutually exclusive, and art was relegated to sensory
involvement and emotions. Since the Renaissance, a necessary condition
of beauty or aesthetic pleasure was the equilibrium of two mutually
counterbalancing forces. As enunciated by Descartes, "among the objects
of every sense, the one that is most agreeable to the soul is . . . so difficult
that it makes the senses suffer in striving to become acquainted with it"
(from M. Rader, *A Modern Book of Aesthetics*, p. 125). As sense and reason
lost their absolute contrast, the association of art and emotionally laden

sense awareness developed into a separate doctrine, imagination, the function of which was to bridge sense and reason.

In Schiller, for instance, there is a 'sensuous urge,' from the nature of human existence in flux, and an 'urge for form,' from the human rational nature. These two urges, life and pattern (Gestalt), converged in a third, the 'play urge,' whose impulse is towards a living pattern, which is identifiable with beauty. Hegel attempted to go beyond the psychological considerations of Descartes and Schiller. For him, beauty was "the imposition of unity on the variety of external phenomena through regularity, symmetry, subordination to laws, and harmony." This principle takes on metaphysical significance: "art is a means of glimpsing the stable world of Ideas behind the shifting heterogeneity of the perceptible world" (Ibid., p. 125).

For Nietzsche, art is related to life and experience. His aesthetics is one theory of art and beauty, in the broad meaning of aesthesis as sense perception. Beauty no longer belongs to Ideas or things themselves, exclusively, but to subjectivity. Art belongs to aesthetics only when it promotes human enjoyment; the beauty is aesthetic only when it pleases someone. Each art has a double source, from two opposing principles, represented by the deities, Apollo and Dionysius. Apollo was god of light, beauty and harmony; Dionysius was god of darkness, drunkenness and chaos. The mutually required interaction of these gods achieved the highest artistic ideal, the tragic. *Tragedy is such an ideal because it concerns the failure *of a cosmology. The union of these dialectical elements is symbolized in art, where the creative act contains them. Thus the aesthetic experience enters into the depth of being and into the chaos of existence, not to embrace Ideas, but to contain pain and joy, creation and destruction, in art. All of life and culture are aesthetic phenomena. Ethics, metaphysics and religion are unified in an aesthetic interpretation of all being.

The tragic view becomes most fully expressed in the "great silence of art," where being is expressed as transcending moral distinctions and responsibility for evil and destruction in its innocence of becoming. "The world is a work of art," proclaimed Nietzsche. Art and life have merged. Humanity celebrates its reunion with nature in aesthetic experience. Art convinces us of the "eternal delight in existence." Art acquires a metaphysical dimension by interpreting the world as an aesthetic phenomenon; metaphysics becomes a "metaphysics of artists." Without agreeing with Schiller, that "man is only man when he plays," Nietzsche expanded the concept of play to include all categories of life.

Holopoesis: Making the World

"When we arrive at the summit of Nietzsche's aesthetics, we have no more aesthetics," said Heidegger. (R. Pfeffer, Nietzsche: Disciple of Dionysius. (Lewisburg: Bucknell University Press, 1972), p. 205) Nietzsche's concept of art becomes metaphysical. His metaphysics is a metaphysics of value, according to Heidegger. These values merge in a total world view, beyond good and evil, beauty and ugliness, and reach into being itself. Heidegger pointed out that Nietzsche carried metaphysics to its ultimate conclusion and therefore to its turning point: The apparent world is the only world that exists; transcendent metaphysics is replaced by a metaphysics of life. Although Heidegger retained Nietzsche's unity of man and nature, where ethics, aesthetics and metaphysics merged, he not only emphasized different points in it, but based it on a different ground. For Nietzsche, humanity was a part of nature and gained meaning only from unity with nature; there could be no complete humanization of nature. Heidegger reversed this important distinction: Human being made nonhuman existence possible, by creating the world with human decisions; nature was a meaningless mass given meaning through human understanding. His unity of man and nature was based on an ontology grounded in existential phenomena.

Dissatisfied with the correspondence theory of truth—that a thing corresponds with what we possess of it—Heidegger asserted that truth was understood from the viewpoint of the openness in which the thing and the person comporting with it found themselves. This openness seemed to be a translucent medium, subject to historical change. Art was defined as what brought about the openness as a possibility for meeting. Art was the "letting come to pass of the advent of truth of beings as such." Heidegger explained: "It is from the poetizing essence of art that it comes to pass that [art] erects in the midst of beings an open place in whose openness everything is different from usual." (in J. Kockelmans, ed., *On Heidegger and Language*, p. 75). The human being seemed to be a passive receiver of what "being" sent, but with the ability to shut off the sending. The effect of a work was not in the working, but a change in the unconcealment of "being."

Poetry is the essence of art, for Heidegger, and poeticizes the openness. Indeed, language as a whole is art. It is more than communication; it brings human being into the opening of "being" with other things and beings. Naming a being makes it appear. It becomes accessible and recognizable. For Heidegger, the being of beings is the primary reality and not the world. Heidegger believed that an analysis of being must be accomplished with terms proper to it. For instance, the analysis of openness in the human subject indicated the primacy of affectivity, according to E. Kaelin (PE 62), which is the perception of ourselves caught in a certain pose before the objects of the world. Affectivity is the modification of our existence in relationship to our world. This is the only world there is, before speech and meaningful gestures.

Once language predominates, it may be mistaken as primary. The works of artists will always seem odd to scientific observers who view those works as thoughtful representations of the natural world; art is really understanding, openness. It is possible to understand our affectivity by having the experience of feeling, by keeping ourselves open to the influence of the world we create. Humans are metaphysical animals, claimed Heidegger, affectively living in the openness of being. Through humanity, being is revealed in language, in poetic and philosophical thought.

The openness of being is the possibility of the appearance of new entities in the process of worlds becoming a world where humans are aware of things becoming things. According to Heidegger, painting and literature are both a means of creating new meaning, which may lead cultural history in new directions. "Painting presents us with a world directly through the medium of vision, and language presents a world in depth that may be sensuous, supersensuous, or however a world may be, indirectly through the ear." (E. Lee and M. Mandelbaum, *Phenomenology and Existentialism.* Baltimore: Johns Hopkins Press, 1967, p. 67). The making of a work of art is the establishment of a tradition, with a gift, a foundation and a new beginning, from the modification of the world.

The origin of a work of art is to be found in its essence as the creative preservation of truth. In his explanation, Heidegger sought the essence of works of art as they functioned. "The setting up of a world and the placement of the earth within are two essential characteristics in the being of a work" (Ibid., p. 83.) Works of art are ontological phenomena in that their creation and appreciation affect a human manner of being in the world. The artist distills a meaning complex to bring forth the earth, that self-contained , newly fixed meaning structure that closes the whole. As the artist introduces new meaning into the world, she modifies the world of others; this meaning sediments to the basis for a common world. Art is a historical process that can unite many different views. In fact, humanity is the poetic species, *homo poeta*, in the words of Becker (in *Structure of Evil*, p. 169). Humans strive for meaning and create their own, playfully.

The Life of Symbols

Plato and Aristotle had initiated a new value, the suspension of the practical and an attitude of detachment. Prior to that, humans lived in a closed, finite world. Husserl called this prereflective, pre-theoretical world the lived-world, Lebenswelt. After the theoretical attitude was adopted, reality or being was only ascribed to changeless essences. Husserl traced the history of the perversion of rationalism through Kant, admonishing that only by using the lived-world as the source of reflection, can a rational world be constructed free from distortions. Instead of focusing his attention on an ontology of the lived-world, as Heidegger did, Husserl attempted, through detachment and the phenomenological reduction, to make the lived-world the basis for a formulation of transcendental phenomenology "which would render the 'Lebenswelt,' through that philosophical method, the universal foundation for all particular sciences" (in E. Schaper, *Prelude to Aesthetics*, p. 59).

Husserl noticed a close affinity between artistic and phenomenological detachment; in different ways, they both illustrated a possible modification of consciousness. The reductions carried out in phenomenology found an automatic fulfillment in art. Husserl distinguished between the neutral modification of art and the neutrality of the representation in every image: The figure in an image had no real being, representing only that the being may be real, but not in the image itself. This substitution is what is meant by the neutralization of the figure. Image modification as such is usually experienced in art or poetry. Husserl considered that it had no aesthetic relevance and was outweighed experientially by proper aesthetic qualities, such as beauty or order. The work of art is not substitutional, but originates from an awareness of existence. It produces and presents a whole experience; it does not represent and reproduce it. Detachment reduces the personal agent to an aesthetic subject in art, and a pure ego in phenomenology. It motivates aesthetic ecstasy. Art and phenomenology are reformations of consciousness. Considering the qualitative richness of experience and the irreducibility of its essential character, Husserl's theory of art concentrated on the exhibition of the inner form, the proper essence of a work of art.

In elaborating the general essence of consciousness, Husserl ignored the brute facts of being that constitute the general order of every possible being. An artist's feeling and expression rose from common life, and then raised that life to a new level, with new experiences. The work of art is simultaneously self-realization and world constitution. It determines the individuality of the artist and the physiognomy of his world. The generic essence of art belongs to a "regional ontology" as the basis for the material object. Meaning in the art object is self-given and wholly in perception. For Husserl, meaning is art is logical meaning, apparently an essence. The artist returns to the "things themselves" as they appear contextually in pretheoretical perceptual experience, as natural meaning structures that are basic to our artificial logic, and which Husserl called the "Logos of the aesthetic world" (Merleau-Ponty, *Signs*. Evanston: Northwestern, 1964, p. xiii).

Apparently, Merleau-Ponty regarded all perception as aesthetic perception, as did Whitehead. The phrase 'aesthetic perception' is redundant, but it will be used to distinguish it from standard notions of perception and from the modern use of aesthetic as a domain of artistic activity. Merleau-Ponty regarded aesthetic perception as a spontaneous reduction, much the way Husserl did. He referred to the best formulation of reduction as "wonder" in the face of the world. The aesthetic image is given in person. The tone of artistic images changes from the middle ages to the renaissance, forming a personal world in a different sort of space. Merleau-Ponty describes such a space: "One could show, for example, that aesthetic perception opens in turn a new space, that the painting as a work of art is not in the space it inhabits as a physical thing and as a colored canvas, that the dance unfolds in a space without ends and without directions, that it is a suspension of our history, that in the dance the subject and his world are no longer opposed, no longer detach themselves each against the background furnished by the other, that consequently, the parts of the body are no longer accentuated in the way they are in natural experience" (Idem, *The Phenomenology of Perception*. London: Routledge & Kegan Paul, 1962, p. 293).

There are many spaces that interpenetrate. The body normally projects an aesthetic spatiality, until the impact of a new experience provoked by a work of art renders it inadequate—the spatiality on canvas is the equivalent of a perceptual world—after which a need for readjustment is felt, and this is the need for expression. Every expression is a creative act, an incarnation of freedom, finite because it is embodied. All creative acts come into being by reference; they are an extension of an already persisting world.

In the presence of a work of art, a style is felt. The image presents itself—it is not representation, but presentation. The presentation is kinaesthetic, an expressive dynamic form that appeals more to the kinaesthetics of the body than to intuition. Merleau-Ponty described the reception of a work of art as a process of reenactment of the vibration of the work by the corporeal perceiver. However, the aesthetic object is not felt as existent; its essence is not necessarily related to existence. The materials only support the image. Therefore, the meaning of the work is intrinsic and related necessarily to the image. Aesthetic knowledge must be prior to conceptual knowledge. For Merleau-Ponty, as for Husserl, art is subsumed under a general theory of linguistics, as the science of symbolic activity.

More than other advanced mammals, human behavior includes the capability of making the things in the perceived-world symbolic. Whereas, in general, the signal to which an animal responds is empirically related to the event for which it stands, the symbol to which a human responds is not just related to an event, but to other symbols. In fact, the relationship of one symbol to other symbols is the same as the relationship of the object signified to other objects. These lateral relations open up the possibility of varied expressions of a same theme. Symbolic behavior must be a necessary condition for human cognition, making it possible to have a unity of an object within a multiplicity of relations.

A biological complexity embedded in a social complexity allows human behavior to express the complexity of the world. Language and painting are primary expressions. Merleau-Ponty called the phenomenon of expression a "Hegelian dialect," "which gathers itself up and launches itself again through the mystery of rationality" (Idem, *Signs*, p. 73). The concept of true history could be recovered, if it were modeled after the examples of language and the arts. Language tends to condense the world, to possess its sense in an independent truth. All literature is engaged in truth when it says something. It always speaks of human relationships— poetic or profane—with the world and other beings. It changes the relationships by its expression and embodied truth; not as propaganda or technique. Therefore the poet or artist is engaged in making.

Art, for Merleau-Ponty, "is supremely responsible to society, not as an arm of propaganda, but as a means of leading us all to a primordial perception of the world, to a contact with things and others that puts us in touch with an open funiverse." (in E. Schaper, *Prelude to Aesthetics*, p. 212). Merleau-Ponty also states, "There is no break in the circuit between human and nature; He concludes that "it is impossible to say that nature ends here and that man or expression starts here" (in "Eye and mind," *The Primacy of Perception*, p. 188). Art is related to the perceived world in which we are in living contact. It puts human beings in touch with the world, awakens them to it and leads beyond what has been to what can be. The artist is unwilling to continue the past through veneration or change it through revolt; she lures it to change. As Merleau-Ponty states, "The novelty of the arts of expression is that they make tacit culture come out of its mortal footnote circle" (*Signs*, p. 79).

Poetic Knowing

In the *Metaphysics* (E.1.1025b25), Aristotle called poetry one of three kinds of intellectual activity:

- Theoretical knowledge (theoretike episteme)
- Practical knowledge (praktike episteme)
- Poetical knowledge (poietike episteme)

The three sciences involved different ends. The theoretical sciences involved necessary propositions and had knowledge as their end; the practical sciences subordinated knowledge to action—as in knowing virtue to act virtuously—and the productive sciences had a product as their end, not knowledge or action. Philosophy was a theoretical knowledge, as was mathematics, physics, and theology. The practical sciences derived many propositions from the theoretical and the productive derived many propositions from both other sciences. Since sciences became less exact as they involved more elements, and became more dependent on the others, poetry was the least exact of all. Yet, in a sense, poetry was more basic than the others, since all sciences produced an end.

Poetic knowledge was inseparable from the power to make. Poetry is a kind of knowledgeable activity with a product for an end. Aristotle defined art at various times as: having to do with creation; using powers; "principles of change in another thing;" and being concerned with the same thing as chance. Poetry was poiesis, a fashioning of random data into a significant statement of universal relevance. The whole is structurally unified into a complex thing. This unity is based on the organic theme in Aristotle. Art is a mimesis of nature, but it does not copy nature's products. It presents unified wholes, in a like manner. Works of art are structured like living things; when things exhibit unity, they have order, and when things have a definite size and order, then they are beautiful, in art and nature. In fact, only by being organically structured can art be mimetic; and only by being mimetic to life can art works be organisms. Poetry imitates, not fragmentary reality, but the essential whole. The poet is a maker, as the etymology of the word indicates. Both Heidegger and Stevens attribute to poetry an ancient, mythic function: it transcends the simple creation of song. E. Sewell stated that the myth of Opheus asked the great question of poetry in the rational world: "What could it do?" One answer is that myth and poetry are considered instruments of knowledge.

Politics & Magic

Poetry is not simply a form of signification, but an activity that makes signification possible, by providing humans with a world. This genuinely create activity can be found in the power of Orpheus to summon things into being. (Ovid, *Metamorphosis*. Baltimore: Penguin, 1955, Book X.) Stevens described the relationship of the world to an individual: (Stevens, *The Palm at the End of the Mind*):

> The world lives as you live,
> Speaks as you speak, a creature that
> Repeats its vital words, yet balances
> The syllable of a syllable.

Poetry acts magically. The poetic attitude collapses the distinction between word and thing. Poetry is immediate synthesis of word and thing; ontologically different relata are collapsed. The primary way of seeing is the original unity of the passive (*pathos*) and active (*poiesis*), of deference and violence.

But *magike* gave way to logos as the principle of the world's intelligibility; the poet-magus lost his reason for being. In place of the identity of poetry and reality, theory instituted the doctrine of mimesis. The magic of poetry came to be understood as rhetoric; the poet no longer built the world in song, but could, through imitation, persuade an audience to follow nature in conduct.

By applying Kantian philosophy, F. Schiller believed that human society could be improved by political means. But after studies on the Thirty Years War in Europe, he became skeptical of the ability of politics. On reading *Reflections on the Paintings and Sculpture of the Greeks*, by J. Winckelmann (1787), Schiller considered the work as historical proof that art can achieve what violence and law cannot—art (paintings, sculptures and poems) educates and liberates the individuals of society in a gradual and peaceful process. In spite of the cultural forces dominant at any moment, an individual has the potential to determine a different course. Unlike the classical humanism committed to lessons of the past and an instructional theory of art, the aesthetic humanism of Schiller was open to possibility.

Humanism started as a revolution against scholasticism in the 15th century, but it has become every bit as dry and reactionary. Classical humanism strives to convert the distant and alien into the comfortable and familiar by reducing it to a moral commonplace (a poem by Horace may exemplify the moral). Humanism does not communicate the past meaningfully because it refuses to acknowledge that the past is different. In its search for a philosophy of universal values in the classic literature of the ages, humanism ignores the otherness of the cultures of the past. The past becomes more distant with academic study, not more accessible. Humanism regards change as the cause of decay, sympathizes with authority, and subverts classical literature for its own justification. Humanists often see their task as the training of an elite for the leaders of tomorrow, who offer the public only skill at public speaking.

A humanism based on Schiller's ideas must have a whole image of the place of humanity within nature, and not a transcendent view. It must confront the past without the baggage of sentiment and the future without the paralysis of dread. The appreciation of the differences of other cultures (the difference of Horace, for instance) will allow us to transcend our present identities. Responding to any art with pre-established values makes one miss the uniqueness of the experience presented. Art would broaden the mental worlds of observers and encourage tolerance and wonder. Education in aesthetic humanism embraces three concepts: liberation, play and community. Liberation is freedom from contemporary limits of identity. Play is imaginative experience, natural learning entered into freely (education should be more like play than work). Society can gravitate into groups to live, but communication across the barriers is necessary for a world community. The wholeness of humanity needs to be affirmed, but from a firm cultural base. The complete surrender of cultural identity is as dangerous as too little openness. Every culture needs its own local, sacred center, which cannot be broken if the group is not to perish.

Poetry took a political path. The real (in Whitehead's sense) could be denounced as constituted and instituted. The poet could change life in the direction of nature as origin, loosening the chains of culture. Culture teaches us to play the game of poetry, giving us directions. But poetry is not limited by this. Poetic praxis could be a revolutionary activity. Poetry is ceremony and ritual, but also reestablishment and regrounding. The learning process of humanity is epicultural. Popular poetry could initiate a counterculture.

The practicing architects of culture have been the historians, artists, propagandists, and poets; often, poets provided the national archetypes. Nation-building wars may provide heroes for popular imagination, but poets and writers make the identities. The real identity of leaders is provided by propagandists and poets; the leaders only provide the horsepower. Their masks are determined by cartoonists and writers.

Radical Language

Benjamin Whorf demonstrated that language is a major element in the formation of thought; culture codifies reality. Edward Hall expanded Whorf's thesis to include all culture—the psycho-cultural basis of perception. Hall's own studies in proxemics made apparent the human personal and social uses of space to structure relationships. Physical relativity was translated into behavioral relativity. Language is like a net, letting much escape unperceived. But this analogy is no good for ecology; it lets too much escape. A more comprehensive language is needed.

In a technical era, language is manipulated as a calculus. But poetry resists and reveals a more fundamental dimension of language. The empirical languages of physics and psychology are opposed and complementary; their synthesis is the language of transcendental philosophy, the comprehensive language of being: poetry. Poetry forms a permanent revolution in language; like dreams to mind and quantum foam to space. An artist works distractingly with both wildness and discipline. Destroying old gestalts, associating and dissociating.

Poetry oscillates between musical knowledge, which is self-defined, and cognitive knowledge, that communicates to others. Fraser stated that poetry is a form of music for the better expression of gnostic feelings. Its shifting to the present changes the observer into a participant. The music analogy is apt; the prairie does sound like a harpsichord, in contrast to the organ sounds of the forest or strings of a brook. *Rimbaud's analogy to music.

Poetry is a form of language used tacitly and by implication that is rich enough to escape subject-verb-object dominance. Poetic language experiments with general impressions of the world and arranges them so they feel right, without invoking truth. Poetic language enforces or changes a world view.

Poetry exploits the natural poetics of language. Only in rational discourse is literal meaning achieved at expense of the figurative. A verse is not a sentence; it is a word image. But the image is not a drawing; it allows the multiplicity, ambiguity and hesitation that are necessary to creativity and dreaming. Poetry maps a landscape. The significance of the wild or domesticated is revealed or simplified in words. The map itself is potentially a landscape. A poem merges with the reality of which it speaks—verbal topology coincides with the real, much as the emperor in one of Borges' fantasies has a map drawn on a scale of 1:1, thus covering the actual empire, until the wind shreds and scatters it.

Perhaps poetry seems like childish babbling; but through their babbling, children become aware of being in a world. They become aware of differences. Saussure pointed out that a language is made out of differences. The phoneme is a distinctive unit whose features are pertinent only in opposition to others; even the meaning of monemes, the signifying unities, is defined by a process of differentiation. The differential elements in a poem result from metaphor.

Metaphor

Language has always had difficulty describing actions and things in the world. If each unique thing or action were named, speaking would become a burdensome impossibility. Paradoxically, in being spoken, language avoids being an inert catalog; it progresses outward from the body of the speaker toward the world, metaphorically. The concept of metaphor has been defined and used for over twenty centuries. Metaphor is used in all advanced languages. In Aristotle, metaphor was a trope, the turning of phrase, derived from tropos, meaning turn. Metaphor, from metaphora, means carrying beyond (meta: into the middle of, phor: to carry). It is defined in *Webster's Seventh New Collegiate Dictionary* as a "figure of speech," a "form of expression," which is an act "of representing in words." Aristotle was one of the first to say what it represented in words: metaphora, in the sense of transference, the process of transferring a word from one object of reference to another. Metaphor consists of applying to a thing a word that belongs to something else; the transference being either from genus to species, or from species to genus, or from species to species, or on grounds of analogy (Wittbecker, "The hologram as metaphor for metaphor," 1974). Subsequently, metaphor was defined as analogy. The transference of a name from the whole to a part, or the reverse, became known as synocdoche, while the naming of an object through association was called metonomy.

At one time, Plato banished poets from his work *The Republic*. In a world of unchanging forms, analogy was considered useless. For Aristotle, art imitated nature, producing things in a natural manner; nature proceeded in a logical order. Poetry was a device to allow human beings to delight in imitation, as well as to learn of nature. Metaphor was a tool of poetry, noble or ignoble, depending on the subject matter.

The early Greeks built logically reasoned philosophies of thought and reality. During that same era, with entirely different values and objectives, Middle Eastern poets and thinkers were using similar stylistic devices. From the Egyptian pyramid texts: (Ibid.)

> Death is in my eyes today:
> As in a sick man beginning to recover
> From a deep illness.
> Death is in my eyes today:
> Like a well-trodden road
> Along which men are returning from . . . wars.

A similar method is employed by the Upanishads to induce the mind toward Brahma by the very inadequacy of the verse; that is, the ultimate cannot be expressed by piling metaphor on metaphor.

> When he shines, everything shines after him; by
> his light, all this is lightened.
> He is the one bird in the midst of the world; he
> is also like the sun that has set in the ocean. A
> man knows him truly, passes over death; there
> is no other path to go. (Yutang)

Lao Tse, in the Tao Te Ching, used such metaphor to represent different angles of vision converging on the hidden unity of the world.

> Thirty spokes unite around the nave;
> From their not being
> Arises the utility of the wheel.
> Mold clay into a vessel;
> From its not being
> Arises the utility of the vessel. (Yutang)

The Roman times and Middle Ages seem to have carried on the Aristotelian sense and use of metaphor. No large works were devoted to proposing new meanings for metaphors. Metaphors were used for religious meanings. As the Renaissance opened, attention to the mundane was renewed. Poems and paintings were embodiments of nature; the arts once again imitated nature. After two hundred years of investigation and celebration, the Reformation and Modern Science altered attitudes toward nature and God; the first found little use for poetic analogy, while the second found it unnecessary.

In Francis Bacon, there seems to be an ambivalence. He who expected the method of science to reveal all knowledge within a mortal lifetime, also referred to true metaphor: "Neither are these only similitudes, as men of narrow observation may conceive them to be, but the same footsteps of nature, treading or printing upon several subjects, or matters" (in Barfield). So these hidden relations between separate objects, and between ideas and objects, already existed. If some had been discovered and described by poets, it was the duty of science to find and define them all.

As science began its task, its findings and assumptions changed the European world view, such that Hobbes admitted poets to his utopia. They were safe, because poetry no longer had validity. Shakespeare was the last of the Renaissance. In Stephen Pepper's terms Formism had been replaced by Mechanism. The world was considered a machine. Locke hypothesized that words were solid chunks, with definite boundaries, to which others chunks could be added in combination. Metaphor was a form of decoration; whatever could be said with metaphor could be better said without. B. Spinoza warned that metaphor was dangerous; uncontrolled emotions might be transferred analogously. Descartes proved that thought was a universal, independent of words, for which words were only correlative clothing. The very structure of language was mechanistic. Each thing had one meaning linked to one word.

These scientific assumptions became so pervasive that scientists and poets soon accepted the fact that all metaphor was willful abnormality of discourse. The poetry of Donne, Pope and others was a trickery of language, meaningless conceits pleasingly arranged. Poetry itself was analyzed scientifically, and in 1730 Lord Kames published a book on the laws of metaphor.

The scientific method multiplied human dividends with the industrial revolution. Darwin cut the divine umbilical cord. Metaphorical attitudes toward nature were changing. Where Wordsworth saw consolation, joy and wisdom in nature, Tennyson saw nature "red in tooth and claw." If, for Shakespeare, our bodies were gardens tended by will, many saw their bodies as machines.

C.S. Peirce and W. James initiated their own world hypothesis, Pragmatism (Contextualism in Pepper's schema), with the argument that the association of ideas, in metaphor, for example, was not based on similarity (as in Formal or Mechanical arguments), but on emotional congruity; if a metaphor worked for a person, it was good.

Hegel was the spiritual father of the fourth world system (after Pepper), Organicism. He regarded metaphor as a device to reasonably create unity in nature. It was also a way of referring to the three stages of unfolding: Logic, Nature, and Spirit. Whitehead is the leading exponent of this system. Each use of a root metaphor by a world hypothesis is worthy of some consideration. Each one describes a different structure.

By contrasting the views of metaphor enumerated by Black with Pepper's four root hypotheses, a rough correlation emerges (see Figure 15). Two other hypotheses can be added to the schema: animism and holocosmology, which considers all views valid to some extent.

Root Metaphor	Function	View
Animism (Mythology)	Identity	Identity
Formism (Rationalism)	Substitution	Similarity
Mechanism	Decoration	Similarity (Error)
Contextualism	Utility	Congruity
Organicism	Wholeness	Interaction (Extension)
Holocosmology	Frame	Star

Figure 15. *The Meaning of Root Metaphors*

Metaphoric Structure

There are two principles governing the creation of a metaphor:
- The just disclosed phenomenon is given the name of a previously identified one that resembles it
- And this resemblance is discovered in the most 'essential' aspect of the new phenomenon, which calls forth a direct perceptual experience, already named.

The metaphor consists of two parts (These terms were contributed by Black; I.A. Richards distinguished them as tenor and vehicle; and, they are similar to the Gestalt concept of figure and ground):
- The focus (=tenor=figure), which designates the figurative term signified through the process
- The frame (=vehicle=ground), which refers to the subject or context.

For example, in the sentence, "Light is a particle," the focus is 'light' and the frame is 'particle.' This relationship is diagrammed in Figure 16.

The focus of the metaphor is the primary system, that which is to be understood, a 'brain' or 'atom,' for instance. The frame is a secondary system which provides a pool of names, such as 'computer' or 'solar system.' The interaction is mutual. The secondary imposes a reorganization of the concepts of the primary ("the brain is a computer"—Popper). Then, the meaning of two concepts is altered; a halo meaning is formed (intention—strain towards). And this 'halo' meaning, in its unique reducibility, permits things to be said that could not be said otherwise.

In the secondary and primary systems—for "the brain is a computer"—opposites interpenetrate and are unified even though the metaphor is initially and cognitively perceived as absurd. This interpenetration is a dialectic, where opposites are unified in a metaphorical synthesis that transcends the initial contradictory conjunction of the two systems. Thus, concept formation in art and science is a working out of contradictions, as in Bohr's metaphor, "The atom is a solar system." Logical opposites logically combined assert nothing: $S+(-S)=0$.

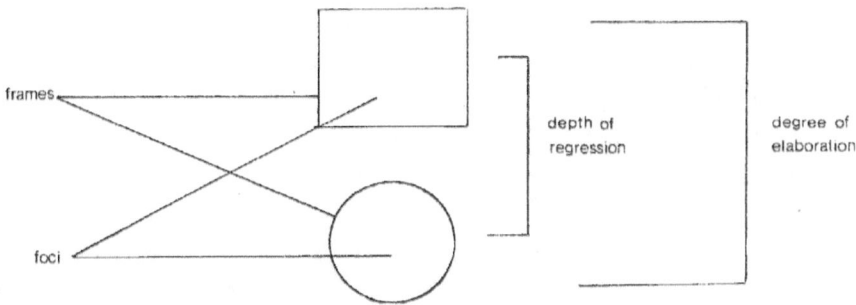

Figure 16. *The Mechanics of a Metaphor.*

Metaphor works because words tend to bring their baggage with them, creating a diffused aura and extending the range of strict terminology; some problems of diction may be avoided. Metaphors are source of creative reflection, in their ambiguity.

Metaphorical logic is not limited to traditional logic. It is more contextual and multivalued. The original meaning of logic in Greek was "gathering up," which is what metaphoric logic does. Metaphorical unity transcends a literal absurdity. Most scientific metaphors exhibit this: "The world is atomic," Leukippus; "The world is mathematical," Pythagoras; "Electricity is a fluid," B. Franklin. Metaphors in science are usually termed models and are used to bestow a more precise meaning to expressions.

The metaphor is a form of discourse where one of the terms is always denotative. The collocation of terms in a metaphor leads to a sort of intercourse, in the Platonic sense, transaction or transference between the associated contexts. The focus is responded to as the frame, in addition to its own original, evoked responses.

The distance between the tenor and the vehicle of a metaphor is necessary; similarity must be accompanied by some disparity. If the two are too close together, then the perspective of double vision may be lost. Johnson claimed that it was useless to compare a tree with a bush. The power of the analogy is also related to the emotive potential of the matrices. It is equally useless to compare a sneeze to a cloud.

This is reasoning by analogy not by differences, which a digital computer does. Metaphorical expression has an analogical unity in human existence. Its central organizing principle is the single person. Imagination is an instrument of perception. It points mind toward broadest meaning. It points, not toward truth, but to an ever-enlarging relational field.

It points to the frame. That which is the frame must be ambiguous. Frames must be used as metaphors. The word nature, for instance, has been used by Western philosophers in thirty nine distinct senses. Under ambiguity many meanings may hide. Nature can be regarded as a puzzle or opponent to be beaten, but both detract from total experience.

Metaphoric Function

Valery claims that the poet is no mad versifier, but a scientist, an algebraist in the service of a subtle dreamer. Wheelwright relied on algebraic ratio to distinguish between the two functions of a metaphor:

- as epiphor
- as diaphor

Epiphor means outreaching, the extension of meaning by comparison. It is transference in the Aristotelian sense, expressing similarity between the concretely known semantic vehicle and the somewhat less known semantic tenor for the purpose of hinting significance. Aristotle called the metaphor "An intuitive perception of the similarity of dissimilars." The epiphor rests on analogy. Its force, however, is increased by novelty. Good epiphors yield fresh insights about the world with a novel juxtaposition that arrests thoughts. As epiphors are used over and over again, they fade into ordinary language. An epiphor is not a symbol. Symbols are normal and literal semantic representation. Symbols are arbitrary; for instance, the word brain has no analogy to what it denotes, although some symbols do have an analogy: hieroglyphics look like what they mean; onomatopoeia sounds as it means. Epiphors necessarily contain analogies that produce grammatical absurdities and psychological surprises. An epiphor may be represented by the following mathematical ratio for the sentence, "Light is a wave."

A : B :: B : C
Light : wave :: wave : water

A pure epiphor would collapse into symbol, without suggestiveness. To name something for the first time, to call a star a star, would be to create a pure epiphor.

The other quality, diaphor, is the production of new meaning by juxtaposition and synthesis. It is a semantic movement through the particulars of experience whereby new qualities and new meanings can emerge from previously ungrasped combinations of elements. The similarity is not so much antecedent, as it is in epiphor, as induced by the poet. The diaphor produces its meaning, beyond analogy, primarily by suggestion. Beyond expressing experiences of which we are not aware explicitly, the juxtaposition of the diaphor suggests new possibilities for experience. The diaphor may be diagrammed as follows for the line by Pound, "The apparition of these faces in a crowd, petals on a wet, black bough."

A : B :: C : D
faces : crowd :: petals : bough

A pure diaphor would be unintelligible, since both referents would be unknown. Abstract painting and 'random' music could be considered almost pure forms of diaphor.

A metaphor must be comprised of both, but in any proportion. According to Wheelwright, the Egyptian pyramid texts and the Upanishads could be described as "a diaphoric succession of epiphorically tended images as a means of inducing the mind to" Ra or Brahma. Conversely, the Tao Te Ching is "a diaphoric juxtaposition of particular epiphors converging on an ever central reality."

Since the vocabulary of emotion is so comparatively underdeveloped, metaphor is necessary to deal with unnamed and unnamable experiences— what words could describe what Wright meant?

Suddenly I realize
That if I stepped out of my body I would break
Into blossom.

Brooks proclaimed that all subtle emotions "demand metaphor for their expression." The synthetic capacity of metaphors can entertain contradictory feelings simultaneously.

A functional metaphor expresses what no declarative sentence can. It states anew, by silence and allusion, economically two ideas transformed into one. Like a myth, the metaphor emerges from its synchronic beginnings and provides continuity of creative thought. Metaphors are formative and constitutive of our life-world. Vico pronounces that imagination is a turning out of one's self. An imaginative metaphysics shows how man becomes all things by not understanding them.

For Nowottny, the metaphor is a set of linguistic directions for supplying the presence of an unwritten literal term. With the metaphor, one can make a complex statement without complicating the grammatical construction of the sentence that carries the statement. However, implicit sentences exist in parallel action or as reflective images. The metaphor allows the sender to supply an uncontaminated image to the receiver from her own experience; for the receiver a physical immediacy is required in order to supply the missing term. These observations provide a more substantive difference between metaphor and simile; the first conveys the relationship figuratively, the second literally. After M. McCluhan, the first is a more involving medium than the second. Many writers have considered both to be figurative.

Jordan distinguishes a number of qualities of a metaphor. *in Wheelwright The metaphor is a formulation of reality as a complex of qualities. It is a process by which a complex of quality becomes individual. It is a word structure that asserts reality through form. This form is a unity of interrelated elements into a whole. The idea that metaphor expresses a likeness or a difference is perhaps a confused perception of the fact that metaphor implies a variety of qualities in the contemplated reality. It appears to overlook the fact that the essential meaning of variety is not difference of quality so much as multiplicity of quality and the presence of unlimited details of available for synthesis.

Origin of Metaphor
There was much concern, however, on how metaphors came about. The prevailing consensus was that primitive humans were not only barren of language, but extremely emotional and imaginative. Happily, according to this theory, the primitive human was able to reconcile these shortcomings by using metaphors to speak—one word referring to several objects. For instance, moving air was a soul-wind or a spirit. This theory was so tenacious that it still appears today. Blake, while implicitly supporting the metaphor theory of language, noted that the ancients animated all objects with Gods and names: Imagination was their savior, who actually created the sensible world. Blake claimed that if it were not for the

poetic character, the philosophical and experimental would soon become the 'ratio of all things,' standing still or moving in circles. Wordsworth attempted a balance of world and thought, but Blake brooked no compromise.

Shelley was so captured by the idea of imagination that he disclaimed that every author was a poet in the infancy of society. He and others felt that language began with simple perceptual meanings and built by metaphor into abstract thought: "Metaphorical language marks the before unapprehended relations of things, and perpetuates their apprehension until words ..." (Ibid).

If this were true, then Macaulay would have been correct in concluding that poetry declines as civilization advances. If Shelley's premise was true, then every author today should be a great poet, and no one would find poetry in Homer, as Barfield suggests. Moving backwards in time, one finds language more and more figurative; moving forwards in time, one still finds it becoming figurative. If both views are correct then these times meet in a golden age of metaphor, making superpoets.

Coleridge rescued imagination by contrasting its concretely real, esemplastic—molding diverse particulars into new perspective—nature with that of fancy, which was only the accidental nature of metaphor.

Embler felt that metaphors were the very stuff that humans used to make sense of the universe. They were principles by means of which we sort our perceptions, evaluate them and guide our purpose. For him, novels, poems, and all designs, were metaphors. Possibly he was using metaphor as a metaphor for models, analogies, paradigms, and metaphors.

Ogden and Richards, in *The Meaning of Meaning*, state that when a term is taken outside of the universe of discourse for which it is defined, it becomes metaphor, which involves the same kind of contexts as abstract thought, i.e., members shall only possess the relevant feature in common, accidental ones cancelling out. They obviously did not consider the accidental ones important. They divided metaphorical language into two types: symbolic, referring to the truth of reference, and emotive, having to do with character or attitude. Interestingly, they regarded primitive language as having a small vocabulary of proper names and having a magical attitude towards words; primitive metaphors were below the level of confusion resulting from abstraction.

Blair addressed the problems of the origins of metaphor (in Barfield). He hypothesized that at first the lack of proper names for every object forced primitive peoples to use one name to represent many things, and to express themselves more fully by metaphor. Naturally, all material objects were named first. For some reason, theorists like Blair, seem to presume the paucity of words for naming not only relationships but objects. The number of words possible would not seem to be as finite as the number of objects. Perhaps primitive thought perceives the many things represented by one word as one. If primitive peoples were so imaginative, thinking up new words would have been easier that making metaphorical connections.

Owen Barfield argued that the roots of speech hypothesis was fallacious. He quotes Jesperson as noting that the "evolution of language shows a progressive tendency from inseparable irregular conglomerates to freely and regularly combinable short elements" (Owen Barfield, *Poetic Diction*. New York: McGraw-Hill, 1964). He concluded that both abstractness and simplicity in words are evidence of a long intellectual evolution, an evolution For instance, Jesperson's statement on the evolution of language toward combinational elements mirrors ideas on biological genetics. that was irreversibly flowing from homogeneity toward dissociation and multiplicity before poets or etymologists became conscious of it. Barfield admitted that etymologically most meanings once referred to sensible objects or animal activities, but the meanings of words changed from context to context from age to age. In fact, the conception of words as names of things is outmoded because facts, as assumptions of reality that shape world views, have changed. The fact that Europeans have three separate words—breath, spirit, wind—while the ancients had one—spirit—shows a difference in reality.

Nowottny stated that a precondition for the existence of metaphor is the completeness of the linguistic system. The attendant terminology of an innovation, iron spear tips or television, for instance, must be in common usage first. It would follow that in a primitive society, metaphor use would not be contemporaneous with naming.

Barfield was also critical of theorists for projecting their logic back to a prelogical time, arguing that human beings do not create language in the same manner as its logical reconstruction. If the relation of primitive to modern meaning parallels that of child to adult, then the primitive speaker may be unconscious of some differences and actually perceive a unity, in spirit. The function of poetry is to discover Shelley's 'unapprehendeds'.

But if primitive people already abound in unities, then what could the function of their poetry be? Or is it poetry? Perhaps Barfield has made an unquestioned assumption or projection, that of projecting poetry back to a prepoetic time, attributing a device to them, metaphor, of which they had no knowledge or need. Archaic songs and epics are communications or ordering codes. Metaphors are more accurately actualities than linguistic terms. Barfield alluded to this problem, writing that "myth is the child of meaning begotten by imagination" (Ibid), but this is the very meaning that changes from context to context. He perceived, after Blake, that without the poetic principle, knowledge would end in algebraic stagnation. He compared the struggle between the rational and poetic principles as two buckets on separate ends of rope above a well, with the rational ascending. Although the principles are inseparable, he is wrong to think them inversely related. They are not. It is possible to become more rational and more poetic.

Hayakawa mentions that art is the ordering of human symbolic processes, and that symbols of symbols, and symbols of symbols of symbols (dissociation?) can be manufactured indefinitely by the human nervous system. To increase the order of anything means to make it describable with less information. *compare with principle of least effort of Ziff. If Hayakawa is right, then the dissociation is historical. Then over time, metaphor would be more and more necessary for synthesizing relations, and science for analyzing them. A scheme of dissociation is shown (in Figure 17).

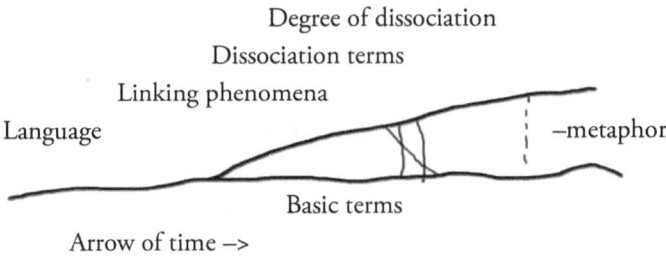

Figure 17. *Dissociation and Metaphor*

As time progressed metaphor would become more necessary for synthesizing relationships (and science for analyzing them). Archaic peoples could make metaphors if linguistic dissociation had occurred. Although a poetic method, like a scientific method, may be considered independent of time, poetry and science are historical methods of knowing.

Philosophical Metaphor

The use of metaphor is marginal in objective philosophy, but it is pervasive in our language and conceptual system, so it must be central to ideas of truth and meaning. It is a basic mechanism for understanding experience. And it can create new meaning, similarities and define a new reality. Metaphor is not merely of language. It is a matter of conceptual structure. Conceptual structure involves all senses, not just intellect.

Freedom, economics and equality are political ways of indirectly getting at the issue of a meaningful existence. Although political and economic ideologies can be framed in metaphorical terms, improper transference can degrade the context. To strictly believe that labor is a resource, like copper or water, is to ignore the meaning of work and to demean its dignity.

Most of our concepts are organized by spatial metaphors: good, virtue and rational is up; bad, depravity and emotional is down. These are systematically related. Happy is wide or high, sad is narrow or low. These are also experiential. The values in a culture are coherent with metaphorical structure. The future is up, for instance. But there are conflicts in subcultures: more is better or small is beautiful.

Rituals are typically metaphorical kinds of activity. Personal rituals are experiential gestalts. Cultural and personal metaphors are partially preserved in ritual. Metaphors and values can be propagated by ritual. There is no culture or person without ritual.

Cosmologies can be understood as having a root metaphor. Stephen Pepper distinguished four root metaphors for world hypotheses, which can be expanded to include animism and holocosmology.

- Animism (Black Elk)
- Formism (Plato)
- Mechanism (Bacon, Newton)
- Contextualism (Peirce, James)
- Organicism (Whitehead)
- Holocosmology

These metaphors should be considered descriptive summaries distilled from centuries of human thought. And they are a useful framework for discussion. Pepper noted that formism and contextualism suffered from an inadequacy of precision, while mechanism and organicism from an inadequacy of scope. For that reason, contextualism and mechanism tended to complement one another, as do contextualism and organicism. Organicism and formism are "hostile;" mechanism and contextualism are simply "eclectic." Furthermore, formism and mechanism are analytic, while contextualism and organicism are synthetic; and formism and contextualism are dispersive, while mechanism and organicism are integrative. Animism is synthetic and integrative. Holocosmology combines all of these views into a complementary matrix. It uses qualitative descriptions, from poetry to catastrophe theory and fuzzy sets, to place humanity in a whole framework. It is systems theory tied to animism.

Scientific Metaphor
According to T. Kuhn, there is no methodological evolution of science; rather, normal science progresses by a succession of paradigms, which he described as noncompetitive and open-ended. He stated that paradigms are the traditions described by the historian under rubrics like: Ptolemaic astronomy or Copernican; Aristotelian dynamics or Newtonian. These examples include law, theory, application, and instrumentation together, and provide models from which the traditions of scientific research spring. In his view, science proceeded by working out problems uncovered by each current paradigm. Should problems occur that could not be ignored, suppressed or resolved, then a revolution would occur to replace the paradigm. The new paradigm would have to include all the old data as well as the new problematical data. Metaphoric systems are the core of structural coherence. For Kuhn, a metaphor is the vital spirit of a paradigm; its best organizing relation. The notion of paradigm includes techniques, examples, community values, and a central metaphor.

Science makes use of the metaphorical process to construct its models. Bacon referred to true metaphor as "the footsteps of nature." The Greek word for universe was to holon, from *holos*, the whole. Cicero transcribed it into Latin as *universum*. Retranscribed, Cicero's word might be *holotrope*, meaning turning whole. Novalis equated man and metaphor, as the blueprint of the world, "Man=Metaphor" (in Robert Bly, *News of the Universe*). Novalis stated, "We are looking for the blueprint of the world—that is what we are ourselves."

Mario Bunge used black boxes as metaphors. The idea of the black box was originally conceptualized by electrical engineers to describe certain unknown systems devoid of structure. Black box theories include kinematics, thermodynamics, information theory, scattering-matrix theory, and circuit theory. The black box approach is useful for all theories whose variables are external and global, that are simple and have a high degree of generality. As theories are supported by observation, black boxes become translucent. The empirical theories listed below with their root metaphors range from black to almost transparent:

> 'Man is an atom,' 'man is an animal' (Pribram)
> 'Man is a system' (Laszlo)
> 'Man is a computer' (Arbib)
> 'The brain is a hologram' (Arbib)

The idea of a hologram as metaphor for the brain will be examined more closely, since it will be proposed as a metaphor for metaphor.

Hologram as Metaphor for Memory & Brain

When an object is illuminated by a light source, each point on the object radiates in a spherical pattern, as though each point was a source of light. If photo-sensitive material is placed before such reflected light, the emulsion will be uniformly exposed. If, however, a board with a small pinhole is interposed between the object and the film, only the light from one specified point on the object will fall on a specific point on the film, such that an image of the object is described, with some diffraction due to the wave-like character of light. The propagation of light energy is a wave form having both amplitude and phase.

Photographic film, being an energy-detection system, records only the intensity (square of the amplitude) in a two-dimensional mapping of the point-to-point brightness of the object. Is there any way to recover, or to record, the information relative to the phase? Since the film has the capability of recording both the amplitude and the phase, it is necessary only to develop a technique to utilize it; that technique is holography. To record a hologram, the amplitude and phase information are converted into intensity variations by using the interference between two interacting sources of light. This is accomplished by providing a second source of illumination incident on the photographic surface, directly, unmodulated by an intervening object. This second source of light is referred to as the reference, and is always split off from the main source so that it will be coherent with it. It is also the reference for the determination of the phase difference between the two beams.

The reference interacts with the light reflected from the object to map, on the two-dimensional film surface, the relative amplitude and phase of each object point into an intensity function. The hologram is essentially an optical computer; a four-by-five inch hologram is essentially an optical computer; a four-by-five inch hologram can store one billion characters at sixty resolution elements per character—this storage capacity exceeds the number of all written symbols ever conceived.

Can the hologram be used as a metaphor for memory, and, if so, how? Arbib compares them as follows. Memory may be described by the following select corollaries (from *The Metaphorical Brain*):

- Memory is a dynamic process, located in an action frame; the perception of a room, for instance, is recalled as more than a two-dimensional perspective, and as more than one instant. We see 3-dimensions instead of isolated 2-dimensional perspectives.
- In some cases, gross brain damage may be experienced without a resulting loss of memory, which implies that memories are not localized, or photographic—in a pictorial sense—in nature.
- Memories of many different events can be stored in the same region of the brain (perhaps this would explain mnemonics and synaesthetic images from releaser stimuli).

Although the hologram is different from the brain in fundamental respects, it may be compared with the preceding corollaries:

- A three-dimensional image is "recalled," and it is equally viewable from multiple perspectives.
- Each part of it can reproduce much of the entire image, although the resolution decreases as the area of the part decreases; a picture by contrast is too sharply localized to be reproduced from a corner. This is because the hologram distributes its record across the whole two-dimensional structure, rather than word-by-word, as in certain types of computer storage, or point-by-point, as in a picture.
- Several images can be superimposed on the same film, using different wavelengths, and later recovered individually since each reference beam restarts only its own wavefront.

If the metaphor is to have any utility, then the reference beams must comprise waves of neural activity. Pribram actually suggests that there is a neural hologram; that it is obtained as a result of interference on neurons between a pattern sent directly (impinging on near end of dendrites) and a slightly delayed pattern (on far end of dendrites). (How would fuzzy sets be related?)

The coherence requirement could be supplied by thousands of parallel fibers in optical tract. Pribram thinks that figure/ground contradictions form interference patterns in optical tract. In the brain one is dealing with electrical discharges between neural synapses that generate standing electromagnetic wave forms of which alpha rhythm is an example. The holographic hypothesis is also good for an explanation of consciousness of the self, the experience of standing out; a mindscape created by synchronized wave forms, projected outward like sound from stereo speakers. Consciousness is heightened by disparities between feedback and feedforward.

In comparing memory to a hologram, we must hypothesize that thinking is the propagation of waves of neural activity rather than a sequential firing of individual neurons (perhaps in a similar way to the McCulloch-Pitts theory of nerve-nets). In a memory wave, fronts of sensory excitation would be frozen into a neural hologram, to be read out whenever that memory experience is recalled intentionally; perhaps associative memories could be explained by the ghost images from a nearly identical reference beam. This metaphor should further allow the possibility of appropriate concepts for modeling adaptive modifications in the action-oriented distributed computations of a layered, somatotropially organized computer.

The problem of remembering may be modeled after a data storage and retrieval system in such a manner: memories are stored in the brain as holograms on film, it is assumed; there must be also an explanation of how memories are matched appropriately with a current experience. To query the current experience, the brain constructs the equivalent of a spatial filter in the form of a Fourier-transform hologram of the experience, to which it simultaneously Fourier-transform holograms of all previous experiences; if the current experience were known, a light would shine through the 'file.' The dawning of an insight has always been represented, at least recently, by a light bulb. Memory loss could be explained by the model as a loss of rotational sensitivity in the stored holograms. This metaphor could be used even to interpret philosophical problems of perception, such as Wittgenstein's duck-rabbit; each a aspect would be constructed from icons into one hologram and the dawning of a new aspect would be tantamount to the switching of filters.

Arbib comments that it would be of less value to the organism to reconstruct a visual input *per se* than to recall vital features of past experience. How are words related to these features? How would it be explained that some people verbalize, others visualize and a few synaesthetize? The appropriate notion for a neural hologram might not be a Fourier transform as Pribram argues, but a nonintrovertible feature transform in which spatial array of intensities is replaced by spatial array of features. In the place of a frequency spectrum in real hologram, an action spectrum in the neural model would have features that would enable an animal to react rapidly. An animal does not need an invertible record from which the original stimulus can be constructed; it needs a nonintrovertible record from which an appropriate response could be made.

Not all information needs to be stored. Efferent control could filter incoming information. That is, the reference beam could negate input; recall would only elicit noise. It would be simpler to store all inputs than to compute which information should be stored. Short-term memory may correspond to current activity around the loops; long-term may correspond to changes in connectivity of neural hologram box. Holography is a useful metaphor if not used literally. Portions of wave activity can help recreate the whole front, with different cuing waves allowing multiple storage. This is quite different from computers with word-by-word memory.

In the neural analog of a hologram, the reference beam could comprise a sampling of ongoing neural activity, both peripheral (for recall of its response) and central (for thoughts related to present). This loop would explain temporal recall of sequences. Miller demonstrated that immediate memory depended more on the number of items to be memorized, than on the information carried. The holographic model of brain does not deny specialization; it is specialized and holographic. Verbal processing is only one memory system. Other, more primitive memory systems may exist also. Since people can recognize much more than they can recall, the distinction between recall and recognition may illuminate the differences between memory modes. Intuition is a holistic system memory. Memory is a function of the organism as a whole, as Bergson recognized.

The metaphor can be extended, using Haber's theory of icon recognition and a simple explanation of the hologram as an energy recording system. The first stage of a central representation in memory might be a visual information store. Neisser named such as store an icon. Icon storage is hypothesized to be the unorganized collection of the primitive features of a visual field. It is probably not photographic. It probably contains only those features that have automatically been extracted from the event by a biological feature detection process, occurring between the retina and the cortex. The information extraction is an active process, subservient to the schemas and programs constructed from prior experience and the expectancy and familiarity of the organism with the event. The iconic storage is brief, but visible to the perceiver, who recognizes only that something is there. Until the perceiver can analyze, integrate or label the icon, it is uncoded, unidentified and unfamiliar; the perceiver does not know what is seen until it is processed. Therefore, it must be of a shorter duration than that for fixing in visual exploration

(250 milliseconds).

Hochberg (Ibid) reported that perceivers do not—cannot—see the entire visual field in a single glance. It takes many glances of an incomplete, indirect and unclear horizon to build a field. An integrated view of a continuous world is constructed from glances, from information in icons. Hochberg argued that figure-ground segregation was constructed because we cannot see the entire figure on the ground in one glance; even figure/ground cannot be a primitive feature. Haber claimed that the figure and ground are built up of icons. The perceiver sees the world before she knows it, since she does not know what she sees as first, at first. In the beginning, according to Haber, before the word, the image. Using such a holographic model, Alex Comfort proposes that in the mystic, oceanic mode of perception, the scan is shut off and the interference pattern itself is intuited. He notes that descriptions of the mystical experience as a lotus, triangular patterns or the music of the spheres, bear a resemblance to holographic interference patterns.

Hologram as Metaphor for Cosmology & Universe

Neil Evernden claims that the camera makes the world atomic, but only the choice of the photographer does that. In acting as a nervous system, the artist can select for perspective and objectivity. The camera has the power to transform the relationship of self to earth; it can show the world as a set of consumable objects or as interrelated feelings. But holography, a technical three-dimensional mapping of the whole, can transform the relationship again. Here the world is interrelated. The laser hologram also gives insight into undivided wholeness; the interference pattern in each region is relevant to the whole—there is no isomorphic correspondence, as from a lens. Fundamental units/particles cannot be isolated as individual. The hologram is produced on a plate from interfering wavefronts, which are divided after the source by an interferometer, which splits the light.

Each point on a hologram receives light from all parts of the subject and thus contains in its coded form, the entire image. Whenever two or more sets of waves intersect, holography is possible. Pribram contends that hologram arises in any system when neighborhood interactions among elements (spatial frequency) become encoded in process of transformation. Some sort of holograph about entire universe could be made at any spot containing information about the whole universe.

Holographic Quality. A holograph possesses field properties; each is understood in relation to a collective. A holographic field could govern the structure of life and thought. The reason for separate 'beings' then is for better resolution, as each reflective part is added. Multiple images can be put on plate by varying wavelength. By altering the angle of the object beam (to the plate) and by altering frequency of laser beam, ten billion codes can be stored in a layered texture of one cubic centimeter of plate. The code can be turned back to an image.

When the hologram is enfolded in a record, it can be unfolded to a recognizable image. The hologram illustrates a new notion of order, the implicate order (of David Bohm), where all is enfolded into all. In the explicate order, science, things are unfolded in particular regions. In the hologram, the physical order is a total order implicated in each region of the whole; the order in each region of space parenthetically extends over the whole universe and its whole past and future.

Holonomic Quality. George Leonard calls holonomic "named for a hologram" (in *The Silent Pulse*). It describes holographic analogues. The holoid is an entity that is holonomic. A human being is a holoid of the universe, but also a unique entity having identity (compare to Koestler's holon).

Like certain holistic physical theories—relativity theory, quantum theory, and the entropy laws—the hologram implies an individual wholeness, in which the analysis of something into distinct parts is no longer relevant. The laser hologram gives insight into an undivided wholeness; the interference pattern in each region is relevant to the whole. There is no isomorphic, one-to-one correspondence of points as from a lens—actually, light from a lens or pinhole is considered a degenerate hologram.

In the hologram, the physical order is a total order implicated in each region of the whole; the order in each region of space parenthetically extends over the whole universe and its whole past and future. All the forms of the universe are inseparable, but can be abstracted, and the universe itself is one turning. The universe is etymologically related to the hologram: the word "universe" (in Latin, *unum versere*, turned into one whole) was derived by Cicero from the Greek work for the whole, *holon*. Hologram comes from the Greek *holo graphien*, meaning whole writing. This reflects the fact that parts of the universe suggest other parts. As Merleau-Ponty phrases it: "The fact is that every fragment of the world—and in particular the sea, so riddled with eddies and waves, so plumed with spray, so massive and immobile in it- self, contains all sorts of shapes of being, and by its manner of reply to the onlooker's attack, evokes a series of possible variants, and teaches beyond itself, a general manner of saying what is" (in *Signs*, p. 70).

The order and measure of a hologram can be enfolded and carried in waves (electromagnetic and other). What carries the implicate order of the hologram is the holomovement, which is indefinable and immeasurable. This implies that it is meaningless to talk of a fundamental theory. Each theory only extracts relevant aspects. No total theory is ever possible because thinking is only necessary from a limited perspective, and a perspective can only extract parts of a whole. The hologram relates one/many and local/global, as well as part and whole. The universe is a unit; parts are related to wholeness in a necessary interrelation. As hologrammatic, the universe is a dynamic web of interrelated events in which the part determines the whole. The field is the unifying character of universe.

Hologram as Metaphor for Metaphor

During the ordering process, more and more is packed into less and less, until miniaturization reaches its greatest level of organic complexity in the human brain. And the brain orders its universe in dreams, through language, and with art. Dreams are a condensation of experience, which the Greeks named *Hyponoia*, a hidden thought with real meaning, but in a secret language. The same condensation is operative in language itself; Wundt termed it the condensation of meanings. As a dream or word may sum up the whole past, present, and future of the dreamer, or speaker, in one event, so may art (poetry, music, or painting) do the same.

A hologram may be read out then by shining a copy of the reference beam across the film; the resulting holographic image is like the freezing of light waves from the object in a window. This provides an interesting parallel to Ortega's definition of art (in C. Otten, *Anthroplogy and Art*, p. 46): Art is a window with a garden behind it: one may focus on the garden or on the window.

Is the hologram, then, an art form? Does it translate the view more accurately than a painting, or only differently?

Art may be the same type of condensation on a window as a hologram. Waddington suggests that there may be an analogy between some modern paintings and a hologram; for instance, Mark Tobey's Messengers may seem chaotic and meaningless, under the wrong reference, as would a hologram. Then again, the hologram must frame a garden, whereas a painting may be of the window itself. The hologram could be used as an art form, like photography, or it could be used to produce new possibilities in art. Since a hologram can be produced from a computer printout, it is therefore possible to generate any object on the printout, even one that has never existed, such as a griffin.

The hologram has been proposed as a metaphor for memory; perhaps it could be offered as a metaphor for metaphor. The two terms of a metaphor, one a pure reference, the other an embodied reflection, interfere with one another to produce the metaphor itself, an interrelated whole. As the hologram captures the phase as well as the amplitude, the metaphor expresses lateral meaning as well as denotative. Literally, the metaphor (carrying beyond, a turning) is a hologram (whole writing) that is capable of describing the universe, that which is turning into one whole.

Mirror & Knot: Imagination & Consciousness

We are misled to believe that our ideas mirror nature; that sets us outside. Alan Watts notes that a tree does not represent fish, though both use light and water. Our ideas are nature, as much as clouds or waves are. Nature pushes through this way also, expressing herself.

But, the outer world is no longer a mirror for humanity. Humans replace nature with their own consciousnesses or bodies. They have neglected one side of consciousness, one side of the brain and body. Necessarily, humans walk bent or folded over, but the right side (brain) may be unfolding now.

Claiming all consciousness for ourselves results in a mental and sensual poverty. Many ecologists and politicians use the language and abstraction of the rational lobe of the brain. We need to take into account other aspects of the human mind—the poetic, mythmaking, metaphorical parts, which operate in systems builders and garbage persons alike. Novalis asserted that because language is abstracted from reality it mirrors aspects of the natural world: "the laughable error whereby people imagine that they speak for the sake of things . . . when someone speaks simply for the sake of speaking, he expresses the most beautiful and original truths . . . It is only thanks to their freedom that they are components of nature and in their free motion alone does the World Soul find expression" (in Bly, *News of the Universe*). Novalis's idea of a secret homology between language and natural phenomena is a fundamental tenet of poetry. Many deep secrets of nature are inaccessible to reason, but can be revealed to poets through gestalt perception.

Wallace Stevens concluded that new expression facilitated new perception: "The freshness of transformation is/The freshness of a world. It is our own./It is ourselves, the freshness of ourselves" (from *The Palm at the End of the Mind*). Robert Bly considers that a certain intensity is based on "night-intelligence," the respect for ancient worlds. The right side unfolds and poetry uses the whole brain. Generally, the products of the right brain are nonverbal—a painting or a symphony—but poetry combines the qualities from both hemispheres. Association and multilogical inference seem to be drawn from the right half and the logical, verbal counterparts from the left. Poetry—the expression after the impulse—crosses into verbal centers in the left hemisphere and back. The transparent view of poetry overlays ideal on real. Poetry intensifies the world; it does not produce a new one from superior authority. The poem is a knot of turbulence, what Pound called a vortex and Yeats a gyre. Gary Snyder relates that the Japanese term for song, bushi or fushi, means a whorl in the grain. The whorl is the world in miniature. The poem is an event in miniature. This miniaturization is an entry to being in the world.

The Order of Imagination

Martin Heidegger claimed that humans were forgetful of experience, that they have full awareness only when confronted with death or poetry. As the adequacy of a habitual view of the earth is questioned, imagination offers alternative ways of seeing. Poetry advances imagination. It feels its way; it presages community consciousness, and it precurses paradigm shifts.

What might come to be is insufficient to poetry, according to Breton. The evidence of the senses can be rejected; the poet can favor an ideal version of things. Rimbaud could change anything into anything else through imagination, e.g., factories into mosques, and found something sacred in this mental disorder. He wrote, "The flag of bleeding meat on the silk of the seas and of the arctic flowers . . ." (in Bly, *News of the Universe*). Vision is always being tricked by imagination and misunderstanding. Coleridge once noted a pretty optical fact: While viewing a soaring kite [bird], he saw two of them floating in unison; but he had mistaken two pairs of leaves on a nearby tree for wings. The magnitude of size was given by his unadjusted gaze. Suzanne Lilar relates a magic transformation of an uninteresting avenue under moonlight to a radiant grand canal. The transformation surprised her, but continued to offer pleasure for weeks after, in spite of its falsity. Maurice-Jean Lefebve contended that the source of fascination of an illusory image lies in the consciousness of its deflection of reality, whether the perception is involuntary or cultivated.

Once this 'disorder' becomes conscious, it can be a means of approaching a cosmological order. A questioning form of expression is needed, a prephilosophical, circular approach through succeeding perspectives. The approach must succeed the concentric problems of metaphysics by incorporating a range of subjects from phenomenological poetry to scientific inquiry, from trees to entropy.

This expression must incorporate the complete range of experience, from the inexhaustible, perceptible universe to the wildest ideality. Expression that is reflexive and indirect would embody transparent expressions that could point to the ground of existence without partitioning or reifying it.

Full Consciousness

According to Novalis, the first step to full consciousness is introspection, exclusive contemplation of the self. But that is only half-way. The second step must be genuine outward observation—spontaneous, sober observation of the external world. Novalis offers: "Self expression is the source of all abasement, just as, contrariwise, it is the basis for all true elevation. The first step is introspection—exclusive contemplation of the self. But whoever stops there goes only half way. The second step must be genuine observation outward—spontaneous, sober observation of the external world" (Bly, *News of the Universe*, p. 48). It does not matter which step comes first. If all of our senses are used only to embody intuitions about ourselves, they atrophy. Psychologists and philosophers may be lodged at the first stage of life; scientists at the second. Poetry can lead them both through a dialectical reconciliation that shifts into a greater awareness of their differences in unity.

Step One: Philosophy. Describing Empedocles' poetic philosophy, Aristotle hinted that, at that time, philosophic wonder had not yet totally emerged from religious awe, so that cosmology and metaphysics were closer to myth. But Plato allowed for the existence of a passage whereby the mind might cross from philosophy to ecstasy, to achieve insight into the purpose and place of human existence in the universe. What he sought as a philosopher was the meaningfulness of things, which modern science has failed to find as an objective feature. Descartes stated that, although poetry had no method, it gives us knowledge through "imaginative force," and makes truth "shine forth the more brightly" than philosophy. A number of German romantic poets and thinkers intended to poeticize philosophy, translate Kant's account of mental activity as a theory of poetic activity; Schelling was a mediating figure. Novalis identified poetry and reality as a central principle, saying "We are on a mission, our calling is to fashion the earth" (in G. Bruns, *Modern Poetry and the Idea of Language*, p. 267). Adumbrations of this idea can be found in Coleridge and Shelley.

Philosophy and ethics are important in creating an atmosphere in which we can act the right way towards our natural surroundings. But they are not enough. We need an aesthetic to help us see, an organized sensibility to polarize our feelings toward the world, outwardly sympathetic and empathetically loving. Poetry can realize the interlinking of human and earth. It can trace morality back to our relations with the world. It can mediate our relations with a sense of the divine. Matthew Arnold turned to the study of poetry from a world apparently dehumanized by science, politics and religion. He suggested that poetry may have to take the place of religion, since religion had materialized itself in the fact and attached its emotions to the fact "and now the fact is failing it. But for poetry the idea is everything . . . The strongest part of our religion today is its unconscious poetry" (in *Matthew Arnold, Complete Prose Works*). But poetry cannot do and be everything. It will never replace science, philosophy or religion, although it can poke and prod, point and lead.

In a sense, philosophy is an individual vision, or perspective of reality determined by temperament and the opportunities of life. The essential vision is communicated in a reflective speech. Merleau-Ponty proposed a creative language for metaphysics. Philosophy is comfortably human-made; poetry is an adventure in nature. Philosophy can use poetry for expression, but a system destroys the poetry. Poetry provides material for reflection for philosophy. that may be transcribed into prose or another creative language.

Whitehead sees poetry as positive evidence for and part of a philosophy of organism: "Thus we gain from the poets the doctrine that a philosophy of nature must concern itself with these six notions: change, value, eternal objects, endurance, organism, interfusion" (in Whitehead, *Science and the Modern World*, p. 89). A philosophy of nature should consider the poetic view. Whitehead recommended that philosophers compare the more concrete intuitions of poets with the abstract formulations of the various sciences. The workings of natural phenomena are mysterious and wonderful. Lucretius and Vergil said that the mysterious actions of nature are best expressed in poetic form. The goal of a philosophical poetry, in the classical Greek sense (from *poietike*, meaning productive science, art and poetics), is to widen the claim of rationality, not yield it to complete irrationality or simple reason. It is not to abolish ratiocination, as Blake attempted, but to diffuse its focus. It is not to ignore poetry as mere decoration, like Johnson, but to use its powers. Poetry is necessary to awaken the power of expression, to transcend things already said. The operative reflexive language of philosophy is inadequate to capture the immediacy or completeness of being.

By forming an internally structured whole, the work of art presented an ordered cosmos. In life and in the world there are not complete actions, but when it conforms to the requirements of organic unity, art can give the mimesis of a complete action. A philosophical treatise may give an account of actions in terms of causes and reasons, but a poem meaningfully relates them into a whole. A philosophical poem combines possibilities into a whole that may be a metaphor of the cosmos.

It is not a question of parts combining into a whole, but of a whole presenting itself in parts. The parts would not hang together if this were not so. The working habit of thought is not unity or synthesis now. Philosophy, religion, economics, and politics are lost because of not thinking in terms of unity. In the presence of nature the feeling intellect of Wordsworth takes over. 'I am, therefore I think.' Wordsworth held that ecstasy is the highest form of thought; it is the nearest we get to communication with truth. Nature has a secret. Shakespeare knew it: "ripeness is all."

Step Two: Science & Art. Art and science share a common fascination for form and structure in nature. But many scientists regard artists' interests as superficial, considering that artists do not have the intellectual rigor to go beyond their dumb wonder. Bronowski refers to their response to nature as "a strangled, unformed and unfounded experience." On the other hand, artists consider the scientists as interested only in dead parts, not having the intellectual courage to go beyond single vision.

Science and art both select, simplify and exaggerate features of the environment in order to understand the whole. A scientist or artist isolates things with clear boundaries; this releases them from confusion of background. Selection is necessary in science and art, although it distorts relationships. Science is obsessed with general truths and functional laws and statistics. It has little time for minor exceptions to general law. But nature, and humanity, are made up of minor exceptions. Art is that branch of science that reaches what science is prevented from reaching by its own methods and tenets—direct experience of existence. Artists find knowledge of the object unique, not statistically articulable. Yet many can repeat the experience through the artist. And repeatability is one criterion of science. To communicate the qualities of things, poetic language is developed as a special language of subjective consciousness, as mathematics is of objective consciousness. Yet again, everything is ultimately subjective. Mathematics deals with relations, poetry with qualities. A sphere results when one can see relations holding between qualities.

In art, great knowledge, taste or intelligence are not essential—otherwise artists would also be most learned of academics. In practice, we wisely reject more knowledge than we gain. It is not necessarily too little knowledge that produces ignorance. Too much can produce the unavoidable result. There is a danger in nature and art in placing the emphasis on the created and not the process of creation.

Poets live as close to the world as any scientist; naked in sheer facts of living. Poetry and science both deal with facts and values from different styles. The focus is different. But poetry can be absorbed through channels other than rational exposition. Nature is an artist: she offers poems, not machines that run on facts. Goethe held that poetry was a product of nature, as did Chinese literati.

Poetry is a way of knowing and viewing nature; it can be used as evidence, as Whitehead did, that there are different ways of looking at nature that are as valid as the scientific view. Auden recommended that poets study the sciences before trying to express facts. Do botanists study landscape painting, astronomers draw hypotheses from van Gogh's stars, or physicists study Picasso or Joyce? Wordsworth considered the problem in his preface to *Lyrical Ballads*. He stated that the remotest discoveries of the chemist, botanist and mineralogist will become subject matters for the poet, no less suitable than any others (in Elizabeth Sewell, *The Orphic Voice*, p. 290). If the facts of science are to be incorporated into art, then they must be facts of direct, meaningful experience.

Science, with its painful vocabularies, will not be felt until it is tinged with emotion. And it cannot be tinged so until it is expressed in poetic form. Shakespeare sums up the idea that we cannot think abstractly without being involved physically in the communities of the earth when he has Hotspur (in *King Henry IV*, Pt. I) say that "thought's the slave of life." The poet is a pontifex. A member of the college of priests in Rome is called a pontifex, from the Latin word meaning "bridge builder." In its religious context, it means one who builds bridges between earth and heaven. A. Huxley used it in the literary sense for one who builds bridges between art and science who joins facts and experiences.

Poetic thought has been a precursor to philosophical and scientific thought. At the beginning of biology, Aristotle used analogies of artists and organisms. Yet poetic thought may sometimes only appear after years of preparation and study. In the early nineteenth century the poet Coleridge differentiated organic forms from mechanical ones according to these criteria: First, the origin of the whole precedes the differentiation of the parts; the whole is primary, the part derived. Second, the form manifests the process of growth by which it arose; form and process are essentially linked, logically and historically. Third, the organism assimilates various components into its own substance; the elements are subordinated to the whole. Fourth, the outward aspect of organism is determined from within, by internal processes. The romantic conception was the starting point for modern biology, without providing biological explanations or laws.

In Goethe's view of organic dialectics, morphology is the study of unity in process. Goethe was among the first to use the term morphology, the study of shape and structure as related to processes governing form and function. Life strives toward archetypal form. Whitehead's organic materialism emphasized the primacy of organism over atom. All are connected with the present undertaking because of their concern from different angles. Pythagorean thought combined poetry and mathematics. Some sciences now show signs of a Pythagorean approach.

In describing the insight that led to Newton's laws, Bohm states that science has the quality of poetic communication of the creative perception of new orders. Prigogine thought that the world was far too rich to be expressed in a single language. Furthermore, the essential parts of experience can not be condensed to a single description. There are many descriptions, irreducible to one another, but they are connected by rules of translation (=transformations, mathematically). Science consists of selective exploration. Poetry, myth and metaphysics are needed for the transformation.

Metaphysics is fundamental to every branch of science, according to Bohm. But it is dangerous because assumptions and inferences are mistaken for observed facts. The proper role of metaphysics is as a metaphor that provides an immediate perceptual grasp of the overall order and structure of thoughts. It is therefore "a kind of poetry," in the words of Bohm and others. A lot of factual science is a kind of poetry, which is indispensable to our general mental functioning.

Full human consciousness depends on the observation of other beings. Human civilizations and sciences depend on the stability and diversity of the biogeochemical systems of the earth. Poetry depends on the complexity and uniqueness of natural events for inspiration. Therefore, as natural habitats and formations are destroyed, or simplified, science and poetry become impoverished. As humanity looses the beings and forms of nature, it looses consciousness.

Holopoetic Image

Poetry, as a vehicle of a metaphorical knowledge of a prerational and metarational character, can still avail itself of any scientific or philosophic reference. Through this blending it achieves its intersubjective communication. It also measures the ratio of cognitive and irrational elements in its own discourse. Poetry needs the hyperreflective awareness of philosophy, which must use a lateral approach. Poetry also needs the exactness of science. Poets live close to the world of primitive people, the naked world fundamental to all of us—birth, love, death. The mind can be domesticated; the savage mind is allowed, in art. Poetry is the vehicle of the mystery of voice, according to Gary Snyder. But not man as the anthropomorphic center, only as a beginning, understanding. Poetic thinking favors a more basic way of living with things in a common world, in an ordinary way.

Poetry attempts to show the present invisible experienced by conscious individuals. Poetry is the skilled use of the voice and language to embody powerful states of mind, both immediate to the speaker and common to the listener. To enable to listener to grasp the perception and capture a significant moment. The poet should perform for the community the function of objectifying in imaginative form experience common to all, but exceptionally vivid, revealing tension and reconciliation of opposite forces in real life. Poetry must be ethical and address urgent issues.

The human body is the "same flesh as the world," noted Merleau-Ponty (*The Visible and the Invisible*, p. 248). It acts and feels the same. Consciousness is in tune with sounds. Through sounding words we communicate with world. Poetry reveals the possible of reality, like Heidegger's truth as unveiling. Poetic knowledge does not copy or imitate reality. Piaget posited that in order to really understand reality it was necessary to invent the structures needed to assimilate it. A person does not simply construct the appropriate images and language; human actions "transform" reality. Kant had argued that the world, as appearance, conformed to our way of representing it. But our representation does not pattern itself after the world "as it is." It cocreates it.

Metamorphosis

Ovid's *Metamorphoses* views the world as a space of flux. In most transformations, as in Actaeon's into a stag, there is a transitional zone of intense quiet between human mind and the inarticulate otherness, which it seeks to own in consciousness. The metamorphosis also moves through ambiguity, as when Daphne becomes a tree, yet Apollo continues caressing her. The metamorphoses demonstrate how identity can be highlighted through a process aimed at suppressing identity; for instance, Daphne the tree still shrinks from Apollo's touch. The metamorphoses represent myths of regeneration as well as destruction. Ovid expressed the cosmic theme of dialectical process of change attributing it to Pythagoras: "Nothing in the entire universe ever perishes . . . things vary and adopt a new form" (in *Metamorphoses*). The earth strives to be invisible in us; this demand is metamorphosis, according to Rilke. We strive to be everything on earth. And everything on earth becomes ambiguous.

Poetry and art mirror the ambiguity of life. No perceptions or feelings are identical. Life is rhythmic movement among opposites. Chinese art is moral symbolism, a persuasion toward harmony, aestheticism, fusion, complementarity, permeability and interpenetration. Ambiguity is necessary to suggest unity of possible meanings and induce new interpretations. Patterns are prior to things, in helixes, light, fields, ecology.

Ambiguity is an essential indispensable element for the transfer of information. For meaning to come through words there must be a strangeness (askewness). Nature is supposed to be strange. Strangeness is necessary to humans to rip them out of their old selves and become new beings. Poetry can embody some of that strangeness. Humans extend their play to other beings. The highest poetic endeavor has its inception in a child's need to be what she wants to understand and to express that knowledge in some outward form. Children are wolves and deer. Poets describe being mice and ravens. The Peregrine by J.A. Baker, describes the author's attempt to participate in nonhuman experience of a wild creature (skillful flight and sharp eyes). Others describe being whales and planets. Wordsworth attempted a more ethereal essence (from Bly, *News of the Universe*, p. 62):

> And I have felt A presence that disturbs me with the joy
> Of elevated thoughts; a sense sublime
> Of something far more deeply interfused,
> Whose dwelling is the light of setting suns,
> And the round ocean and the living air,
> And the blue sky, and in the mind of man;
> A motion and a spirit, that impels
> All thinking things, all objects of thought,
> And rolls through all things.

Only recently has nature been conjoined with human history. Before that poetry constructed archetypal images. C. Brooks makes the division

of poet perspectives. One group of poets is preoccupied with history
(and possibly evolution); Tennyson, Crane, Lowell, Tate, and Whitman,
who stressed participation in the ongoing work of the universe, go here.
Another is preoccupied with nature (cf. cyclism); Thomas, Lawrence,
Graves and Yeats go here. The last with the aesthetic moment; Joyce,
Stevens, Aiken, Williams, Wright, and Bly go here. Walter Ong judges that
Whitman lacks Teilhard's 'inwardness' of things. And Crane retreated into
Ouspensky's eternal present. Ong cites G.M. Hopkins as the poet most at
home in a historical and evolutionary cosmos. Hopkins was devoted to the
"instress" of things, uniqueness itself; he was a proto-existentialist, with a
love for variety. His themes have an open-ended development, but tend
to be underdeveloped. Poetry, like evolution, needs repetition in rhythm
and rhyme. In modern poetry, the celebration of nature is not tied to a
cyclic theory. Human evolution needs to improve harmony. This can be
done by ideals, new modes of thought. Waddington believes that new ways
of thinking are being developed in terms of instructions and normative
modes, and that these are beginning to provide methodologies capable of
achieving the necessary, challenging tasks.

The Secret of Ecology

Modern civilization disengages from nature; truth is relegated to
impersonal propositions. But objectivity is not the only route to
knowledge and it pulls counter to the self. A poetic language could go a
way to including a view of the infinite interpenetration of all existence
in a sublime ecology. C. Sherrington noted that nature dealt with the
individual body and mind as a unity. Biological science does not. Sewell
claimed that biology needed poetry rather than mathematics to think
with (Elizabeth Sewell, *The Orphic Voice*. New York: Harper & Row,
1960, p. 44). Ecology requires a combination of aesthetic perception and
disciplined thinking, as does poetry. Huxley notes that Elton remarked in
his work on animal ecology that there is more ecology in Old Testament or
Shakespeare than in zoological texts.

Ecology contains a secret: attention to detail. A metaphorical ecology
has more than a scientific or political meaning. The whole can be seen by
the part, because it is implicit in every part—this is why hologram can be
reconstructed from a small piece. Intimacy does not necessarily require
details.

Poetry is communicative of the quality of things. Like philosophy
and science, it discriminates the unsuspected in the commonplace. It pulls
in; showing is not simply mirroring. The poet accepts ontological parity;

aspects of the world are not negated or reduced by one another. In Greece the Eleusinian Mysteries embodied resistance to human domination of nature; they evoked a sense of awe, a sense that we shared a consciousness with plants animals and minerals; and all shared it with the soul of the world. 'As above, so below' denies the validity of superior and inferior.

The poet is willing to grant consciousness to trees and hills or other living creatures. After Descartes, a gap develops that lets us emphasize perception rather than the object. Our energy circulates in the house of the body. The circuit is truncated. When the gap is large enough, when people tire of perceiving words or judgments, perception changes. Rilke sees that if we leave our locked in interior and use imagination to see a tree, we grant the whole world its being. (from Bly, *News of the Universe*):

> Whoever you are: some evening take a step
> out of your house, which you know so well.
> slowly, slowly, lift one black tree
> up, so it stands against the sky: skinny, alone.
> With that you have made the world. The world is immense,
> and like a word that is still growing in silence.

Poetic ecology contains a secret: attention to the detail of a tree. Blake wrote of seeing the world in a grain of sand; that is the secret expanded. We can see using our entire imaginative power if we can avoid the fear of being swallowed by the immensity of the cosmos. Is it truer to life to know that a tree has its own life; its own assertive existence and relatedness? Or is marketable lumber or warmth in a campfire? This is G.M. Hopkins' notion of inscape: a perceived individual form constituted by shape and texture of an object; a cluster of qualities and perceptions; the organic beauty of a tree, as well as poetic uniqueness.

D.H. Lawrence announced that speech is the death of Pan. A conquered world is no good for humanity; conquest is boring—we have nothing to live with. The connection to allness has been severed. In the living universe there is no boredom, because everything is alive and active; danger is inherent in every movement. Contact between things is wary and keen; wariness is a kind of reverence or respect. Nothing can be taken for granted. Life itself consists in a live relatedness between man and animals, flowers, rocks and stars. Lawrence concluded that we need to sustain the pan relationship. Lawrence noted that in Whitman's Song of Myself: "I am All, and All is Me."—or I am Pan and Pan is Me—is not true; Walt is not All; All is not Walt. The self cannot contain the all in more than a metaphorical sense; an individual can be no more than one perspective.

Gary Snyder presented poetry as an ecological survival technique. Poetry is then defined as the skilled and inspired use of language and voice to embody rare and powerful states of mind common to the singer and all who listen. But the poet has the power of Orpheus, to call up a world from nowhere for "man to dwell," in Heidegger's words. Poetry has an ancient, ontologically mythic function. Not different from science, but more diffuse; not better than science, but more comprehensive.

Percy Shelley tried to express in poetry the thoughts suggested by science. He refused to accept the abstract materialism of science and held that nature cannot be divorced from the aesthetic values that arise from the presence of the whole. Whitehead interprets Shelley as expounding that a philosophy of nature must concern itself with six notions: change, value, endurance, ideals, organism, and interfusion (in *Science and the Modern World*, p. 75-94).

Poetic ecology is housekeeping on earth. As Bachelard stated, the poet's occupation makes the universe into a habitable cosmic house. Only when we are comfortable can we study the house; that study is called ecology. The poetic imagination, with a primitive awareness and scientific knowledge, may save our world.

Poetic Cosmology

Poetry can measure a whole qualitatively and mimetically, a cosmos with its imagery. As J. Dewey states: "A poem presents material so that it becomes a universe in itself, one, which, even when it is a miniature whole, is not embryonic" (*Art as Experience*, p. 241). In Steven's "Planet on the Table," (*The Palm at the End of the Mind*, p. 386) a life's poetry, like the model globe, reproduces the whole world in miniature.

> His self and the sun were one
> And his poems, although makings of his self,
> Were no less makings of the sun.
> It was not important that they survive.
> What mattered was that they should bear
> Some lineament or character,
> Some affluence, if only half-perceived,
> In the poverty of their words,
> Of the planet of which they were part.

Edgar Allan Poe was more ambitious. His Eureka is patterned after the cosmos of Humboldt, a universe of pure extension in space. The atoms of material and spiritual character are fragments of an original unity Poe calls God. The business of poets is to change chaos into form. But where Orpheus creates an environing world, Agathos (in Poe) creates a pure poem in space.

In a cosmos, perhaps it is not details, or knowledge of the operation, that is critical, but an understanding of the wholeness, of order. Plato acknowledged the limitations of verbalization in expressing the essence of a thing; only a vision through and beyond language could claim knowledge of a thing, by reaching through particularity and even intelligible patterns to another order.

Novalis understands that "We dream of travelling through the cosmos;" and asks, "but does not the cosmos lie within ourselves?" The depths of the human spirit are unknown. Exploring either limit produces insights. Mallarme defined the poet's duty as the Orphic explanation of the earth. The microcosm and macrocosm are revealed in reciprocal patterning. A. Beguin thought that inner exploration would be convincing if the structure of the mind (or total being) and its rhythms were identical with the structure and rhythms of the universe. Novalis's *Die Lehringe zu Sais* proposed that reality was a vast poem, whose signs could be construed.

Perhaps we are too removed to read them. In another poem by Stevens, a man rides through Connecticut in a glass coach. We have created a hard glass between the mind projecting itself and the object desired. Sometimes we doubt if there is a space on the other side that can be seen through this window of consciousness. Poetry offers confirmation that we are not trapped behind glass. That we are in the world.

The function of poetry is to nourish the spirit of humanity by giving it the cosmos to suckle (suggested Bachelard). We need only to lower our standard of dominance and raise our standard of participation in nature to allow reconciliation. Hope lies in a poetry through which the world so invades the spirit of humanity that they become almost speechless and later reinvent languages. Ponge charges that society puts poets at the bottom; love of things keeps them there. They are ambassadors of the silent world. And they stammer, murmur and sink into the dark of logos, until they reach the roots where things and formulas are one.

The license to frame metaphors in translation of the ineffable is what sets the poet apart from the historian and philosopher. Metaphor is imaginative reality. a tool for comprehending partially what cannot be totally: feelings, aesthetic experiences, moral practices, and spiritual awareness. People need to be made aware of the power of self-determination, and the possibility. Poetry intensifies this function over politics. A great poet can express herself in words that cause others to understand glimpses of a timeless reality.

For Heraklitus, cosmos names the manner in which the world comes to radiate order. Heidegger argues that Logos means, not rational discourse, but gathering, the act of gathering the flux into unity by virtue of which the world emerges. This gathering has the fundamental character of opening. The act of disclosure is a poetic act. The Logos is a poetic act that calls the world into the unconcealment of being. The Heraklitean unity of Logos and being is a unity of poetry and being. While the persona of the poet may be regarded as immature, foolish and neurotic, the poet also celebrates the unity of existence by sharing it with everyone. The poet reconnects the real world and the thought-world (or perhaps heaven and earth) in a poem. The Chinese symbol for a prince may also represent the poet.

The poet creates new forms and myths to make the earth sacred again. The richness hidden in thoughts, places and beings is revealed. Ponge said that (in *The Voice of Things*): "What is completely spontaneous in man as he touches the earth is an immediate feeling of familiarity, sympathy, or even veneration, of a filial kind." We need to feel the immensity of nature. People need to feel things, before they can act on them. Poetry can help them feel themselves as part of the web of life, or on an oasis in space. Then people may act with wisdom, or as if they were wise.

We need a strategy for emergence to a healthy planetary culture; and this strategy must use a science, religion and art with a profound and holistic view of nature and life. We would be wise to undertake an orderly radical change in civilization before it is forced on us by an unbalanced environment. We need a creative language to express a new vision of man and nature, based on ignorance and feeling, as well as knowledge and thought—we need a poetry of the earth.

The primitive world view, radical scientific knowledge, and the poetic imagination are related forces that may help to save whales, maybe humanity, possibly the earth. Poets are needed to make a blueprint or code into a dream, so that one may feel the Arcadian wood or the warmth of a home. The dream is more than a code—it is ideal reality. As poets transform these codes, they are, as Shelley said, the unacknowledged legislators of the world.

The Masks of Being

Tragedy

Aristotle defined tragedy as "the imitation of an action that is serious and also, as having magnitude, complete in itself; in language with pleasurable accessories [i.e., rhythm and harmony], each kind brought in separately in the parts of the work [i.e., some in verse, others in song], in a dramatic, not a narrative form; with incidents arousing pity and fear, wherewith to accomplish its catharsis of such emotions" (W. Ross, ed., *The Works of Aristotle*. Oxford: Clarendon, 1952, p. 677). For Aristotle, tragedy The usual explanation of tragedy is that is means a goat song; W. Kaufmann notes that G. Murray concluded that it was the title of the contestants in the tragedy and perhaps the original prize was a goat. is the mimesis of a good or noble action. Tragedy is defined in terms of its formal characteristics and emotional effect. Reversal (peripeteia), the change of a situation into its opposite, is an important plot mechanism. This aspect of Greek tragedy is inherent Dionysius: joy and plenitude, but also compassion and emotional excess. There is a rhythmic universe of contrasting joys and pain. Disaster results from breaking the principle of sophrosyne (temperance, or nothing in excess). The principle of peripeteia held that when sophrosyne failed, the actor would see 'the transformation of his action into its opposite.' This antinomy is the Heraklitean notion of enantiodromia (the return swing of the pendulum). Human ideals are in dynamic opposition, swinging back and forth. Tragedy is enantiodromia; a single element of value grows cancerously and kills the whole. The Greeks acted out on a metalevel the process by which absolute values buckle beneath peripeteia into antithesis. This could be diagrammed in Catastrophe Theory.

Values are sharply contrasted in state of contest. The Greek word to use here is agon, meaning contest; from agein, meaning drive. But the anomolies in tragedy can call forth a creative response. Higher level of moral awareness born in dialectic clash of opposites. Virtue requires steering between intellect and impulse. Folly is the misjudgment in combining values, missing the just proportions. The tragic hero triumphs and overlearns a winning value combination and employs it disastrously in new circumstances. In this sense, perhaps natural selection in evolution is tragic (the tragedy of reality). M.W. Fox and G. Hardin hold this view.

Many Japanese legendary heroes, like Yamato Takeru, have a time of success followed by failure from application of the strategy that made them successful previously. This behavior is the Nobility of Failure, *mono no arvare*, the pathos of things. Another good example of the heroic parabola was Japan's use of kamikaze during a world war. The Shikishima Unit exchanged the lives of 24 pilots for 1 American vessel sunk and 6 others damaged. Encouraged by the relative success, more pilots were trained. Within a year, about 5000 more had died in suicide raids but only two more ships were sunk. This was an exercise in heroic futility.

The tragic error in Greek tragedy is a mistake of being, of individuation, of an evil predicament. Oedipus did not sin; he was caught in contradictory circumstances. The fundamental notions of tragedy are hubris and nemesis; hubris is an arrogance that arises from blindness, and nemesis is the eventual consequence. The hero can build up an interpretation of events that conforms to his ideal. Hybris allows a decision on the basis of the hero's mistaken interpretation, and the decision results in ruin. The quality of irony brings recognition of the situation, a decree of necessity. The hero recognizes herself and her ideas in terms of laws. This is purgation.

The Greek tragic hero was a typical man isolated and projected onto larger background of fate. Tragedy stresses the price of consciousness. Tragic heroes are unique egos. J. Meeker does not seem to distinguish between uniqueness and ego. He confuses uniqueness with importance. Uniqueness cannot be denied; everything is unique. Importance is a personal and cultural choice. For Ortega, the will is the tragic theme; the tragic character is tragic so only as long as he wills (in Otten, *Art and Anthropology*). Tragedy results from the failure to give up a chosen part or role. The choice results in great loss.

Cultural Tragedy

By contrast, cultural heroes represent peoples. Cultural heroes are often mythical beings, of human birth, who restore balances. Also by contrast, many Japanese heroes changed their roles. The hero becomes multi-faceted, ferocious, then poetic, after success and loss.

Cultural heroes are declining. Thompson states that today's tragedy is one of collectivization; tragedy is impossible without a true and known self. Scott Buchanan claimed that after the late middle ages, humans substituted animals for heroes, in the controlled experiment. There fate made its pronouncement. That pattern of tragedy is still in science: Purgation is elimination of false hypotheses; irony is verification.

Rank believes that human problems arise from attempts to deny mortality, from fear of life or death. Becker claims that the tragedy of evolution is that it created a limited animal with unlimited horizons.

Tragedy is wanting an earth that is perfect, a heaven abstracted from imperfection. Enantiodromia ensures that humans will create no place perfect. Recent definitions of tragedy have linked it to cosmology, the image of the place of humanity in the universe.

Tragedy & Cosmology
The essence of tragedy for Ophuls is the moral impotence of reason. Knowing good but unable to act on it. He recommends adopting the tragic perspective. Meeker judges that the tragic view of life, as embodied in Greek tragedy, is based on a deep conviction that man has no part in nature, that human behavior must conform to moral laws that are extranatural. The tragic view assumes human superiority over nature. The tragic view also assumes that we are in conflict with greater powers. Obviously, the assumption of human superiority is what causes the conflict. Humanity can be part of nature and still be tragic, however. Even if moral laws are natural. The conflict of tragedy is more than ethical, as Hegel held.

Tragedies imply conflicts larger than the individual or even society. The external order of things or cosmic plan is challenged, even if the cosmos is the size of the polis. A. Bradley saw the character-flaw as the source of tragedy. But the fatal flaw of the character is a fatal flaw of the world-view. This is the root of Hardin's tragedy of the commons. The tragedy of the commons occurs only when people are locked into a system of self-interest through economic gain. Hardin's definition of tragedy is the working of fate. But this tragedy results from the failure of a cosmology: humans are responsible, not chance or fate. We can choose between the tragedy of the commons or that of Leviathan, or expand the cosmology. We are tragic because we accept responsibility for our actions (cf. Roszak).

Tragedy is an expression of the failure of a cosmological view. The hero's problems may be unresolvable, but they are communicated. The continuity is provided by the viewer. The reidentification of the viewer with his or her lives is a reemergence to a higher order; this is an essential element of tragedy. The higher order may be a more adaptive cosmology.

In *The Birth of Tragedy*, Nietzsche suggested that tragedy was dead. But the Socratic spirit needs tragedy as Anteus needed earth. Socrates was tragic because he was one-sided, in denying the claims of poetry. So is modern science tragically the same. The attempt to avoid enantiodromia, without understanding the way of nature, ends in tragedy.

Comedy

Western images are tragic because death does not imply rebirth or a living continuity. Indian images are comic because death does imply rebirth; as rebirth implies further death. The comedy depends on surprise—death is really illusion. Immortality is the shift of identity from ego to universe, the one universal rhythm that exists in all beings of all sizes. This is the Indian rhythm of the juggler, balancing worlds; and if one seems to fall and shatter, hundreds of new jugglers are born.

The moment after tragedy can be a comic moment; the actor steps out of tragic action and observes herself and former universe and laughs. The actor is then free of evil, restraint, body, and death. Laughter involves detachment, which is a fundamental form of freedom; and freedom is the central value of comedy.

The comic actor tries to create a new and better universe. It is a celebration of human freedom. Farce opposes aging and death; it affirms life. It is comic recognition of the impossible. Comedy tries for freedom. The farcical hero demands the universe to be changed; the comic hero demands that society accommodate itself to his will; and the absurd hero sees the universe as a hoax and makes no demands. Comic heroes lack self-awareness; if they had it the collision of will and act would be tragic. Comedy does not trivialize what is important, though it deflates the overinflated.

The comic mode is a genuine affirmation of instinctive patterns necessary for biological survival, as defined by Meeker (in *The Comedy of Survival*). Comedy is concerned with muddling through, not progress or perfection. He argues that evolution shows all the flexibility of comic drama. Evolution is a shameful, opportunist comedy whose object is the proliferation of life without regard to morals. The participants must adapt, diversify, and accommodate. He contends that events in tragic literature could not occur if comic principles are observed. Comedy encourages necessity and acceptance; tragedy avoids necessity to try to accomplish the impossible. Comedy assumes that all choice is likely to be in error. To comedy or evolution, nothing is sacred but life itself.

Evolution and ecology cannot be compared to comedy or tragedy, which are descriptions of the fitting of human images to a changing environment. In the end both tragedy and comedy encourage the acceptance of human limitation. Meeker emphasizes that comedy is immoral, like evolution, but he is wrong. Comedies of manners and types have a lesson to teach: moderation and control are affirmed; rascality and immorality denied. High comedies show that the world is basically good and that evil is introduced by humans who lack moderation and control. Furthermore, the comic mode is an incomplete strategy for living. If the comic attitude is necessary for survival then it must be moral at least in the etymological sense. The comic mode, as described by Meeker, cannot be reconciled with natural patterns of reproduction and death. Life is no more sacred than rock or air. What Meeker has described is not comedy, which is an analogue of complete freedom, which cannot occur, but compliance, acceptance of partial freedom and partial conflict. The reduction to a comic mode as a model of behavior would be tragic, in the Socratic sense, because it refused just proportion, and was single-sided.

Tragedy proceeds by analogy and homogeneous substitution in the rationalization of the hero. Events are controlled to be consistent with an idea; the direction of expansion is integration; it ends in cumulative catastrophe and purgation.

Comedy proceeds by wide variation and heterogenous substitution. Every action discovers inconsistency. Expansion holds discrimination. Ideas have continual purgation. Comedy plays with the ideas that tragedy discovers. But the play of ideas is hedged with the mystery of tragic issues. Reason moves between tragic pain and comic disillusion. Comedy offers a rebirth. Tragedy also offers a way out, but it is through death. Tragedy confronts evil; comedy avoids it. In comedy, frames of reference collide and shatter harmlessly; in tragedy the frames conflict.

The mask is seen by the audience as tragic and comic. The mask offers a surprise. The surprise catches the hero or the audience and the audience laughs or cries. The play is tragic or comic only from perspective. the difference between comedy and tragedy is in the point of view, not the subject matter. The single mask of tragedy and comedy reflects duality: The acceptance or refusal of the inevitable; detached indifference (comedy) or compassionate concern (tragedy). Both are combined in one mask. From the holocosmological perspective, there is no tragedy or comedy: everything simply is. M. de Montaigne wrote that "Our great and glorious masterpiece is to live appropriately" (in *Complete Essays*). That is, according to Michael W. Fox, to live responsively and responsibly.

The Tao of Cosmology

When geometric diagrams and digits
Are no longer the keys to living things,
When people who go about singing or kissing
Know deeper things than the great scholars,
When society is returned once more
To unimprisoned life, and to the universe,
And when light and darkness mate
Once more and make something entirely transparent,
And people see in poems and fairy tales
The true history of the world,
Then our entire twisted nature will turn
And run when a single secret word is spoken.
                Novalis (in Bly, *News of the Universe*, p. 42)

Our dream of nature, our modern cosmology, was the dream of order and beauty. As Aldous Huxley noted, the dream of order begets tyranny, the dream of beauty, monsters and violence. The dreams become nightmares because they are not complete. Thinking and valuing are separated from nature. The nightmares are symptoms that reflect an unbalanced and immature cosmology. Modern cosmologies are unconnected. The origins of ecological crises lie deep in cultural traditions that have been unchanged for thousands of years. A traditional cosmology evolves with people's needs, fears and knowledge. If it is incomplete, it may fail. Many early cosmologies were defective. They failed to fit the earth. People constructed their own worlds from preconceived notions. Many of these worlds did not survive because of problems in adapting to the ambihuman environment. Failure is not unavoidable. These traditions, however, describe what we may be and helps us become what we are. The world tends to be how we imagine it, as spaceship or garden. Our view of the earth is ambiguous. It is spaceship, island. oasis, boat. But it is not any of these images; we need to learn to imagine it as wild/garden/city complement. There are traditions that have value systems capable of guiding thought toward integration with natural processes. Any cosmology is only one of many possibilities. Every good cosmology is a way, a tao. One of the first translations of "tao" from the Chinese was as "logos," which has been translated as word or image. There is no single way or one correct way. We need to return to the facts and feelings of all beings and dream again. The self-reflexive mind relates the whole world to the individual and the individual to the whole world.

Neither art nor science can let us understand life or nature itself. Scientists have experimented with biological processes behind glass (*in vitro*) in the laboratory. We have made an experiment of ourselves; our mentality has evolved behind glass. C.P. Snow has commented that watching megadeaths by starvation in Africa on television screens could mark the end of any moral community of humanity. Augustine remarked to the Romans: "What glory is there in the largeness of empire, bright and brittle like glass, and forever in fear of breaking." We are behind glass and fear it will break. Reason alone cannot cure what it caused. Glass cannot divide humanity and nature; nor can we humanize the planet without dehumanizing ourselves. We need a sanctified vision of life from a deep participation in culture.

A culture rises out of individual social actions. Culture contains languages, skills, attitudes and ideas. One set of the ideas is termed cosmology; it is concerned with the nature of the universe. The visible world is made sense of in terms of an invisible background, which is presumed to exist but not directly observed. A cosmology includes a set of myths in an aesthetic logic. Aesthetic logic is lived logic, a broader category than intellectual logic. This logic requires balance and symmetry. Mythology requires this logic.

Myths are accounts of past events. Myths serve to explain the universe as it exists. And to order the place of humanity within. To be understandable to members of a culture, the elements of a myth must be taken from the features and values of that culture. Myths explain that which is otherwise incomprehensible, like death and disorder. Campbell noted that when the tribe was the relevant social unit, it was possible for mythology to represent all those beyond its bounds as inferior. The young were trained to respond positively to tribal members to love their home and project hatred outward. The concept of tribe and state is growing toward an ecumene, an inhabited earth.

Today, there is no outward on earth. Our mythology has to grow also, to include the whole planet. There is no practical 'elsewhere' anymore. A global mythology cannot afford to teach of elsewheres. It must teach of a multiplicity of cosmologies. The difference between cosmologies is not due to the number of phenomena taken into account; it is due to the difference in basic postulates of thought. The difference is not a matter of truth or falsity. Truth and falsity are meaningless for cosmologies.

Primordial water is no less true than six-dimensional phase space or primordial ylem. No one group's image is more true or accurate than any other's. Each group views and reconstructs the world through their experiences and values. Codifications are true to reality; they represent different facets, not exhaustive catalogs. Inconvenient truths, like the germ theory of sickness or the vengeance of Coyote, are usually disregarded when they conflict with the direct beliefs of the cosmology. The balance of freedom and necessity ensures that no cosmology will ever fit perfectly. Perfection is not important.

A cosmology will coalesce, which unlike astronomy, which deals with prosaic aspects of stellar relationships, will try to encompass the whole, as a child discovers the image of her own soul in any whole being. This cosmology will translate the poetry emerging from life and from which humans find inspiration. The voices of beings. Pascal faced the implications of humanity in an immense universe, in its vast indifferent silence. But the silence of the universe is only the absence of human noise; the universe speaks on all wavelengths, from hydrogen lines to a human voice. We need only listen to the whole field, whole in energy, mass, space and time.

All that has been said is an interim report on the history of the idea of nature. Hegel observed that "That is as far as consciousness has reached." The study of nature is not a thing that exists on its own. Natural science is a form of thought that depends on the existence of some other form of thought, which is history. Natural science consists of facts and theories. A scientific fact is a class of historical facts. One cannot understand the first without understanding the second. No one can answer the question what nature is unless he knows what history is. Every cosmology includes ideas of the past, present and future. An ontology of temporal process would provide a global perspective on world order, on the coming to be of higher levels of meaning in the universe as a whole.

As mysticism, with its synchronal sight, regards all beings as equal, science, with its diachronal sight, regards all equal through time. A complete cosmology needs science and mysticism. The proper attitude of such a cosmology is care, by which Heidegger meant the abandonment of the neutral attitude of consciousness. Care is an attitude that moves beyond its own preoccupations towards the beings of the world. It means letting be. It means reacting spontaneously to nature; loving, fearing or fighting when appropriate. If all nature were tamed like Europe, there would be no adventure; just introspection becoming shallower. Reverence can only be felt at the alienness of nature, not its comfortable conquest. Evernden suggests that commitment to a self-constrained role in relationships of the life-world are of fundamental importance. Compliance may be the Janus-face of caring—the acceptance of place and concern for life in general. It is a kind of wisdom.

The Intestines of Day

The Hawaiian phrase for wisdom is 'the intestines of day,' referring to an awareness of the obvious and hidden. Awareness opens a way to understanding. Understanding fuses ends with means, and wisdom (the timeless realization of suchness) with compassion, which is wisdom in action. Bateson defines wisdom as knowledge of the larger interactive system. Wisdom is a perception of relationships and relativity, an awareness of the wholeness of things without losing sight of the unique particularities. It joins the left and right brains in a union of logic, poetry and feeling. It reintegrates knowledge with values. It implies making judgments in advance, infusing elements of older wisdom into a new expression. The wisdom of cultures forms a *philosophia perennis* of the human race. Gary Snyder discerned an undercurrent in civilization since the late Paleolithic. He considered Buddhist Tantrism to be its finest and most modern statement: "that Mankind's mother is Nature and Nature should be tenderly respected; that man's life and destiny is growth and enlightenment in self-disciplined freedom; that the divine has been made flesh and that flesh is divine; that we not only should but do love one another . . . these values seem almost biologically essential to the survival of humanity." (from *Earth House Hold*, p. 105).

Salk defined wisdom as the art of disciplined use of imagination in respect to alternatives, exercised at the right time and in the right measure. Judgment is required as to what is right, and judgment may be an innate art. It is a new kind of fitness, supplanting the biological kind of evolution. Humans have made radically different conditions that they must now accommodate. If the mind is exposed to economy of nature, as revealed through living systems, humans will recognize the necessity of balancing values. Total win-lose conflicts are unwise. Value systems concerned with dynamic equilibrium, aesthetics, complementarity, reciprocity, justice, interdependence, reconciliation, and intuition are the language that biology speaks. Myths (with transformations) and metaphors (with structure of integrated differences) are modes for conveying ecological wisdom; they are less concerned with survival than the survival value of a good fit between dualisms of life. Equilibrium is needed between self-restraint and self-expression, between self-protection and self-restriction.

245

Not self-expression or self-restraint, or exponential growth or plateau, but all in the finest fit. Fitness attunes us to limits. Wisdom cannot be dependent on perfect knowledge–it does not exist. Humans must act "as if" they were wise, circumspectly, with caution and respect.

We are self-congratulatory that we understand evolution, and we are proud to be a recent product of evolution, assuming we are higher and more complex. But if we really understand or respect evolution, then we are bound to let it continue and not try to control it by converting all wild systems into domestic or to end it by destroying all other wild species.

Of course, humans continue to evolve in their domesticated, technological environments. Artificial evolution is a form of the continuity of evolution as it applies to humans and their inventions, but it does not replace the evolution of wild species in wild ecosystems. Both are possible, and we have to limit our impacts for the wild to continue. It is not necessary to bring human order to the planet–it is self-ordering–we only need to order our own 'worlds' so they may renew as limited, balanced, social systems. Our modern culture is not the last, not the be-all and end-all of development. It has to be understood in context, understood in its limits as a form for an optimum population to live in self-defining places.

This book urges that we create a framework to allow other, local cosmologies to continue, and the processes of a wild environment to continue, and to limit the machine cosmology that tries to replace all others with a final, evolution-ending, impossible attempt at complete control of biological processes.

A holocosmology, that preserves traditions and limits human impacts to a human part of the planet, is a positive vision that can be meaningful for people trying to avoid consuming every last plant or bird. A cosmology is a mutually constructed image of the earth that inspires effort, compromise and coordination in applying it.

Every day the earth is new, and that is exciting to us. Designing the future is exciting, especially if it is a healthy future for every living being. We need to convince others of this way, this disciplined path. Not that we will save the earth, or preserve it, but that we can remember to share it with all the other wild inhabitants, even as we make part of it a technical paradise, with other embedded virtual worlds.

The Last Word

William I. Thompson wrote (in *Evil and the World Order*): "If we withdraw our projections on our enemies and take them back into ourselves, we learn compassion in the contemplation of our own shadow; and in that compassion we begin to get a glimmering of what Jesus meant when he counseled us to love our enemies. Out of that initiation into compassion through pain and terror comes an understanding of the true mystery of human love; and if we try to create a just world order with anything less than this mystery, all our clever problem-solving will be in vain, and our very efforts to do good will create a planetary evil beyond anything we have experienced before in human history."

But we fear to try. Fear casts out love. And with love, goodness, beauty, truth, and intelligence. Until all that remains is fear of other beings and the unknown; fear of the smiling science and technology that take away more than is given; fear of fellow human beings, who are trying to regain what was taken. But love casts out fear. In the Upanishad it was written that "Who sees all beings in his own Self, and his own Self in all beings, loses all fear." Love is the problem of an animal who must find the world compelling and symbolic. We confuse our symbols with the natural world, the present with the represented. Sometimes the image of love is loved more than the actual. As fears and unconscious motives are understood, the awareness of all feelings intensifies. Feelings that are dualistic at one level—fear and courage, pride and humility—are combined at a higher level, for instance, as *saudade*, the Portuguese word for sweet sadness (suggested by M.W. Fox). Unconditional love blends many feelings that cannot be understood at the level of the intellect. A holocosmology can only be effective with the dimension of love, in a field of being.

Four elements in loving have been identified by E. Fromm (quoted in Hampden-Turner):

- Care, the active concern for life and growth
- Responsibility, the desire to respond to others needs
- Respect (meaning to look at), to recognize others' uniqueness
- Knowledge, combining objectivity with participation and intimate identification.

These elements define a loving relationship. The inexhaustibility of a being or our relationships constitutes much of the nature of love. Human beings are compelled to seek other beings and love is the only approach. Seeking in their hearts with wisdom, even the sages in the *Rig Veda* (X. 129) found that love was the first seed of the soul. Nature has evolved the seeds, as

Pope understood (in *An Essay on Man, Poetical Works*, p. 259):
Look round our world; behold the chain of Love
Combining all below and all above.
See plastic Nature working toward this end . . .

Love exists in the conversation itself—Buber referred to a dialogue between humans in the present as an example. But, conversation is not limited to two individuals or to the present—it can be between human beings and other beings, across lifetimes. In the sense of living together (symbiosis), it is ethical. Binswanger takes from Scheler the assumption that 'I and Thou' (of Buber) are secondary derivations from the primary 'we.' This sharing of being and place is beyond mere being-in-the-world. Care and compliance are limited kinds of being compared to love. Maslow presents "love-knowledge" as unlimited. Love creates an openness to experience, without judgment. Beings unfold. Contradictions can abound in love's wholeness. Love expands the awareness of the self and other beings. And its intensification of feeling pulls the frame through the focus, in a metaphor, yet preserves the original distance. Love binds space and time in miniature. Its intimacy permits distance. Its duration reaches future generations of beings. Love personalizes the universe, but keeps it free (the word free is from the Greek, *frijon*, meaning to love or beloved. It seems to be a natural connection).

We cannot approach beings through our personal and economic interests, but only on their own terms, in relation, through respect and love. Any other approach separates us from other beings and truncates our aesthetic responses with boundaries. The word animal means endowed with spirit (animus). Our spirituality places sacredness in everything. We are part of the cycle, woven into unity.

The world is a living symphonic poem. The score does not fully determine the music, the passion and intensity. The present movement gives no clue as to how it will finish. Each voice fits in with others, but is not limited. We can be aware of the symphony as a whole and the individual voices. When we are attuned to it, control is not a problem. If we can trust ourselves to improvise as the need arises, we can trust nature, and not follow some rigid plan. Every cosmology has limits, of incompleteness, indeterminacy, and of locality. A holocosmology recognizes its limits with love.

Aldous Huxley has the last word on love (*Adonis and the Alphabet.* London: Chatto & Windus, 1956, p. 72): "Of all the worn, smudged, dog's-eared words in our vocabulary, 'love' is surely the grubbiest, smelliest, slimiest. Bawled from a million pulpits, lasciviously crooned through hundreds of millions of loudspeakers, it has become an outrage to good taste and decent feeling, an obscenity which one hesitates to pronounce. And yet it has to be pronounced; for, after all, Love is the last word."

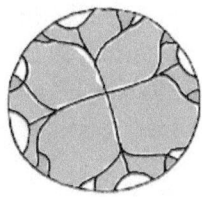

Figure 18. *Logo for the G. P. Marsh Institute.*

End Matters

Special Terms

The words listed herein are terms used throughout this work. The definitions are specialized and usually end with the etymological meaning of the word.

- Accommodate to settle, 'conform with right measure'
- Actual occasion Whitehead's term for a being; also called actual entity
- Adaptation, the process of adjustment to the environment
- Aesthetics, the theory of the beautiful, in philosophy; 'perceiving'
- Alchemy a miraculous change for the better
- Ambiguity, uncertain, being open to multiple interpretations; 'wandering around'
- Ambihuman, everything that is not human; nonhuman; ultrahuman; 'surrounding the human'
- Analogy, a correspondence based on similarity; in computers, based on similar electric charges
- Anamorphosis, a distorted image that can only be viewed from a certain perspective or with a special instrument; 'to form anew'
- Animism, the belief that all things have a soul; in Pythagoras, an immaterial force
- Anthropocentrism, the assumption that humanity is at the center of the universe or the final aim
- Anthropomorphism, the attribution of human characteristics to natural phenomena; inclusive of feelings
- Aristocentrism, the belief that humans are superior to other beings
- Assimilate, absorb, incorporate, 'to make similar'
- Autopoiesis, self-making, as used by F. Varela
- Being, the ground of existence, similar to the tao; not capitalized
- Beings, individuals perspectives, unities
- Care, Heidegger's term for 'letting be,' similar to Goethe's nonintervention
- Cognitive dissonance: Failure to absorb conflicting positions, ending in a form of self-deception; Festinger's term
- Comedy, a humorous play; 'singer in the revels'
- Complementarity, Bohr's term for the idea that two descriptions are needed to understand the whole reality; mutual completion
- Conversation, the communication between two or more beings; 'turning with'

- Culture, the symbolic social codification of reality
- Dialectic, the process of change whereby two opposites are resolved at a higher unity, Hegel's term; 'gathering across [warp and woof]'
- Diaphor, the production of new meaning by juxtaposition and synthesis
- Difference, the condition of being unlike or dissimilar; 'carrying apart'
- Digital, relating to a digit or finger; in computers, the performance of operations with discrete quantities (digits)
- Dualism, the condition of being two-fold, having two basic natures
- Dyad, two units regarded as a pair; being two-fold
- Earth, the entire planet, including all life forms
- Ecology, the study of the planet; 'study of the house'
- Ecstasy, 'to stand out from'
- Ektropy, the fundamental ordering process of the universe; Hirth's term 'turning in'
- Emergence, the unpredictable appearance of new characteristics in a process
- Enantiodromia, the production of the opposite of intention; 'running opposite'
- Enchant, to sing magic words; to charm a savage place
- Entropy, the fundamental disordering process of the universe; Clausius' term 'turning out'
- Epiphor, the outreaching extension of meaning by comparison
- Epistemology, the theory of the nature of knowledge; 'to stand upon'
- Ethics, the principle of right conduct for a society; 'custom'
- Evolution, a gradual process of change; 'turning out; unfolding; rolling open'
- Feeling, the reaction to touch; emotion
- Field, a region of space characterized by a physical property; a set of operations
- Fitness, being the proper size and shape for; adaptability
- Flesh, the ground of existence; being; Merleau-Ponty's term
- Foam, the effect of process of virtual quanta on existence; the froth of process
- Focus, point of convergence; equal to tenor and figure
- Form, the contour or structure of something; mode; essence; 'shape'
- Frame, something enclosed or encircled; equal to vehicle or ground
- Gaia, the hypothesis of the living earth; Homer's term
- Gestalt, a unified configuration having properties that cannot be derived from the parts
- Gnosis, augmentative knowledge; intuitive apprehension; 'to know'

- Harmony, the simultaneous occurrence of tones; agreement in feeling
- Heterarchy, a hierarchy of values; ambiguous order
- Hierarchy, sacred order; a vertical arborizing process
- Holarchy, a whole order
- Holocosmology, the whole ecological and cultural framework of human cosmologies
- Hologram, pattern produced on photosensitive medium; a three-dimensional image of an object; equal to holograph; 'whole writing'
- Holomovement, the motion of the universe as a whole; Bohm's term
- Holon, a Janus-faced entity, simultaneously a part and a whole; Koestler's term
- Holonomy, naming the whole process
- Horizontal, a planar dimension; one level in a hierarchy
- Identity, the unique collective aspect of a set of characteristics by which a being is recognized
- Ideology, a body of ideas reflecting the needs or aspirations of a culture or individual
- Image, the reproduction of an appearance of something; 'imitation'
- Indeterminacy, a state of being not quantitatively determined; lacking precision or clarity
- Lebenswelt, the lived world; Husserl's term
- Logos, word; reason; 'choose or collect'
- Love, an intense feeling; mysterious, emotive force
- Macrocosm, the larger image of the universe
- Magic, a sorcerer's (=enchanter) art to control natural events by invoking the supernatural
- Matrix, a situation in which something develops; in computing, a network of intersections; 'mother'
- Melody, motion and rhythm
- Mesocosm, the middle image of the universe; human society
- Metalysis, the process of renewal by discrete units; 'loosening change'
- Metamorphosis, a change in appearance or structure; transformation by magic; 'changing shape'
- Metaphor, a figure of speech involving transference; 'transference or bearing change'
- Microcosm, the individual image of the universe
- Miniature, a complete assimilation in a whole
- Moral, acting in accord with standards; individual behavior; 'doing together'
- Morphic, relating to shape (see Ektropy)

- Motion, the process of change of position
- Music, the art of organizing sounds in a coherent sequence to elicit a response; art of the Muses
- Mythology, a cosmological account of the past; an explanation of the natural by the supernatural
- Negentropy, (see Ektropy)
- Net, an openwork fabric of woven threads forming a mesh in various sizes
- Order, a condition of comprehensible arrangement among elements of a group; a number of successive differentiations
- Organism, a living individual or living whole
- Panethic, the human recognition of the importance of interrelations of all beings
- Paradigm, a model or example
- Participation, joining or sharing with others
- Phenomenology, the study of appearances in human experience
- Poetry, the making of images in words
- Polarity, separation; opposition
- Process, ongoing movement; a series of changes
- Proposition, that which is expressed in a statement having logical constants
- Quality, a characteristic of something; a feature; 'of what kind'
- Quantity, an amount of something; the character of a proposition
- Quantum, a quantity of something; indivisible unit; 'how great'
- Radical, referring to root
- Reverence, Schweitzer's 'honor-fear' a feeling of respect, awe or love
- Religion, the institutional expression of belief in the supernatural; 'to bind back'
- Rhythm, durational quality; a regular movement
- Rights, in accordance with law or morality; just claims
- Ritual, a religious ceremony; the technique of constituting an order
- Sacred, worthy of reverence; made holy
- Set, a collection of elements
- Sign, the suggestion of a presence of a quality; a gesture to convey meaning; 'seal'
- Signal, a sign serving as a means of communication
- Star, a respresentation of a process and element in process
- STEM, the universal field of space-time/energy-matter
- Symbiosis, a close biological association; 'living together'
- Symbol, a representation by association, resemblance or convention;

'thrown together'
- Synergy, the emergent effects of two or more organisms
- Syntropy, (see ektropy)
- Symmetry, a relationship among the constituents of a system; 'of a like measure'
- Systems, a group of interacting, interrelating or interdepending elements forming a collective entity; a functionally related group of elements
- Tao, way; way of the universe; uncapitalized
- Texture, horizontal and vertical relationships
- Thermodynamics, the study of the relationships between heat and other forms of energy
- Tone, sound of a well-defined pitch and quality
- Totemism, the belief in kinship with animals, plants or natural objects through identification with a symbol
- Tragedy, a dramatic work of struggle ending in ruin; 'goat song'
- Triad, a group of three
- Triune brain, McLean's theory of evolutionary distinctions in the human brain
- Unity, a condition of accord; the state of being one
- Umwelt, a perceived world; von Uexkull's term for animal world
- Universe, all existing things; 'turning into one'
- Vagueness, not clearly expressed; indefinite; lacking definite shape
- Version, the universal process of turning (see ektropy, entropy, evolution)
- Vertical, extending from a plane; composed of levels
- Warp, to twist; running vertically in a fabric
- Wild, pre-reflective, undomesticated
- Woof, threads that run crosswise in a fabric; horizontal
- World, the image of a group in a place; a subset of the earth.

Bibbliography

Alexander, Samuel. 1920. Space Time and Deity. 2 vols. London: Macmillan & Co.

Aristotle. 1952. The Works of Aristotle. trans. I. Bywater. W. Ross, ed. Oxford: Clarendon Press.

Arbib, Michael. 1972. The Metaphorical Brain, New York: John Wiley and Sons.

Arnheim, Rudolf. 1971. Entropy and Art: An Essay on Disorder and Order. Berkeley: University of California Press.

Arnold, Matthew. 1927. Prose and Poetry. A. Bouton, ed. New York: Scribners.

_____. 1960-77. Complete Prose Works. R. Super, ed. 11 Vols. Ann Arbor: University of Michigan Press.

Bachelard, Gaston. 1971. On Poetic Imagination and Reverie. trans. C. Gaudin. Indianapolis: Bobbs-Merrill Co. Inc.

_____. 1969. Poetics of Space. trans. M. Jolas. Boston: Beacon Press.

Bacon, Francis. 1901. Novum Organum. J. Devey, ed. New York: P. F. Collier.

_____. 1974. The Advancement of Learning and New Atlantis. Oxford: Clarendon Press.

Baker, Richard St. Barbe. 1980. "A man of the trees." Coevolution Quarterly 25: 66-70.

Barfield, Owen. 1964. Poetic Diction: A Study in Meaning. New York: McGraw-Hill Book Co.

Barrett, William. 1978. The Illusion of Technique: A Search for Meaning in A Technological Civilization. New York: Doubleday.

Bateson, G. 1979. Mind and Nature: A Necessary Unity. New York: E.P. Dutton.

Beardsley, Monroe C. 1968. "Order and disorder in art." In The Concept of Order. Seattle: University of Washington Press. Pp. 191-218.

Becker, Ernest. 1968. The Structure of Evil. New York: Braziller.

_____. 1973. The Denial of Death. New York: The Free Press.

Beckner, Morton. 1971. "Teleology." In Man and Nature: Philosophical Issues in Biology, pp. 92-100. R. Munson, ed. New York: Dell Publishing Co.

Bell, J. S. 1964. On the Einstein Podolsky Rosen Paradox. Physics 1:195-200.

Benedict, Ruth. 1934. Patterns of Culture. Boston: Houghton Mifflin.

Benedict, Ruth. 1970. "Synergy: Patterns of the good culture." American Anthropologist 72: 320-333.

Bergonzi, B. 1969. Great Short Works of Aldous Huxley. New York: Harper & Row.

Bergstraesser, Arnold. 1962. Goethe's Image of Man and Society. Freiburg: Herder.

Berlyne, D.E. 1971. Aesthetics and Psychobiology. New York: Appleton Century Crofts.

Bertalanffy, Ludwig von. 1952. Problems of Life: An Evaluation of Modern Biological Thought. New York: John Wiley and Sons.

_____. 1975. Perspectives on General Systems Theory. New York: G. Braziller.

Bestor, H. 1971. The Outermost House. New York: Ballantine Books.

Binswanger, L. 1963. Being-in-the-world. New York: Basic Books. Black, C. A. 1968. Soil Plant Relationships. New York: Wiley.

Black, Max. 1962. Metaphor In: Models and metaphors. M. Black, ed. Ithaca: Cornell University Press.

Bly, Robert. 1975. Leaping Poetry. Boston: Beacon Press.

_____., ed. 1980. News of the Universe: Poems of the Twofold Consciousness. San Francisco: Sierra Club Books.

Bohm, David. 1951. Quantum Theory. New York: Prentice-Hall.

_____. 1980. Wholeness and the Implicate Order. London: Routledge and Kegan Paul.

Bonifazi, Conrad. 1967. A Theology of Things: A Study of Man in His Physical Environment. Philadelphia: Lippincott.

Bonner, J.T. 1952. Morphogenesis: An Essay on Development. Princeton: Princeton University Press.

Borges, Jorge. 1964. Labyrinths: Selected Stories and Other Writings. New York: New Directions.

Boulding, K. 1956. The Image: Knowledge in Life and Society. Ann Arbor: University of Michigan Press.

Brandon, William. 1971. The Magic World: American Indian Songs and Poems. New York: Morrow.

Bridgman, P. W. 1941. The Nature of Thermodynamics. Cambridge: Harvard University Press.

Brillouin, L. 1949. "Life, thermodynamics and cybernetics." Am. Sci. 37:554-568.

Bronowski, J. 1965. Science and Human Values. New York: Harper & Row.

_____. 1978. The Visionary Eye: Essays in the Arts, Literature, and Science. Cambridge: The MIT Press.

Brown, G. S. 1979. Laws of Form. New York: The Julian Press.

Brown, Norman O. 1966. Love's Body. New York: Random House.

Bruns, Gerald. 1974. Modern Poetry and the Idea of Language. New Haven: Yale University Press.

_____. 1980. "Poetry as Reality: The Orpheus Myth and its Modern Counterparts." NJ NV: 263-286.

Buber, Martin. 1958. I and Thou. trans. R. Gregor. New York: Scribners.

_____. 1965. Between Man and Man. trans. M. Friedman and R. Gregor. New York: Harper & Row.

Bunge, Mario. 1973. Method, Model and Matter. Boston: Synthese Library.

Burnor, David. 1980. "Ed Ricketts: 'From the Tidepool to the Stars." Coevolution Quarterly 28: 14-21.

Calhoun, John B. 1962. "Population density and social pathology." Sci. Am. 206: 139-148.

Campbell, Joseph. 1969. The Flight of the Wild Gander. New York: Viking Press.

_____. 1972. The Masks of God: Primitive Mythology. New York: Penguin Books.

_____. 1972. The Masks of God: Creative Mythology. New York: Penguin Books.

_____. 1972. Myths To Live By. New York: Viking Press.

Capra, Fritjof. 1975. The Tao of Physics Berkeley: Shambhala.

_____. 1982. The Turning Point. New York: Simon and Schuster.

Caratheodory, A. 1976. Wild Apples. Wilmington: M&RW, Ltd.

_____. 1982. Amphibian Dreams. Wilmington: M&RW, Ltd.

Cardinal, Roger. 1981. Figures of Reality: A Perspective on the Poetic Imagination. Totowa, NJ: Barnes and Noble Books.

Charter, S. P. R. 1970. Man on Earth: A Preliminary Evaluation of the Ecology of Man. New York: Grove Press.

Chew, G. F. 1970. Hadron bootstrap: triumph or frustration. Physics Today (October):23-28.

Churchman, C.W. 1968. The Systems Approach. New York: Delacorte Press.

Cicero, M.T. 1933. De Natura Deorum. trans. H. Rackham. London: Wm. Heinemann.

Clark, Grahame. 1977. World Prehistory. Cambridge: Cambridge University Press.

Cobb, John B., Jr. 1965. A Christian Natural Theology. Philadelphia: The Westminster Press.

_____. 1971. Is It Too Late? A Theology of Ecology. New York: Glencoe.

Coleridge, Samuel Taylor. 1971. Coleridge on Shakespeare. Folger monograph no. 3. R. Foakes, ed. Charlottesville: The University Press of Virginia.

Cook, R.J. and K. Baker. 1982. The Nature and Practice of Biological Control of Plant Pathogens (in press).

Daly, Herman E. 1977. Stead-State Economics. San Francisco: Freeman.

Darlington, Cyril D. 1958. The Evolution of General Systems. New York: Basic Books.

Darlington, Philip J. 1957. Zoogeography: The Geographic Distribution of Animals. New York: Wiley.

Dasmann, Raymond. 1972. 3rd Ed. Environmental Conservation. New York: Wiley.

Darwin, Charles. 1859. The Origin of the Species by Means of Natural Selection. London: Murray.

_____. 1896. The Descent of Man and Selection in Relation to Sex. New York: D. Appleton & Co.

Daubenmire, R. 1947. Plants and Environment. New York: Wiley.

De Bono, Edward. 1968. New Think: The Use of Lateral Thinking in the Generation of Ideas. New York: Basic Books.

Dewey, J. 1958. Art as Experience. New York: Capricorn Books.

Dicke, R. H. 1961. "Dirac's cosmology and Mach's principle." Nature 192: 400.

Diole, P. 1974. The Errant Ark: Man's Relationship with Animals. New York: Putnam.

Doolittle, W. F. 1981. Is nature really motherly? Coevolution Quarterly 29:58-62.

Dubos, Rene. 1965. Man Adapting. New Haven: Yale University Press.

_____. 1968. So Human an Animal. New York: Charles Scribner's Sons

_____. 1972. A God Within. New York: Charles Scribner's Sons.

_____. 1974. Beast or Angel? Choices That Make Us Human. New York: Charles Scribner's Sons.

_____. 1980. The Wooing of Earth. New York: Charles Scribner's Sons.

_____. 1981. Celebrations of Life. New York: McGraw-Hill.

Dyson, Freeman. 1979. Disturbing the Universe. New York: Harper.

Eddington, Arthur. 1928. The Nature of the Physical World. Cambridge: The University Press.

Edie, James. 1973. Expression and Metaphor Philosophy and Phenomenological Research. Vol. 23: 538-561.

Edie, J. 1969. New Essays in Phenomenology. Chicago: Quadrangle.

Ehrlich, P. and A. Ehrlich. 1972. Population, Resources, Environment. San Francisco: Freeman.

Ehrlich, P. 1981. An ecologist standing up among seated social scientists. Coevolution Quarterly 31:24-35.

Eibl-Eibesfelt, I. 1970. Ethology: The Biology of Behavior. New York: Holt, Rinehart and Winston.

Eigen, Manfred, and P. Schuster. 1979. The Hypercycle: A Principle of Natural Self-Organization. Berlin: Springer-Verglag.

_____. 1981. Laws of the Game. New York: Alfred A. Knopf.

Einstein, Albert, and L. Infeld. 1960. The Evolution of Physics. New York: Simon & Schuster.

Eiseley, Loren. 1970. The Invisible Pyramid. New York: Scribners.

Eliade, Mircea. 1963. Myth and Reality. trans. W. Trask. New York: Harper & Row.

Emerson, Ralph Waldo. 1950. Selected Writings of Ralph Waldo Emerson. New York: Modern Library.

Evernden, Neil. 1981. Out of Place (in press).

Festinger, L. 1957. A Theory of Cognitive Dissonance. Stanford: Stanford University Press.

Fiebleman, James K. 1968. "Disorder." Pp. 3-13 In The Concept of Order. P. G. Kuntz, ed. Seattle: University of Washington Press.

Finkelsten, D. 1972. The space-time code. Phys Rev 50, no. 12:2922.

Fowles, John. 1970. The Aristos. New York: The New American Library, Inc.

_____. 1979. Seeing Nature Whole. Harper's. 259:49-56.

Fox, Michael W. 1974. Concepts in Ethology: Animal and Human Behavior. Minneapolis: U. of Minnesota Press.

_____. 1976. Between Animal and Man. New York: Coward, McCann and Geoghehan Inc.

Fox, Michael W. 1980. One Earth, One Mind. New York: Coward, McCann and Geoghehan Inc.

_____. 1980b. Returning to Eden: Animal Rights and Human Responsibility. New York: Viking Press.

Frankel, Charles. 1956. The Case for Modern Man. New York: Harper.

Frankel, Otto. 1975. Crop Genetic Resources for Today and Tomorrow. New York: Cambridge University Press.

Frankena, William. 1973. Ethics. 2nd Ed Englewood Cliffs: Prentice-Hall.

Fraser, J.T. 1975. Of Time, Passion and Knowledge. New York: George Braziller.

Fromm, Erich. 1956. The Art of Loving. New York: Harper.

_____. 1976. To Have or To Be. New York: Bantam Books.

Frye, N. 1957. The Anatomy of Criticism. Princeton: Princeton University Press.

Galdston, Iago, ed. 1963. Man's Image in Medicine and Anthropology. New York: International Universities Press, Inc.

Gazzaniga, M.S. 1967. The split brain in man. Sci. Am. 217:24-29.

Gazzaniga, M.S. and J.E. LeDoux. 1978. The Integrated Mind. New York: Plenum Press.

Georgescue-Rogen, N. 1971. The Entropy Law and the Economic Process. Cambridge: Harvard University Press.

Gibbs, J. W. 1960. Principles in Statistical Mechanics. New York: Longmans, Green and Co.

Glacken, Clarence. 1967. Traces on the Rhodian Shore. Berkeley: Univ. of California Press.

Globus, G., G. Maxwell, and I. Sarednik. 1976 Consciousness and the Brain. New York: Plenum Press.

Goethe, Johan W. von. 1957. Poems. trans. NN. Chapel Hill: University of North Carolina Press.

Goldsmith, Edward et al. 1972. A Blueprint for Survival. Boston: Houghton Mifflin Co.

Gould, Stephen J. 1977. Ontogeny and Phylogeny. Cambridge: Belknap Press.

_____. 1977. Ever Since Darwin. New York: W.W. Norton.

Grant, Verne. 1977. Organismic Evolution. San Francisco: Freeman.

Grene, M., ed. 1971. Interpretations of Life and Mind. New York: Humanities Press.

Gustavson, Carl G. 1976. The Mansion of History. New York: McGraw-Hill Book Company.

Haeckel, Ernst. 1905. The Wonders of Life. trans. J. McCabe. New York: Harper & Bros.

Hall, Edward T. 1969. The Hidden Dimension. Garden City, New York: Doubleday & Co.

Halprin, Lawrence. 1969. The RSVP Cycles: Creature Processes in the Human Environment. New York: George Braziller.

Hampden-Turner, C. 1981. Maps of the Mind. New York: Macmillan.

Haraway, D. J. 1976. Crystals, Fields, and Fabrics. New Haven: Yale University Press.

Hardin, Garrett. 1969. Population, Evolution, and Birth Control. San Francisco: Freeman.

_____. 1977. The Limits of Altruism: An Ecologist's View of Survival. Bloomington: Indiana University Press.

Harper, J. L. 1961. The Evolution and Ecology   Evolution, Vol. 15: 209-227.

_____. 1977. Population Biology of Plants. New York: Academic Press.

Harrison, Edward R. 1981. Cosmology: The Science of the Universe. Cambridge: Cambridge University Press.

Hayakawa, Samuel. 1978. 4th ed. Language in Thought and Action. New York: Harcourt, Brace, Javonovich.

Hebb, D.O. 1958. "Alice in Wonderland." In The Biological and Biochemical Bases of Behavior. Madison: U. Wisconsin Press.

Heidegger, Martin. 1960. Being and Time. 9th ed. Tubingen: Max Niemeyer Verlag.

Heisenberg, W. 1958. Physics and Philosophy. New York: Harper Torch Books.

Heminger, Jr., S. K. 1974. Touches of Sweet Harmony. San Marino, California: Huntington Library.

Henderson, Hazel. 1980. Creating Alternative Futures: The End of Economics. New York: Putnam.

Hofstadter, Douglas. 1979. Godel, Escher, Bach: An Eternal Golden Braid. New York: Benjamin Books.

Holling, C. S. 1973. "Resilience and Stability of Ecological Systems." In Annual Review of Ecology and Systematics, R. F. Johnston et al., eds., Vol. 4: 1-24.

Homer. 1956. The Iliad. Middlesex, England: Penguin Books.

Hoyle, Fred. 1977. Astronomy and Cosmology. San Francisco: Freeman.

Huizinga, Johan. 1955. Homo Ludens: A Study of the Play Element in

Culture. London: Routledge & Kegan Paul.

Humboldt, Alexander von. 1897. Cosmos: A Sketch of a Physical Description of the Universe. trans. E. Otte. London: H. G. Bohn.

Huxley, Aldous. 1945. The Perennial Philosophy. New York: Harper.

_____. 1948. Ape and Essence. New York: Harper & Row.

_____. 1956. "Knowledge and Understanding." In Adonis and the Alphabet. London: Chatto and Windus.

_____. 1977. The Human Situation. P. Ferrucci, ed. New York: Harper & Row.

Huxley, Julian, and Huxley, T. H. 1947. Touchstone of Ethics. New York: Harpers.

James, William. 1950. The Principles of Psychology. 2 Vols. New York: Dover Publications.

Jantsch, E. 1975. Design for Evolution. New York: Braziller.

Jantsch, E. 1980. The Self-Organizing Universe. New York: Pergamon Press.

Jaynes, Julian. 1977. The Origin of Consciousness in the Breakdown of the Bicameral Mind. New York: Houghton Mifflin.

Jeans, James. 1932. The Mysterious Universe. New York: The Macmillan Co.

Jonas, H. 1974. Philosophical Essays: From Ancient Creed to Technological Man. Englewood Cliffs: Prentice-Hall Inc.

Jouvenel, Bertrand de. 1968. "The stewardship of the earth." In: The Fitness of Man's Environment. pp. 99-118. Smithsonian Annual II. New York: Harper Colophon Books.

Kaufmann, Walter, ed. 1960. The Portable Nietzsche. New York: Viking Press.

_____, ed. 1968. Philosophical Classics. Volume 1: Thales to Ockham. 2nd ed. Englewood Cliffs: Prentice-Hall.

Kieffer, George H. 1979. Bioethics: A Textbook of Issues. Reading, MA: Addison-Wesley Publishing Co.

Klein, David. 1972. "Toward an ecophilosophy." Tomte Symposium on Ecology and Land Use, Steinsgard, Norway.

_____. 1976. "Wilderness Part 1. Evolution of the Concept." Landscape 20: 36-41.

Klopfer, P. H. 1962. Behavioral Aspects of Ecology. Englewood Cliffs, NJ: Prentice-Hall.

Kockelmans, J., ed. 1972. On Heidegger and Language. Evanston, IL: Northwestern University Press.

Koestler, A. and J.R. Smythies, eds. 1969. Beyond Reductionism: New

Perspectives in the Life Sciences. London: Hutchinson.

Koestler, A. 1978. Janus: A Summing Up. New York: Random House.

Kohler, I. 1962. Experiment with goggles. Sci. Am. 206:62-86.

Kohler, W. 1947. Gestalt Psychology. 2nd ed. New York: Liveright Publishing Corp.

Kohr, Leopold. 1977. The Overdeveloped Nations: Diseconomics of Scale. New York: Schocken Books.

Kropotkin, P.A. 1972. Mutual Aid: A Factor in Evolution. New York: New York University Press.

Lacan, J. 1968. The Language of the Self: The Function of Language in Psychoanalysis. Baltimore: Johns Hopkins Press.

Lamarck, Jean. 1963. Zoological Philosophy. trans. H. Elliot. New York: Hafner Publishing Co.

Lao Tse. 1963. Tao Te Ching. trans. D. C. Lau. Middlesex, England: Penguin Books.

Laszlo, Ervin. 1972. Introduction to Systems Philosophy: Toward a New Paradigm of Contemporary Thought. New York: Harper Torch.

Lee, E.N. and M. Mandelbaum. 1967. Phenomenology and Existentialism. Baltimore: Johns Hopkins Press.

Leonard, G. 1978. The Silent Pulse. New York: E. P. Dutton

Leopold, Aldo. 1949. A Sand County Almanac. And Sketches of Here and There. New York: Oxford University Press.

Levi-Strauss, C. 1963. Structural Anthropology. New York: Basic Books.

Levy-Bruhl, Lucien. 1975. The Notebooks on Primitive Mentality. trans. Peter Leenhardt. Oxford: Basil Blackwell.

Lewin, K. 1951. Field Theory in Social Science. D. Cartwright, ed. New York: Harper & Row.

Lorentz, H. A., Einstein, A., Minkowski, H., and Weyl, H. 1952. The Principle of Relativity. trans. W. Dennett and G. Jeffery. New York: Dover Publications, Inc.

Lorenz, Konrad. 1952. King Solomon's Ring: New Light on Animal Ways. trans. M. K. Wilson. New York: Crowell.

_____. 1974. Civilized Man's Eight Deadly Sins. trans. M. K. Wilson. New York: Harcourt, Brace, Javonovich.

Lovejoy, Arthur O. 1964. The Great Chain of Being: A Study of the History of an Idea. Cambridge: Harvard University Press.

Lovelock, J. E. 1979. Gaia: A New Look at Life on Earth. Oxford: Oxford University Press.

MacLean, Paul D. 1969. A Triune Concept of the Brain and Behavior. Toronto: University of Toronto Press.

McArthur, Robert H. 1972. Geographical Ecology: Patterns in the Distribution of Species. New York: Harper & Row.

Malinowski, B. 1944. A Scientific Theory of Culture and Other Essays. Chapel Hill: University of North Carolina Press.

Margalef, R. 1968. Perspectives in Ecological Theory. Chicago: University of Chicago Press.

Margulis, L. 1974. Five kingdoms—classification and the origin and evolution of cells. Evol Biol 7:45-48.

Maruyama, Magorah. 1978. Cultures of the Future. The Hague: Mouton.

_____. 1980. "Toward Cultural Symbiosis." In Evolution and Consciousness, pp. 198-213. Reading, MA: Addison-Wesley.

Maslow, A. H. 1968. "Effects of Aesthetic Surroundings in Faces." In Interpersonal Communication. Boston: Houghton Mifflin Co.

_____. 1968. Toward a Psychology of Being. 2nd ed. New York: D. Van Nostrand Co.

_____. H. 1971. The Farther Reaches of Human Nature. New York: Viking Press.

Mayr, E. 1942. Systematics and the Origin of the Species. New York: Columbia University Press.

Mazrui, Ali Al Amin. 1976. A World Federation of Cultures: An African Perspective. New York: Free Press.

McKeon, Richard. 1973. Introduction to Aristotle. Chicago: University of Chicago Press.

McLean, G.F., ed. 1978. Man and Nature. Calcutta: Oxford University Press.

Meeker, Joseph. 1974. The Comedy of Survival. New York: Charles Scribner's Sons.

Mehra, Jagdish. 1973. The Physicist's Conception of Nature. Boston: D. Reidel Publishing Co.

Merleau-Ponty, Maurice. 1962. The Phenomenology of Perception. trans. C. Smith. London: Routledge and Kegan Paul.

_____. 1963. The Structure of Behavior, Alden Fisher, trans. Boston: Beacon Press.

_____. 1964. The Primacy of Perception. James Edie, ed. Evanston, IL: Northwestern University Press.

_____. 1964b. Signs. trans. R. McCleary. Evanston, Illinois: Northwestern University Press.

_____. 1968. The Visible and the Invisible. trans. A. Lingis. Evanston, Illinois: Northwestern University Press.

Merriam, Thomas. 1977. The Disenchantment of the World. The Ecologist, Vol 7, Pp. 22-29.

Merton, Thomas. 1971. Contemplation in a World of Action. Garden City, NY: Doubleday.

Mill, John S. 1963. Collected Works. 5 Vols. Toronto: University of Toronto Press.

Miller, G. 1956. The magic number seven plus or minus two. Psych. Rev. 63:81-97.

Mills, Charles W. 1959. The Sociological Imagination. New York: Oxford University Press.

Montaigne, Michel E. de. 1958. Complete Essays. trans. D. M. Frame. Stanford: Stanford University Press.

Morgan, Conway Lloyd. 1925. Emergent Evolution. New York: Henry Holt and Co.

Mourelatos, A. P. D., ed. 1974. The Pre-Socratics. Garden City, New York: Anchor Press/Doubleday.

Mumford, L. 1973. Interpretations and Forecasts: 1922-1972. New York: Harcourt, Brace, Jovanovitch.

Munson, R., ed. 1971. "Man and nature: Philosophy." In Issues in Biology. New York: Dell Publishing Co.

Naess, A. 1972. The shallow and the deep, long-range ecology movement. A summary. Inquiry, 16: 95-100.

_____. 1978. Self-realization in mixed communities of humans, bears, sheep, and wolves. Inquiry, 22: 231-241.

Neihardt, J.G. 1959. Black Elk Speaks. New York: Pocket Books.

Nicolis, G., and Prigogine, I. 1977. Self-organization in Non-equilibrium Structures. New York: Wiley.

Norberg-Schulz, Christian. 1971. Existence, Space and Architecture. New York: Praeger.

Nowottny, W. 1962. The Language Poets Use. London: Athlone Press.

Odum, Eugene. 1971. Fundamentals of Ecology, 3rd ed. Philadelphia: Saunders.

Ogden, Charles and I. A. Richards. 1923. The Meaning of Meaning. New York: Harcourt, Brace.

Ong, Walter J. 1967. In the Human Grain. New York: MacMillan Co.

Ophuls, William. 1977. Ecology and the Politics of Scarcity. San Francisco: W. H. Freeman & Co.

Ornstein, R., ed. 1973. The Nature of Human Consciousness. San Francisco: Freeman.

Ortiz, A. 1972. New Perspectives on the Pueblos. Albuquerque: University of New Mexico Press.

Otten, C., ed. 1971. Anthropology and Art. Garden City, New York: American Museum of Natural History.

Ovid, P. 1955. The Metamorphoses. trans. M. Innes. Baltimore: Penguin Books.

Pagels, H. 1982. The Cosmic Code: Quantum Physics as the Language of Nature. New York: Simon and Schuster.

Passmore, J. 1974. Man's Responsibility for Nature: Ecological Problems and Western Tradition. London: Duckworth.

Peacock, James L. 1975. Consciousness and Change: Symbolic Anthropology in Evolutionary Perspective. New York: Wiley.

Pearce, J.C. 1971. The Crack in the Cosmic Egg: Challenging Constructs of Mind and Reality. New York: Julian Press, Inc.

Peirce, Charles Sanders. 1955. *Selected Writings of Peirce*. Edited by J. Buchler. New York: Dover Publishing Company.

Pepper, Stephen C. 1958. *Sources of Value*. Berkeley: University of California Press.

_____. 1961. *World Hypotheses*. Berkeley: University of California Press.

Pfeffer, R. 1972. *Nietzsche: Disciple of Dionysius*. Lewisburg: Bucknell University Press.

Piaget, J. 1968. *Logical Thinking in Children*. I. Sigel, comp. New York: Holt, Rinehart and Winston.

Pico della Mirandola, Giovanni. 1943. *Of Being and Unity*. trans. V. M. Hamm. Milwaukee: Marquette University Press.

Planck, M. 1959. *The New Science*. New York: W. W. Norton and Co.

Plato. 1961. *The Collected Dialogues of Plato*. E. Hamilton and H. Cairns, eds. trans. L. Cooper et al. New York: Pantheon Books.

Poe, Edgar Allan. 1909. *The Works of Edgar Allan Poe*. 10 Vols. New York: The Century *Co.*

Poincare, Henri. 1905. Science and Hypothesis. trans. W. S. G. London: The Walter Scott *Publishing Co.*

Polanyi, Michael. 1958. Personal Knowledge: Towards a Post-critical Philosophy. Chicago: University of Chicago Press.

Polunin, Nicholas, ed. 1980. *Growth without Ecodisasters?* New York: Wiley.

Ponge, Francis. 1972. *The Voice of Things*. trans. B. Archer. New York: McGraw-Hill Book Company.

Pope, Alexander. 1966. Poetical Works. H. Davis, ed. New York: Oxford University Press.

Popper, K.R. and J.C. Eccles. 1977. The Self and Its Brain. Berlin: Springer-Verlag.

Portmann, Adolf. 1964. New Paths in Biology. New York: Harper & Row.

Pribram, Karl. 1977. "Problems concerning the structure of consciousness." In Consciousness and the Brain. New York: Plenum.

_____. 1977. No Title Brain\Mind Bulletin. (July).

Prigogine, Ilya. 1980. From Being to Becoming. San Francisco: Freeman.

Radcliffe-Brown, A.R. 1952. Structure and Function in Primitive Society. London: Cohen and West.

Rader, M. 1973. A Modern Book of Aesthetics. 4th ed. New York: Holt, Rinehart and Winston.

Rapoport, A. 1969. House Form and Culture. Englewood Cliffs: Prentice-Hall.

Redfield, R. 1956. Peasant Society and Culture. Chicago: University of Chicago Press.

Reichel-Doklmatoff, G. 1977. Cosmology as Ecological Analysis: A view from the Rain Forest. The Ecologist, Vol 7, Pp. 4-11.

Riedl, Rupert. 1978. Order in Living Organisms. trans. R. P. Jafferies. New York: J. Wiley & Sons.

Rifkin, J. 1982. Algeny: The Last Magic. (in press).

Riggs, L.A., et al. 1953. The disappearance of steadily fixated test objects. J. Op. Soc. Am. 43:495-501.

Rilke, Rainer Maria. 1938. Later Poems. trans. J. B. Leishman. London: Hogarth Press.

Rimbaud, Arthur. 1975. Arthur Rimbaud: Complete Works. trans. P. Schmidt. New York: Harper & Row.

Rodman, John. 1977. "Theory and practice in the environmental movement." In The Search for Absolute Values in a Changing World. Tarrytown, New York: International Cultural Foundation.

Roszak, Theodore 1972. Where the Wasteland Ends. New York: Harper & Row.

_____. 1975. Unfinished Animal. New York: Harper & Row.

_____. 1979. Person/Planet. New York: Harper & Row.

Rothenberg J. and G. Quasha, eds. 1974. America A Prophecy New York: Vintage Books.

Salk, J. 1973. Survival of the Wisest. New York: Harper & Row.

Sallis, J. 1978. Radical Phenomenology: Essays in Honor of Martin Heidegger. Atlantic Highlands: Humanities Press.

Salm, Peter. 1971. The Poem as Plant. Cleveland: Press of Case Western Reserve University.

Sapir, E. 1949. Selected Writings of Edward Sapir in Language, Culture and Personality. Berkeley: University of California Press.

Sarfatti, J., and B. Toben. 1975. Space-Time and Beyond. New York: Dutton.

Schaper, E. 1968. Prelude to Aesthetics. London: Allen and Unwin.

Scheler, M.F. 1954. The Nature of Sympathy. trans. P. Heath. London: Routledge & Kegan Paul.

Schiller, Ferdinand. 1968. Riddles of the Sphinx: A Study in the Philosophy of Humanism. no trans. New York: Greenwood Press.

Schrodinger, Erwin. 1946. What is Life? The Physical Aspect of the Living Cell. New York: Macmillan.

Schumacher, E.F. 1973. Small Is Beautiful. New York: Harper & Row.

Schweitzer, Albert. 1949. Out of My Life and Thought. New York: Henry Holt and Co.

_____. 1957. The Philosophy of Civilization. trans. C. T. Campion. New York: Macmillan Co.

Searles, H. 1962. The role of the nonhuman environment. Landscape (Winter 1961-1962):31-34.

Sewell, Elizabeth. 1960. The Orphic Voice: Poetry and Natural History. New York: Harper & Row.

_____. 1964. The Human Metaphor. Notre Dame: University of Notre Dame Press.

Sheldrake, Rupert. 1981. A New Science of Life: The Hypothesis of Formative Causation. Los Angeles: J. P. Tarcher, Inc.

Shepard, Paul. 1967. Man in the Landscape. New York: Alfred Knopf.

Shepard, Paul and D. McKinley, eds. 1969. The Subversive Science. Boston: Houghton Mifflin.

Shepard, Paul. 1978. Thinking Animals. New York: Viking Press.

Sherrington, Charles S. 1951. Man on His Nature. Cambridge: University.

Simpson, G.G. 1944. Tempo and Mode in Evolution. New York: Hafner Publishing Co.

Singer, Peter. 1981. The Expanding Circle: Ethics and Sociobiology. New York: Farrar, Strauss & Giroux.

Skolimowski, Henryk. 1978. "Eco-philosophy versus the scientific world view." Ecologist Quarterly 3 (Autumn): 227-248.

_____. 1980. "Evolutionary illuminations." NJ NI: 3-9.

_____. 1981. Ecophilosophy. Boston: Marion Boyars.

Slater, P. 1974. Earthwalk. New York: Bantam Books.

Smith, Maynard J. 1968. Mathematical Ideas Biology. Cambridge: Cambridge University Press.

Smuts, Jan C. 1926. Holism and Evolution. Ann Arbor, MI: University Microfilms.

Snyder, G. 1969. Earth House Hold. New York: New Directions.

Soleri, P. 1969. Arcology: The City in the Image of Man. Cambridge: The MIT Press.

_____. 1978. A response to "Fields of Danger". The North American Review, Spring: pp. 71-72.

Spiegelberg, Herbert. 1972. "Ludwig Binswanger: Phenomenological anthropology." In: Phenomenology in Psychology and Psychiatry. pp. 193-233. Evanston: Northwestern University Press.

Stanley, S. 1981. The New Evolutionary Timetable: Fossils, Genes and the Origin of Species. New York: Basic Books.

Stevens, Peter S. 1974. Patterns in Nature. Boston: Little Brown Co.

Stevens, Wallace. 1974. The Palm at the End of the Mind: The Collected Poems of Wallace Stevens. H. Stevens, ed. New York: Vintage Books.

Stone, Christofer D. 1974. Should Trees Have Standing? Towards Legal Rights for Natural Objects. New York: Avon Books.

Stratton, G.M. 1896. Some preliminary experiments on vision without inversion of the retinal image. Psych. Rev. 3:611-617.

Susser, Bernard. 1981. Existence and Utopia: The Social and Political Thought of Martin Buber. Rutherford: Fairleigh Dickinson Press.

Tagore, Rabindranath. 1961. Towards Universal Man. New York: Asia Publishing House.

_____. 1961. A Tagore Reader. A. Chakravarty, ed. New York: The Macmillan Co.

Taylor, Walter P. 1936. "What is ecology and what good is it?" Ecology 17:335-336.

Teilhard de Chardin, Pierre. 1959. The Phenomenon of Man. trans. B. Wall. New York: Harper.

Thakur, S.C. 1978. "A Touch of Animism." In Man and Nature. G.F. McLean, ed. Calcutta: Oxford University Press.

Theobald, Robert. 1972. Habit and Habitat. Englewood Cliffs: Prentice-Hall.

Thines, George. 1977. Phenomenology and the Science of Behavior. London: George Allen & Unwin.

Thom, Rene. 1975. Structural Stability and Morphogenesis: An Outline of a General Theory of Models. trans. D. C. Fowler. Reading, MA: W. A. Benjamin.

Thomas, David H. 1979. Archaeology. New York: Holt, Rinehart and Winston.

Thomas, Lewis. 1975. Lives of a Cell. Toronto: Bantam Books.

Thompson, William I. 1974. Passages About Earth. New York: Harper & Row.

_____. 1976. Evil and World Order. New York: Harper & Row.

_____. 1981. The Time Falling Bodies Take to Light. New York: Harper & Row.

Tillich, Paul. 1952. The Courage to Be. New Haven: Yale University Press.

_____. 1963. The Eternal Now. New York: Scribners.

Todd, John. 1977. "Towards a sacred ecology." In Earth's Answer. Pp. 170-183. M. Katz et al., eds. New York: Harper & Row.

Toynbee, Arnold J. 1976. Mankind and Mother Earth: A Narrative History of the World. New York: Oxford University Press.

Turnbull, C.M. 1961. The Forest People: A Study of the Pygmies of the Congo. New York: Simon and Schuster.

Tylor, E.B. 1958. The Origins of Culture. New York: Harper Torchbooks.

Uexkull, J. von. 1957. "A Stroll Through the World of Animals and Men." In Instinctive Behavior. New York: International Universities Press.

_____ 1957. The Upanishads. trans. S. Prabhavananda and F. Manchester. New York: New American Library.

Varela, Francisco. 1976. "Not one, not two." Coevolution Quarterly. Fall.

_____. 1979. Principles of Biological Autonomy. New York: North Holland.

Vico, Giovanni B. 1968. The New Science of Giovanni Vico. trans. T. Bergen and M. Fisch. Ithaca: Cornell University Press.

Waddington, C. H., ed. 1969. Towards a Theoretical Biology. Chicago: Aldine Publishing Co.

_____. 1975. The Evolution of an Evolutionist. Ithaca: Cornell University Press.

Wallace, Anthony F. C. 1966. Religion: An Anthropological View. New York: Random House.

Walsh, R. 1981. Towards an Ecology of Brain. Jamaica, New York: Spectrum Publishers.

Weber, Max. 1976. The Protestant Ethic and the Spirit of Capitalism. trans. T. Parsons. London: Allen and Unwin.

Weiner, Norbert. 1967. The Human Use of Human Beings. New York: Avon Books.

Weiss, G. 1975. Campa Cosmology. Anthropological papers, Vol. 52, Part 5, Pp. 217-588. New York: American Museum of Natural History.

Weiss, Paul A. 1973. The Science of Life. Mount Cisco, New York: Futura.

_____. 1967. "One plus one does not equal two." In The Neurosciences. New York: Rockefeller University Press.

_____. 1969. "The Living System: Determinism Stratified." In Beyond Reductionism: New Perspectives in the Life Sciences. A. Koestler and J. Smythies, eds. New York: The Macmillan Co.

Weizsacker, Carl F. von. 1951. The History of Nature. London: Routledge & Kegan Paul.

Weltfish, Gene. 1965. The Lost Universe. New York: Basic Books.

Wheeler, J., W. C. Misner, and K. Thorne. 1973. Gravitation. San Francisco: Freeman.

Wheeler, W. M. 1939. Essays in Philosophical Biology. Cambridge: Harvard University Press.

Wheelwright, P. 1962. Metaphor and Reality. Bloomington: Indiana University Press.

White, Leslie A. 1959. The Evolution of Culture. New York: McGraw Hill.

Whitehead, Alfred North. 1920. The Concept of Nature. Cambridge: Cambridge University Press.

_____. 1925. An Enquiry Concerning the Principles of Natural Knowledge. Cambridge: Cambridge University Press.

_____. 1933. Adventures of Ideas. New York: Macmillan.

_____. 1938. Modes of Thought New York: Macmillan Co.

_____. 1954. Religion in the Making. Cleveland: Meridian Books.

_____. 1958. The Function of Reason. Boston: Beacon Press.

_____. 1967. Science and the Modern World. New York: Free Press.

_____. 1969. Process and Reality. New York: Free Press.

_____. 1978. Process and Reality. (corrected edition) New York: Free Press.

Whitman, Walt. 1962. Complete Poems and Selected Prose. J. Miller, ed. Boston: Houghton Mifflin.

Whyte, Lancelot Law. 1965. Internal Factors in Evolution. New York: G.

Braziller.

Wigner, E. 1963. The problem of measurement. Am J. Phys. 31: 6-15.

Willard, B. E. et al. 1977. "Ethics of Biospheral Survival: A dialogue." In Growth Without Ecodisasters? pp. 505-535. N. Polunin, ed. New York: John Wiley & Sons.

Wilson, E.O. 1975. Sociobiology: The New Synthesis. Cambridge: Belknap Press.

Wimsatt, W. K. 1954. The Verbal Icon. Knoxville: University of Kentucky Press.

Wordsworth, William. 1957. The Preface to Lyrical Ballads. W. Owen, ed. Copenhagen: Rosenkilde and Bagger.

Worringer, W. 1963. Empathy and Abstraction. New York: International Universities Press.

Wright, John K. 1966. Human Nature in Geography: Fourteen Papers, 1925-65. Cambridge: Harvard University Press.

Zeleny, Milan, ed. 1980. *Autopoiesis: A Theory of Living Organisms*. New York: North Holland.

About the Author

During a brief career in astrophysics and astronomy at the University of Arizona, where he worked on mathematical models of stars and on spectrometric analysis, Alan Wittbecker spent his daylight hours climbing trees and trying to track mountain lions. He shared a trailer with a mouse, cockroach, squirrel, and bat (but did all the cooking himself).

Encouraged by research cuts to pursue a different direction, Wittbecker went to graduate school in psychology, anthropology, philosophy, and ecology (his degrees are in these fields). As a graduate student in 1970, he was a cofounder of the G. P. Marsh Institute for Research in Ecology, where he worked for 22 years, including 3 as Director by rotation. When projects were sparse, he worked in other occupations, such as ditchdigger, janitor, gardener, auto mechanic, appliance repair, diving coach, gymnastics teacher, artists model, librarian, systems engineer, editor, graphic artist, typesetter, forester, and math instructor.

In 1976, with three partners, Wittbecker cofounded Nieman Ryan Community Designs, specializing in private and urban local landscape design—but, also designing books, posters, journals, packages, landscapes, and buildings. In 1992, he founded SynGeo ArchiGraph, a firm specializing in global and regional ecological designs; he created designs for several bioregions, as well as international frameworks. A year later he set up the educational program for the Ecoforestry Institute, becoming an Instructor in 1994, journal Editor in 1995, and Director in 1997. He has worked on public and private forests from British Columbia to California, and on large predator wildlife projects, from Siberia to Norway.

A veteran of the US Air Force, Wittbecker is also a returned Peace Corps Volunteer from Bulgaria, where he monitored wolves in the Central Balkan Mountains. He has written newspaper columns and articles on ecology. He is the author of eight books, including *The Poetic Archaeology of the Flesh: An Investigation into the Phenomenology and Ecology of Being, Good Forestry*, and *Redesigning the Planet*. He has published over 100 articles on wildlife ecology and forestry.

Colophon

Type: Adobe Garamond Pro 11/14
Display Type: Palatino
Book Design: Rian Garcia Calusa Designs
Cover Design: Rian Garcia Calusa
Photographs & Graphics: Alan Wittbecker
Author Drawing: Merissa Nieman
Editing: J. Garcia B. of Rian Garcia Calusa
Hardware: Macintosh G5
Software: AzTex, Photoshop, InDesign, Acrobat
Furious Charge & Entertainment: Pippi Frog
Spiritual & Material Support: Precious Woulfe